AN OVERVIEW
OF ORTHODOX
CANON LAW

ORTHODOX THEOLOGICAL LIBRARY

Protopresbyter George Dion. Dragas
General Editor

Daryle R. Lamoureux
Technical Editor

Other Titles in this Series:

1. Protopresbyter John S. Romanides. *An Outline of Orthodox Patristic Dogmatics*. Translated, edited and introduction by Protopresbyter George Dion. Dragas

2. Panagiotes K. Chrestou. *Greek Orthodox Patrology: An Introduction to the Study of the Church Fathers*. Translated, edited and introduction by Protopresbyter George Dion. Dragas

ORTHODOX THEOLOGICAL LIBRARY 3

AN OVERVIEW OF ORTHODOX CANON LAW

Professor Dr. Panteleimon Rodopoulos
Metropolitan of Tyroloë and Serention
Ecumenical Patriarchate

Translated from the Greek original by W. J. Lillie

Edited by Protopresbyter George Dion. Dragas
Professor of Patrology/Patristics,
Holy Cross Greek Orthodox School of Theology

ORTHODOX
RESEARCH
INSTITUTE

Rollinsford, New Hampshire

Published by Orthodox Research Institute
20 Silver Lane
Rollinsford, NH 03869
www.orthodoxresearchinstitute.org

Original Greek title: Ἐπιτομὴ Κανονικοῦ Δικαίου

Library of Congress Control Number: 2005927534

ISBN10 1-933275-15-4
ISBN13 978-1-933275-15-4

Editor's Foreword

This is the first full manual of Eastern Orthodox Canon Law to be published in English. The Orthodox Research Institute offers it to Orthodox clergy, students of Theology, and all Orthodox laity that have responsible positions in the Church in the USA and abroad with much gratification and a sense of achievement. "The Orthodox Theological Library," sponsored by the Orthodox Research Institute, is definitely enriched by the addition of this volume, and therefore I want to express our gratitude to His Eminence for giving us this single privilege to include it in this series. The name of the author is a guarantee for the accuracy and excellence of this volume. Professor Dr. Panteleimon Rodopoulos, Metropolitan of Tyroloë and Serention (Ecumenical Patriarchate of Constantinople) is well known in the Orthodox world and especially to the Orthodox in America. He not only served in the past as Dean of Holy Cross Greek Orthodox School of Theology in Brookline, Massachusetts, but has also been the Special Envoy of the Venerable Ecumenical Patriarchate to several Clergy-Laity Conferences of the Greek Orthodox Archdiocese of America. As a professor at the Aristotle University of Thessalonica and specialist in Canon Law he is also world renowned and his expertise has been recently celebrated with the publication of the volume, Kirchenrecht und Ökumene: Gestgabe Panteleimon Rodopoulos, Verlag Roman Kovar, Eichenau 1999, which comprises essays written in his honor by experts in the field of Canon Law. See also his Eminence's fuller biography provided by Dr. Athanasios Arvanites at the end of the volume. The translation was undertaken by a British scholar who teaches English in

Thessaloniki. It is more literal than literary due to the technical nature of the original text. This attachment to the original Greek was the wish of the author. We respected this preference and did not attempt any restructuring of the sentences to comply with American literary convention.

Protopresbyter George Dion. Dragas

Prologue

This Overview of the Canon law of the Orthodox Catholic Church is a précis of the lessons on Canon Law which I taught to undergraduate students of the Theological School of the Aristotle University of Thessaloniki from 1968; and, after the division of the School into two Departments in 1982, to the undergraduates of the Department of Pastoral and Social Theology from that year until today. With the passage of time, the content of my lessons underwent adaptations and improvements because of what had in the meantime become my established ecclesiological and canonical views on certain matters of Canon Law. These changes were small but nonetheless of the essence.

The present edition does not constitute a complete system of Canon Law, but, as its title declares, is an overview thereof. If God grants me life, I shall attempt to compose as full a system as possible of the Canon Law of the Orthodox Catholic Church.

I should like to thank my student and colleague, now Assistant Professor of Canon Law at the Theological School of the University of Thessaloniki, Mr. Theodore Yiangou, for the interest he has shown and for correcting the proofs of the Greek edition.

Professor Panteleimon Rodopoulos
Metropolitan of Tyroloë and Serention
The Holy Patriarchal and Stavropegic Monastery of Vlatades
Pascha 1998

Prologue to the English Edition

Some years ago my colleague in professorship and good friend, Dr. Elias Patsavos, Professor of Canon Law at the Theological School of Holy Cross, Brookline, Mass., published a favorable review in a local Boston newspaper concerning the textbook of Canon Law "*An Overview of Canon Law*," which contains, in brief and summarized form, my lectures to the students of the Theological School of the University of Thessaloniki.

During the Clergy-Laity Congress of the Holy Archdiocese of America in Philadelphia, PA, USA, in the year 2000, favorable reference was made to this textbook in the competent Committee for Administrative Matters of the Archdiocese during discussions of the draft of the new Charter of the Holy Archdiocese. The wish was expressed by Emmanuel Demos, Eleni K. Huszagh and the members of the Committee, as well as by Professor Patsavos, that it be translated into English and that the publication be undertaken by the Theological School of Holy Cross. This suggestion was agreed to by His Eminence Archbishop Demetrios of America, presiding over the Clergy/Laity Congress.

The translation was undertaken by an Englishman, W. J. Lillie, head of an English language school in Panorama, Thessaloniki, who is familiar with theological terminology.

Unlike the Greek original, the English edition of this textbook does not include the Constitutional Decrees concerning the Church of

Greece and its Charters, nor the Patriarchal and Synodal Tomes and Acts which refer to this Church. In their place the Charters of the Holy Archdiocese of America, which have been granted by the Ecumenical Patriarchate from the founding of the Holy Archdiocese until today, have been included.

I would like to thank Professor Elias Patsavos, the Committee for Administrative Matters of the Clergy-Laity Congress of the Holy Archdiocese of America in Philadelphia, PA, USA (2000) for their kind and generous proposal, which does me great honor, and also His Eminence Archbishop Demetrios for agreeing to it.

The Theological School, for technical reasons, delayed the publication. Thus, the Very Rev. Professor Protopresbyter George Dion. Dragas, my colleague also in Professorship and co-representative with me of the Ecumenical Patriarchate of Constantinople in international Theological Dialogues, and the Orthodox Research Institute, Rollinsford, NH, have undertaken it. I thank them.

I hope that the publication of this textbook in English will prove useful for English-speaking students of Theology, the clergy and all those interested in the Canon Law of the Orthodox Church.

> Professor Dr. Panteleimon Rodopoulos
> Metropolitan of Tyroloë and Serention
> November 30th, 2006
> Feast Day of Saint Andrew the Apostle
> Founder of the Church of Constantinople (Byzantion)

Table of Contents

PART ONE

GENERAL

CHAPTER ONE

Introduction

Canon Law is a core subject in the Theology Syllabus. It investigates in an academic way the law of the Church and presents it systematically. Through this law, the internal life of the Church is regulated, as a visible organization, on the basis of what was ordained by Christ and the Apostles, and also on the basis of the Sacred Canons, ecclesiastical regulations, practice, custom and state laws.

Canon Law is a theological science because the Sacred Canons and the ecclesiastical ordinances, which define matters relating to the Church's system of government and administration to the life and position of the faithful within it, and even to things concerned with the most practical matters, are certainly formulated in the shape of laws, but necessarily have a theological basis and theological presuppositions. The Church aims at its basic goal, that is the salvation of people and the world, also through the Sacred Canons and other ordinances. Although Canon Law is a branch of Theology, it nevertheless touches upon the science of law, too, because it uses its legal method.

In particular, any system of Canon Law is founded on two basic concepts: that of the Church, on the one hand, and of law, on the other, insofar as its content has been influenced and formed by Christianity.

1 THE ECCLESIA (CHURCH). The term *ecclesia*, in Ancient Greek phraseology, meant a gathering of the people, an assembly, in which,

in the pre-democracy period of the Greek states, not every citizen took part, but only those who were "called out" by the herald (from the verb ἐκκαλεῖν, "to call out").

According to the Septuagint, the term *ecclesia* referred to the chosen part of Israel, that is to the real Israel.

In the Gospels, and in particular that of Matthew, the Lord twice speaks of the Church (Matt. 16:18 and 18:17): "You are Peter and on this rock I shall build for Me the Church…" as a society of those believing in Him, as the Kingdom of God on earth. The term Church (Ἐκκλησία) is also encountered in the Acts of the Apostles, in the Epistles and in the Revelation and sometimes means all Christians wherever they are, the whole Church, and sometimes all the Christians in a local Church (Thessaloniki, Corinth, Rome, etc.) or even the Church in a single house (e.g. that of Philemon).

In the New Testament, the Church is called the "Church of God" because it was created by Him and belongs to Him, being the appearance or epiphany of God on earth. It made its appearance as "the communion of Jesus Christ our Lord" (I Cor. 1:9), the members of which are closely connected with Christ and among themselves, so that through the power of the Holy Spirit, they constitute one body — "the body of Christ." The Apostle Paul speaks of "the body of Christ, which is the Church," and says "He is the head of the body of the Church" (Col. 1:24; 18).

The Church in its essence is closely linked to the mystery of the Triune God Who was revealed in Christ and in the Holy Spirit (Eph. 5:32). It is "the treasury of the secret mysteries."[1]

Of course, in the Holy Scriptures and in Sacred Tradition, no immediate and full definition of the notion of "Church" is provided, but there are many depictions and descriptions from which it is possible to construct directly what the Church is in its essence.

According to Holy Scripture, as was said above, the Church is "the body of Christ" (Rom. 12:4ff.; I Cor. 12:13; 27), the "people of God" (I Peter 2, 10), the "house" or "temple of God" (I Tim. 3:15; Eph. 2:21;

---

[1] John Chrysostom, *Homily on 1 Cor. 16:3*, Migne *PG* 61, 134.

I Cor. 3:16ff), "a royal priesthood" (I Peter 2:9), a "holy nation" (I Peter 2:9), the "bride of Christ" (cf. Mark 2:20; Matt. 25:1ff; Rev. 21:2), the "vine of God" (Is. 5:7; Jn. 15:1ff).

Descriptions are also given in Sacred Tradition, each extolling one or another aspect of the Church, such as, for example, its episcopal system, its priestly and charismatic character, its character as a communion of the faithful, its constitution by all the Orthodox of all ages and as humanity united in the God/Man Jesus Christ.

Thus, the Church, in its essence, is not merely a human community and organization, nor a passing phenomenon in the history of mankind. It existed in the pre-eternal will of God concerning the world and Man, was initially prefigured in Israel, during the period of the Old Testament, and heralded by the Prophets as the future people of God, the people of the New Testament, among whom God would found His definitive, indissoluble kingdom on earth, extending over all (Is. 2:2; Jer. 31:31). Later, in the fullness of time, the Church became reality in the incarnation of God the Word through preaching, through the call and election of the Apostles[2] and the delegation of authority to them,[3] through the Last Supper, the Crucifixion and the Resurrection, as well as by the sending of the Holy Spirit on the day of Pentecost for both the sanctification of the Church and for the empowerment of the Apostles to perform their task and of their mission to preach the Gospel of the Kingdom of Heaven.[4]

The Church, which was founded on earth by the Lord, then, is the body of Christ and a theanthropic organization, whose head is Christ. It is a tangible community, capable of description, but it is also an internal and spiritual relationship of its members both toward its Divine Founder and among themselves.

---

[2] Matt. 4:18 – 22; Mark 1:16 – 20, Luke 5:1 – 11; 9:59 ff; 10:1 – 12. "As He walked by the Sea of Galilee, He saw two brothers, Simon, who is called Peter and Andrew his brother, casting a net into the sea…and He said to them, 'Follow Me, and I will make you fishers of men.' Immediately, they left their nets and followed Him." Likewise, on the election, see Matt. 10:1 – 5, Mark 3:13 – 19, Luke 6:12 – 16.
[3] Matt. 16:13 – 19; 18:18; 18:28; Mark 16:15 – 16; Luke 22:29 ff.; Jn. 20:21; 21:15 – 17.
[4] Matt. 9:35 – 10:14; Mark 6:7 – 13; Luke 9:1 – 6 and 10:1 – 24.

The Church, as the people of God in progression, lives on the earth in expectation of its Lord until the fulfillment of the Kingdom of God. It lives and exists in heaven as the Church Triumphant, through those who have already passed on, and also on the earth as the Church Militant, through the faithful, through those who are engaged in the good fight (cf. II Tim. 4:6 – 7).

It is celestial and invisible in its first aspect, terrestrial and visible in its second, a communion and organization which has a priesthood linked canonically and successively, without interruption, to the Apostles. It also has stable and unchangeable dogma and ethical principles, clearly defined and ordered worship, and a body which is distinguished into clergy and laity.

In the Church, the new life in Christ and in the Holy Spirit is perfected and in it the grace and the divine life of Christ, that is, its head, is conferred on all its members for their sanctification and salvation.

The essence of the Church found its dogmatic expression in the Creed of Nicea-Constantinople. In this Creed, belief in the Triune God is followed by belief in "One, Holy, Catholic and Apostolic Church."

These four dogmatic properties of the Church formulated in the Creed, being mutually in *perichoresis* and indissolubly unified, allude to its indestructible character and indicate the infallibility of the Church as "a pillar and bulwark of the truth" (I Tim. 3:15).[5]

The Orthodox Catholic Church lays greater stress on the mystical and invisible element, which is why it has not assigned a secular and legalistic, but rather a spiritual mystical, character to its organization. As a palpable and visible society of living beings, however, it also had the need to be organized through the enactment of canons and laws which would regulate its life and activities, as well as the relationships between its members. In this way, the visible Church was formed into a society and spiritual authority with spiritual powers, with its own organization and government. It was distinguished from all secular

---

[5] The introductory text concerning the Church, of the joint Theological Committee of Orthodox and Old Catholics, in Ἐπίσκεψις, no. 173, 1-9-1977, pp. 13 – 15.

authority and polity by its spiritual nature, its content, its goals and its means. The visible Church, then, as a communion of people and as a living body consisting of many members, contains the human as well as the divine element and is imbued with certain principles and by canon law which is of divine provenance. It has been provided by Christ with triple ecclesiastical authority — to instruct, to celebrate/sanctify and to administer/shepherd — with visible means of sanctification and other instruments and sacraments accessible to all people, through which it aims to confer on people salvation in Christ and to establish the Kingdom of God on earth.[6]

Within the Church, the will of Jesus Christ prevails and is sovereign, not as the will of one standing outside the Church, but as the will of the Head of the body of the Church, through whom the faithful are united in the communion of the new people of God. This property of the Church, thus, leaves no room for defining the essence of the Church through legal concepts.

In brief, we note that for the perfection of the Church as a visible institution, the Lord performed the following actions:

1. He established the apparatus of the Church through the call and mission of the twelve Apostles initially and through the bishops who continue the triple function and office of the Lord.

2. He preached the divine word, through which the Lord enlightened people and which to this day guides the ministers of the Church, to teach correctly the word of truth.

3. He laid down the fundamental legislation of the Church.

4. He inaugurated the Divine Eucharist, through which the mystery of the Church is realized in place and time.

5. On the day of Pentecost, He sent to His disciples and Apostles the Holy Spirit, who "welds together the whole institution of the Church."

Principally through these acts of the theanthropic Lord, the Church became an organized society with its own legislation, hierarchy and wor-

---

[6] I. Karmiris, article Ἐκκλησία in Θρησκευτικὴ καὶ Ἠθικὴ Ἐγκυκλοπαιδεία, vol. 5, col. 456.

ship, distinct from all other human institutions and accomplishing the
redemption and salvation of mankind through its own means.

2 LAW. Throughout the ages, philosophers, lawyers, sociologists and
particularly those concerned with the philosophy of law have giv-
en a variety of answers to the question: "What is law?" None of these
have, however, been generally accepted so far by the science of law or has
gained preeminence within it. Even today the philosopher Candius' iron-
ic remarks holds true: that lawyers are still seeking to find a definition for
their discipline. The more the student of jurisprudence devotes himself to
its study, the more he understands the difficulties that surround the ap-
parently simple question of what is just. Because of the nature of justice,
which does not belong to the tangible world but rather to that of spiritual
values, finding expression in life, it has been claimed by many law experts
who have specialized in the philosophy of jurisprudence, that any full
definition of law from the point of view of its essence is not feasible.

Hence, only a descriptive definition is possible, and this is why the definitions of jurisprudence given so far are so very different among themselves. Aristotle writes: "So what is just is lawful and equal, what is unjust
is unlawful and unequal;" "Laws wish for what is just, good and beneficial,
and this is what they seek... and when it is found, it is equal and the same
for everyone... Law was devised and given by God, it is the conviction of
wise men, the correction of conscious and unconscious sins and a common pact by which it is fitting that everyone in the polis should live." Cal-
licles affirms that: "Law is nothing but the advantage of the better," while
Celsus describes it as "the art of the good and the equal" (*jus est ars boni et
æqui*). It would be difficult to enumerate all the definitions of law.

But what is the fundamental meaning of the term "just"? In common
parlance, what is meant is the right thing in every circumstance. According to the Roman jurist, Ulbian, the term "just" derives from "justice."[7]
According to this lawyer, justice is "the unwavering and perpetual desire

---

[7] *Pandectes* a, 1.

to render to each his own right" (*justitia est constans et perpetua voluntas jus suum cuique tribuendi*).[8] What is just, therefore, is whatever corresponds to or reflects justice, while whatever opposes justice is unjust. But the content of justice and its criteria are defined and formed by religion and its ethical teaching, by the philosophical and spiritual convictions and experiences of the people within a society. However that may be, "just" and "justice" form the basis of all societies under law (*justitia fundamentum regnorum*).

Aristotle says in his *Politics* that man is a social animal, which means that he is unable to live without communion with his fellow men, since — as Aristotle goes on to say — those who do not live with others may be one of two things: either wild animals or a god. In other words, they may be so savage as to be unfit for coexistence with others; or they are so perfect, like God, that they have no need of others. Living together with others, therefore, is part and parcel of human nature. There must, however, be some rhythm to this coexistence: that is to say, there must be rules to govern the way people live together. It is not possible to cast ourselves upon the good will of individual persons and to be dependent on how they regulate their behavior toward others, but rather there must be clear-cut rules laid down, on the basis of which this coexistence will be ordered. The axiom of Roman law is well-known, according to which wherever a human society has been established, there, of necessity, will also be found law: "*ubi societas ibi jus*." Without law and legitimate order, anarchy and chaos would reign in human society, that is, a war of all against all: "*bellum omnium contra omnes*."

Through the order of the law, the interests of individuals and groups are harmonized with the whole social entity, so that all may be brought under the same rule of government and the same code of law. It is self-evident that in the course of achieving this harmonious coexistence through the law, there must be some limitation of the unbridled freedom of the members of society. It is not possible for members of a soci-

---

[8] Ulbian L 10 DI, I.

ety under the law to act selfishly and to do as they wish, without regard for the harm their behavior may be causing to the interests of the other members of society. Rather, they are obliged to act in accordance with the established order of the law.

It goes without saying that this restriction, in the final analysis, also constitutes the guarantee and surety of people's relative freedom. That is to say, peaceful coexistence among people demands the harmonization of freedom, on the one hand, and of obligations to the social entity as a whole, on the other, and this is achieved through the regulatory function of law in human societies.

Enforced compliance, for the sake of the social entity as a whole, presupposes a certain independent source of authority, which must be equipped with the power to govern. The final and supreme source of power in human societies under the law is God. Naturally, in any specific society, human authority must also have independent powers. In the exercise of its authority, however, and in the adoption of its laws, it must conform totally to the natural law implanted by God in people's conscience and of which St. Paul speaks in his Epistle to the Romans (2:14 – 15): "When the Gentiles, who do not have the law, do by nature that which the law requires, they are a law unto themselves, even though they do not have the law. They show that what the law requires is written on their hearts, while their conscience also bears witness."

Therefore, every law and every human judicial institution must be formulated in accordance with divine justice (*jus divinum*), that is with unwritten divine justice or natural justice (*jus naturale*) or the natural law (*lex naturalis*) and with the written divine law. In any instance where a law is in conflict with divine justice, then it is wanting in ethical character. We are, then, no longer dealing with true justice, but rather with legalized injustice, which is not able to obligate or bind the human conscience.

3 CHURCH AND LAW. There is an initial problem of the essence of relations between the Church and law. The problem is how to reconcile the notion and theory of the Church as an organized communion of the faithful, which is conditioned by Canon Law and other laws, with the fundamental teaching of the Church, according to which Christ became incarnate in order to free mankind from the "curse of the law," from the bonds of the legal polity and so on, i.e. the Synagogue (Pharisees and the legalistic way of conceiving and living religion), and to bring people to the freedom of the spirit, to the communion of love, to the Church, in which it is not the law but "grace which has worked everything." This is a very serious problem and continues to exercise Canon Law scholars to this day. Because of it, according to the essence of the Church, it is doubtful whether a legal system, and therefore, the science of Canon Law, can exist at all.

This problem was created and became acute mainly because of the extreme positions into which the western Churches and Confessions, the Roman Catholic and the Protestants, were led at the time when they were being organized.

The Roman Catholic Church became a very powerful organization, in which, however, the spiritual element was combined with the secular, while the Protestant Confessions, from the point of view of the legal system, are purely secular organizations.

In the Roman Catholic Church, its visible aspect is underlined and its exterior dispositions as an organization are stressed. And, in keeping with the Latin mindset, form is emphasized at the expense of substance and the law, the legal system, at the expense of freedom of the spirit and of the Church as a communion in which the new commandment of love prevails.

This is why the Roman Catholic Church is characterized by the Protestants as the Church of law, which is opposed to the Church of love.

The Protestant Confessions, on the other hand, overlook the visible Church and ascribe to it only external significance, considering it a secular organization from the point of view of the legal system. They emphasize the invisible Church, which they consider, as the true Church, to be "a communion of faith and the Holy Spirit in the heart." They also claim that this Church is called — and in its essence is — a communion of love, largely irrespective of external organization, and hence of Canon Law, which is a human construct.

These departures and the resultant disharmony between the essence of the Church and the canonical order, action and life of the heterodox Churches were instrumental in the creation of a movement at the end of the 19th century, represented by the famous Protestant Romanist and canonist Rudolf Sohm. This movement, using positivist and intellectual criteria, claimed that it was not possible for there to be Canon Law in the Church. "The essence of the Church and the essence of law are at odds," or, in other words, "By its very nature, the Church has no need for Canon Law."

However, through his work, Sohm made a great contribution to the science of Canon Law. He believed that the incarnate Word of God was God and Man and that the Church founded by Him was founded on the Word of God as God/Man. Sohm was able to comprehend the great problem of the relationship between Church and law in great depth.

By his refusal to acknowledge the possibility of the existence of Canon Law, in accordance with the essence of the Church, however, Sohm threatened to shatter the foundations of the canonical order of the Churches. His theory, as was natural, provoked a storm of protest, which resulted in a flowering of the science of Canon Law. In order to refute Sohm's theory, canonists enquired systematically and *ab initio* into this most important topic of the relations between Church and law. Sohm's basic premises were overturned because of the exaggerated and absolute terms in which they were couched. Despite this, and though this theory is often considered a dead letter, it continues, as Mörsdorf observes,[9] to constitute a thorn in the side of the science of Canon Law and is a constant irritation. The problem of the relationship between the Church and the law remains and will continue to absorb those concerned with Canon Law for many years to come.

---

[9] Klaus Mörsdorf, *Kirchenrecht*, I, 37ff, Paderborn, 1964.

From the Orthodox side, very little has been written in any systematic form concerning the relations between the Church and law. In practice, however, the answer to this question is contained in the long legislative synodal tradition of the Orthodox Church, in the works of the Fathers, particularly those dealing with matters of order, administration and the life of the Church and in Patriarchal and Synodal Acts. Moreover, as heterodox theologians confess, the Orthodox Church has retained unadulterated the organization and the spirit of the ancient Church, in its basic principles, while the Roman Catholic and Protestant Churches have departed from this organization and from the ecclesiology of the ancient, undivided Church, so that objective research on the matter is difficult. In the Roman Church, the institution of the Papacy has intruded, while with the Protestants, there is denial of the Sacrament of the Priesthood and disregard for the visible Church. Any investigation from the Orthodox point of view, however, and any attempt to resolve the problem of the relationship between the Church and the system of law also requires knowledge of the findings of Canon Law in the heterodox Churches and a study of their organization during the course of their historical evolution, since in this way ample light will be cast on the whole subject, as also on the causes of the departure of the heterodox Churches from the ancient, undivided Church, in regards to its theology and organization. The problem, then, may be posed as follows: "How can we come to terms with the existence of Canon Law in the Church, which, as a *par excellence* spiritual and supernatural organism, is, in its deepest essence, a communion of love and in which the spirit of freedom in Christ is paramount?" The answer to this, as was mentioned above, is given by the ancient, undivided Church's spirit and teaching, which is stored in the treasury of the writings of the Fathers of the Church.

The Lord, as the Lawgiver of the Old and New Testaments, does not merely overturn the law of the Old, but, on the contrary, fulfills the Mosaic law, completes it and perfects it.

The fulfillment of the law was accomplished by the Lord in three ways (St. John Chrysostom):

a) through the implementation of the provisions of the law.

b) through His sacrifice on the Cross. Through His sacrifice, the Lord made a reality of the will of the law, which was that mankind might be justified through the implementation of its provisions. The faithful who take part in the redemptory sacrifice of the Lord are justified, and in this way, the aim of the law is accomplished without the scrupulous observance of its provisions.

c) through the introduction of the legislation of the New Testament. This does not repeal the law of the Old Testament but rather completes and perfects it. "But if anyone will inquire accurately, he will find also another, a third sense, in which this has been done. And what is this then? In the sense of that future law, which He was about to deliver to them. For what He said was no repeal of the former, but a protraction and completion of them. Thus, 'Do not commit murder' is not annulled by 'Do not become angry,' but is rather completed by it and established more firmly. And this is true of all the others. Therefore, indeed, He had inconspicuously sown the seeds of His teaching well before, so that at the time when, from His comparison of the old and new commandments He would be more openly suspected of contraposing them, He could correct this."[10]

The perfection of the law, however, is achieved principally through the new commandment of love, which is the hallmark of the New Testament and which gives to the Church the characteristic of a communion of love.

But what does the perfection of the law by love consist of? What is the connection between love and the freedom of the Spirit and the bonds of the law?

Saint John Chrysostom directs the attention of the faithful particularly to the correct interpretation of the Gospel's law, so that they will not be brought into misconduct and heresies by altering the true spirit of the revealed truth. The occasion for this was the promulgation of a view similar to that which claimed that the Church is merely a communion of

---

[10] Chrysostom, *Homily on Matthew* 16, 2, *PG* 57, 241.

love and which was opposed to the organization of the Church through divine law.

It is true that the Lord freed us from the curse which was entailed in the transgression against the law, as well as from the way in which the law was conceived and applied by the Jews of His time. The Jews paid particular attention to the legal provisions of their religion, so that by the time the Lord came, they had completely distorted the true spirit of the religion revealed in the Old Testament. The Prophets, who constitute the soul of the Old Testament, were, for the most part, ignored. What was stressed, then, and what was sought was the formal observance of the religious provisions, the result being that religious life was completely external, superficial and hypocritical, while the spirit and the internal element of religion were neglected and ignored. Liberation from "the letter of the law, which kills," and the call to the freedom of the Spirit, which gives life, do not, however, mean unrestrained freedom. "But do not use your freedom as an occasion for the flesh … Christ has delivered us, he says, from the yoke of bondage, He has left us free to do what we will … but that we may have ground for receiving a higher reward, advancing to a higher philosophy."[11]

The liberation of mankind by the Lord from the letter of the law does not mean the abolition of legal order within the Church. The perfection of the law by love consists, on the one hand, of the liberation of mankind from the exclusive and Pharisaical devotion to the external and formal provisions of the law and, on the other, by the introduction of a more perfect and spiritual law. "But because He calls the law above and below a yoke of bondage, and grace the loosing of the curse, in case people suspect that He is urging abandonment of the law so that they can live lawlessly, He corrects this notion. What He has said was not so that our course of life might be lawless, but that our way of life might surpass the Law. For the bonds of the law have been broken. And I say this not so that we may be humbled, but rather exalted. For both the fornicator and he who leads a virgin life step outside the measures of the law, though

---

[11] John Chrysostom, *On Galatians*, 5, 4 *PG* 61, 669.

not in the same way: the one transgresses against the law, while the other transcends it" (*ibid.*).

Jesus redeemed mankind from guilt, but did not make us irresponsible people who would simply act according to our own wishes. Love is the expression of perfection in the life of the Spirit, which is, above all, a responsible life. Love is the new law of grace, the implementation of which is the prerequisite for the justification of mankind. "But not only redemption, but after redemption, law, too, so that we shall demonstrate the worth of the State of grace."[12]

Love is not merely the new commandment, the new law, but is also the fulfillment of the law, in the sense that the whole of the legal order is inducted into the new commandment of love, which constitutes, according to the authentic interpretation of the Lord, the supreme law. Applying it in practice leads to the implementation of the other commandments: "If you love Me, you will keep My commandments." "We need everywhere works and actions, not a mere show of words ... This is love: to convince through works."[13]

Love is the prerequisite for the perfect implementation of the law.

Through love, the main cause of transgression against laws and of disorder in the Church in general is removed.

It would have been impossible for the Lord, as the All-Wise Creator, who knows human nature and its imperfections perfectly, to overlook the need for the acquisition of spiritual freedom to be supported by external laws through the "certainty of justice," which "is not merely the law telling us what to do, but grace delivering us from what has gone before and acting as certainty for what is to come."

The organization of the Church, then, is based on the commandment of love, which must be the reason behind the creation of every canon and law within it. This truth is seen by Chrysostom as having been implemented by the Lord when He assigned to Peter his pastoral function: "'He who loves Me will keep My commandments.' But His

---

[12] John Chrysostom, *On the Psalms*, 110, PG 55, 289.
[13] John Chrysostom, *On John*, Homily 75, 1 PG 59, 403.

commandments, and the sum of them, are: 'To love God is to love one's neighbor.' For if you love me, Peter, He says, tend My sheep. To love one's neighbor makes for keeping the commandments, so it is fair to say, 'On these hang all the law and the prophets.'"[14] We may, therefore, draw the conclusion that the Church is a fully organized institution on earth, with its own means of achieving the sublime purpose at which it aims. The nature and character of the Church, as a theanthropic institution, specify that its earthly organization is, above all, spiritual.

For as long as the Church has its earthly form, as the Church Militant, calling all, the righteous and unrighteous, to struggle within it to enter the ranks of the Church Triumphant in heaven; as long as the Church contests against the dark forces of this world, against its external and internal enemies; as long, that is, as its members bear the weakness of the flesh and of the old Man — in other words, until the end of the ages — the Church on earth will have the form of an organized communion of people, in which justice and the laws will constitute the secure external framework within which the free life of the Spirit will develop under the supreme authority of the Holy Trinity. The laws of the Church in no way exhaust the religious life of Man, but constitute an auxiliary but necessary feature in the perfection of the spiritual life of the faithful. It follows from this that the Church is neither a mere communion of love (*Liebeskirche*), opposed to the organization of the Church through divine law, nor yet a mere ordinary legal organization (*Rechtskirche*).

Love and the law are not opposed to each other. On the contrary, it is the synthesis of the two that gives the ecclesiastical organization the character of a spiritual institution. Law and love will be found in harmonious synthesis in Christ's Church Militant until everyone finds themselves in the kingdom of the love of God at the Second Coming.

4 LAW AND ETHICS. The law and ethics, with rules of custom or proper behavior, are the factors that govern the way in which people live to-

---

[14] John Chrysostom, *On Matthew*, Homily 71, 1, *PG* 58, 661.

gether. Ethics, insofar as it is concerned with cohabitation within society, coincides with the law at least in part, in regards to content. It coincides in part because ethics makes greater demands of people than the law, both in terms of the depth of its severity and the extent of its demands.

Besides, the rules of ethics have a broader scope of implementation than the provisions of the law, since they tend to govern the relationship of individuals toward God, toward themselves and toward all people in general.

Despite the coincidence of the rules of ethics and the provisions of the law in regards to human cohabitation, i.e. the relationship of people with their fellow men, there is nevertheless a difference between them.

1. Ethics is more concerned with judging people's inner way of thinking, while the law concentrates more on the external expression, without which inner thought does not fall within the sphere of the law.

There is, for example, the rule, the law against blasphemy. The provision of the legal code merely requires people not to blaspheme, i.e. it requires that their external behavior should be such as to avoid offending the religious sensitivities of their neighbors, of society as a whole. The code of law demands a particular kind of behavior from people, but is indifferent as to their reasons or disposition in complying with these provisions of the code.

In the above example, the provision does not examine why someone refrains from blasphemy. No doubt one person does so because he fears the punishment of the law, while another refrains for religious or spiritual reasons, or because he fears the consequences that might befall him in the life hereafter. A third may consider it barbaric, rude and unbecoming, and yet another because it pleases him to use other swear words in his contentions with his neighbor. The law is indifferent to the reason why each of these four people refrains from blasphemy and is content with the fact that blasphemy has been avoided, that in their external behavior, people have conformed to its provisions.

Ethics, on the other hand, addresses people's inner beliefs, their conscience, their thought. While the provision in the law prohibits blasphemy, the ethical rule is interested in the reasons and the intention of those who do not blaspheme. On the subject of theft, the provision in the code of law requires people not to steal, while the ethical rule goes further and says: "Do not covet that which is your neighbor's." It is not satisfied with external behavior, but states further that you are not to covet the belongings of your fellow man, thereby addressing the ethical rule to the inner person.

2. However, the feature which distinguishes the provisions in the code of law from the rules of ethics is that the provisions in the law, unlike the rules of ethics, are enforceable, either *manu militari,* enforcement in the narrow sense, or by the threat from the legal order of other unpleasant consequences on those who act to the detriment of the provisions in the law. Ethics, however, cannot exist without personal freedom. Enforced behavior has neither moral merit or demerit. The law, on the other hand, cannot respond to its mission as a factor in the harmonious coexistence of people and societies unless it has the element of enforcement, through which the legal order in societies is assured after a case of transgression. Certainly, however, enforcement is not part of the authority of the code of laws, but it appears as a substitute, as a corrective function and a disciplinary measure. Proof of this is that there are laws of the state which do not impose any sanction in the event of infraction (Constitution of Greece).

However, these distinguishing features do not correspond entirely to the nature of things, since, in regards to the former, we would observe that codes of law are not always concerned merely with people's external behavior, but are often also interested in the inner way of thinking (e.g. the distinction between malice and negligence in punishable offenses or conventional violations, or good or bad will in private law). By the same token, ethics is not always concerned simply with intentions. It does not judge with equal severity the coveting of one's neighbor's wife and actual adultery with her. A real code of law is not limited to external expressions but also monitors inner intentions through them and so arrives at a judgment on an action. Since, however, the "species specific difference" between these two summæ of rules (those of the legal codes and of ethics) has not yet been defined by philosophy in such a way as to achieve broad recognition,[15] we will stay with the above distinction for Canon Law as well, both because it serves us well enough in most instances and also because it has not been replaced by anything better.

A rule of etiquette is not a provision of a legal code nor yet a rule of ethics, but one that regulates the polite address and good manners which should inform relations between civilized people.

In conclusion, we would observe that the rules that govern the way people live together are of three kinds: those of law, those of ethics and those of etiquette. Provisions in codes of law mainly address people's external behavior. It may be possible for people to be forced by the State to comply with implementation of the provisions of the law with the aim of achieving harmonious cohabitation for all. The rules of ethics, apart from external behavior, are mainly interested in people's morals and their inner way of thinking and belief.

5 CANON LAW. After what has been said above about the basic concepts of Church and law, on which, as has been noted, Canon Law is founded, we are now able better to understand what Canon Law is. It has its place, on the one hand, in the general nature of law, but on the other, acquires its particular character from the fact that it is the law of the new people of Christ, which lives not of itself but of God. The law of the Church, then, is characterized by its divine provenance as being divine and sacred law in its fundamental ordinances and as expressing basic ecclesiological positions in the form of law.

The name "Canon Law" came from the word "canon," which originally meant a carpenter's or stonemason's rule, the stem of a straight reed or a relatively long straight piece of wood that was used in chopping and smoothing wood or stone. Thereafter, it came to mean, metaphorically, an example or prototype, a standard of excellence and a grammatical rule.

---

[15] G. Kousoulakos, "The Provenance of the Teaching of Law as 'Minimum Ethics," (in Greek), in *Μελέταις Φιλοσοφίας, γενικῆς θεωρίας καὶ τεχνικῆς τοῦ δικαίου*, vol. 1, Athens 1948, p. 135.

In Christian parlance, it also serves as a technical term denoting the authentic catalogue of the books of Holy Scripture. According to the Church Fathers, as Vlastares testifies, it denotes the ecclesiastical ordinances, the provisions of ecclesiastical law which have a legislative content and which are agreed upon by organs of the Church, and in particular by the synods. These canons, which have been formulated by the Church and which should operate within it as having the force of commands with universal validity, are different from the traditional customs of the Church[16] and from civil laws.[17]

Canon Law in the Orthodox Catholic Church is, in the strict sense, the Canons and Laws which are contained in the Nomocanon (in 14 titles), a collection compiled in the last quarter of the 9th century. In the Roman Catholic Church, the term was used for the chief collection of Canon Law known as the *Corpus Juris Canonici*, before the promulgation of the *Codex Juris Canonici* in 1917, and, since 1983, for the collection of the new *Codex Juris Canonici* based on the decisions of the Second Vatican Council. From this point of view, Canon Law is different from Ecclesiastical Law, by which is understood the sum total of the laws passed by the Church and the State, through which the life of the Church in general is ordered. Ecclesiastical Law is, therefore, broader than Canon Law, since the contents of Canon Law consist only of the ordinances and canons passed by the Church, including those in Holy Scripture and Sacred Tradition. This distinction is of great importance for the Western Church, which has a whole system of law which is independent of and uninfluenced by State legislation.

---

[16] "It has come to the notice of the holy and great Synod that in some regions and cities Deacons are giving the Eucharist to Presbyters, which is something neither the Canon nor custom has allowed..." (Canon 18 of the First Ecumenical Synod).

[17] "If for the general welfare, We have taken measures to render the civil laws more effective, with whose execution, God, through His good will toward men, has entrusted Us, how much more reason is there not for Us to compel the observance of the sacred canons, and Divine Laws, which have been promulgated for the safety of Our souls? For those who observe the sacred canons become worthy of the assistance of Our Lord God, while those who disobey them render themselves liable to be punished by Him" (Proeme of *Novella* 137 of Justinian).

For us, this distinction would lose its importance if, as in Byzantium, because of the system obtained in the relations between Church and State, the State brought its ecclesiastical laws into line with the Sacred Canons and if the Church were to accept State laws on ecclesiastical matters as being in complete agreement with the Sacred Canons. The difference between Canon and Ecclesiastical Law would, then, simply be terminological.

In any case, according to the Constitution of the Greek State now in force, the position of the Sacred Canons is safeguarded and laws concerning the Church published by the State have to be in accordance with the Sacred Canons, or else they are unconstitutional.

Another essential difference between Canon and State Ecclesiastical Law concerns the whole notion of the Church. Orthodox Canon Law teaches that only the Orthodox Church is to be considered as the Church, while State Ecclesiastical Law, which acts freely and does not have dogmatic considerations such as Orthodox theology, also places alongside the Orthodox Church other, heterodox Churches which exist in the Greek State.

Moreover, there is a difference in the way Canon Law, on the one hand, and State Ecclesiastical Law, on the other, are produced. Canon Law is for the most part shaped by the Sacred Canons, the Ecclesiastical Synodal Ordinances and the Holy Tradition of the Church in general, also by the whole theological foundation of the given canons. State Ecclesiastical Law, however, is based on the State law concerning the Church. In State Ecclesiastical Law, legal understanding and the exposition of its contents in accordance with the general principles of Civil Law are overriding, while in Canon Law theological understanding dominates.

6 CANON LAW WITHIN THE WHOLE SYSTEM OF LAW. The whole system of Law is divided into two basic branches: Public Law and Private Law (*Jus publicum; Jus privatum* or *jus civile*).

Public Law (*jus publicum*) is that branch of the law which regulates through its provisions the organization of the State and includes, for example, Constitutional Law, Administrative Law, etc.

Private Law (*jus privatum*) is that branch of the law which regulates through its provisions the relations between persons, as persons.

What is the significance of "as persons"?

In the legal relations of Public Law, one party ("legal person") is the civil power, which always appears as the bearer of some authority, while the rules of Private Law have as their principle the equality of the "legal persons" (parties) which are involved in the relationship. In other words, if the parties in the legal relationship present themselves as equals, then the relationship falls within Private Law. But if, on the other hand, one (the State) appears in a position superior to the other, then the relationship is one of Public Law.

If, therefore, we want to tell whether a provision belongs to Public or Private Law, we have to examine the position of the parties in the legal relationship they have entered upon (legal relationship is that social relationship which the law covers and regulates). If the parties are of equal authority, if they are on the same level, then we have a provision of Private Law. But if one party has a dominant position as against the other, that is, if it wields sovereign power, then we have a provision of Public Law, such as the sequestering or requisitioning of transport in the case of mobilization.

To which of these two branches of the law, then, does Canon Law belong? Public or Private?

The answer is to neither one nor the other, but rather that it is *jus sui generis*, a branch of the law parallel to but not subject to the others. The Church is complete in itself, it depends on no earthly institution, and therefore, Canon Law occupies a self-sufficient and independent position. The actions and activities of people are expressed either in relation to their own personal entity or in relation to their position as members of the State. It is in this that the legal relations of the persons have their origin, and it is this that forms the two branches of the law, Public and Private. Not all aspects nor everything that concerns them, however, are included in these two branches.

By their very nature, people are religious; they believe in God; they have a leaning toward eternity, to union with God; and this is not con-

tained either in Public or Private Law, nor is any human law able to sat-
isfy it. This proclivity toward union with God is satisfied in combination
with other people who are also imbued with this tendency, with those
in society who also feel the need for unity with God. This proclivity and
communion with those of the same aims is inherent in every person.

In pre-Christian antiquity, religion was identified with the interests
of each State, and the religions of those years were state- or nation-ori-
entated, restricted, by and large, to the borders of the nation or the state.
For this reason, the code of laws that regulated the religious organization
could hardly be independent from the civil code of the country which
confessed the religion in question.

In Ancient Rome, for example, the will of the Roman emperors was
the source of the divine and human legal codes which constituted the *jus
publicum* of the Roman Empire. The *jus sacrum* formed part of the *jus
publicum*. Among the Jews, on the other hand, the *jus sacrum* was itself
the *jus publicum*, just as the Koran is for the Muslims.

The incarnation of the Savior, however, and the foundation of His
Church as His kingdom on earth, which is not limited to one nation
alone nor, even less, to one single State, brought a radical change in the
notion of law.

The Christian faith is the common possession of all people, everywhere on earth, without discrimination in regards to ethnicity and system of government. As such, in its fundamental principles, it is not subject to any law defined by the nature of one people. Those who confess
the Christian faith are united in a single, self-regulatory and independent whole.

While, until the time of Christ, the source of law was the State, from
the time of its foundation on earth, the Church has also been a source of
law, in particular Canon Law. It follows, therefore, that since that time
both State and Church have been sources of law. The Church, founded
by Christ as a worldwide organization embracing all people, cannot be
dependent on any unilateral code of laws, but needs its own in order to
regulate its internal affairs.

Canon Law is derived from its own independent sources, and, in the first place, from Christ the Savior, the incarnate Word of God, the Founder of His Kingdom on earth, the Church. It is not dependent on any earthly power at all.

"All authority in heaven and on earth has been given to Me. Go, therefore, and make disciples of all the nations, baptizing them in the name of the Father, the Son and the Holy Spirit, teaching them to observe all that I have commanded you. And behold, I am with you all the days until the end of the age" (Matt. 28:18 – 20). The founder of the Church passed on this authority to His disciples, the Apostles, who then exercised it in His name. From the Apostles, this authority came down to the bishops, to the Church, which exercises it freely and independently, as did its Founder, Christ.

On the strength of this power alone, the form of government of the Church was composed according to the principles set out in the Gospels, its administration established, the necessary offices appointed in the Church, the way of life within it confirmed and, in general, those regulations were given which deal with matters of the Church and which constitute Canon Law.

The independence of the sources of Canon Law and of Canon Law itself are also perfectly apparent from its history. The period during which the Church was shaping its own organization was a time of persecution and martyrdom. Not only did the state refrain from any contribution to the creation of Canon Law, it did not even recognize the legal existence of the Church, which it wanted to disband and abolish. When the Roman State later became linked to the Church, Canon Law not only retained its independence, but as it developed further, from its already firmly-established bases, it had a beneficial effect on the progress of law and of justice.

From what has been said, we may conclude that according to the essential difference in legal relationships in which people engage as parties in themselves, as members of the State and members of the Church, there are three corresponding spheres of legal relationships, according to which the law is then divided into Public, Private and Canon Law.

Canon Law is derived from its own positive and self-sufficient sources, the authority of which does not trace back to any earthly power, but to the power of Christ. It is self-sufficient and independent law, parallel to both Private and Public of any State.

7 **THE METHOD OF PRESENTING CANON LAW.** The contents of Canon Law are enormous in extent, and in order to make it possible for it to be interpreted and presented systematically, it must be constructed in one comprehensive system with a well-defined method.

The systematic presentation of Canon Law varies, depending on the particular version and concept involved and on the purpose to be served. So far, a number of different methods, such as the empirical, the historical, the philosophical, the historical-philosophical and the historical-theological have been employed in its presentation.

The empirical method confines itself exclusively to the external parts of law, which refer to it simply as it is, without any investigation into its genesis nor to the fundamental principle that pervades it. If the historical method is to be beneficial to the subject, it must be linked to the other methods. If it restricts itself merely to the genesis of law and deals unilaterally with the way in which it has been shaped over time, then it impairs understanding and the precise investigation of the internal force and theological presuppositions of law, which is then judged solely on its historical presuppositions and consequences, with no reference to the foundations of theological teaching and dogma, of which it is the expression in life. The philosophical method is also unilateral, because it does not lead to any real understanding of the genesis and development of Canon Law, nor of its positive value, but to a subjective notion of it, that is of a Canon Law which, created in this way, is "philosophical" or "natural."

The historical-philosophical method need not be rejected, although the philosophical elements should be used with caution and without departing from the dogma of Orthodox theology. Of all the methods, however, the one to be preferred is the historical-theological, the most reliable, which, on the one hand, investigates and comprehends the dogmatic and theological presuppositions of Cannon Law and, on the other, its history, the historical framework within which it developed.

In regards to the classification of the material of the Canon Law of the Orthodox Church, there is no generally accepted method, and it might be said that each author attempts to make his own divisions. The same was true until recently for the law of the Roman Catholic Church.

Historically, the problem exhibits the following evolution. In the first works of Canon Law, the material was classified either by chronological order, or by importance or by the subjects dealt with by the respective canons. These systems, however, did not have internal, organic unity and were, thus, devoid of any academic value. During the Middle Ages, a system partially gained currency in the West whereby there was a five-way division of the material of Canon Law, denoted by the terms: *Judex, Judicium, clerus, sponsalia, crimen*. By the first of these was understood the priestly authority, by the second, procedure, by the third, clergy, by the fourth, marriage and by the fifth, everything referred to in the chapters concerning ecclesiastical violations. This system, by and large, has been abandoned in more recent times.

Another system also made its appearance, in imitation of Justinian's *Institutions*, in which the material of Canon Law was divided into three parts, of which the first had to do with persons, the second with things and the third with judicial acts. However, this too was soon abandoned. Today, Western canonists usually follow the division as defined by the *codex juris canonici*, that is *norme generalis, de personis, de rebus, proces sibus, de poenis*.

For the law of the Orthodox Church and especially for the autocephalous Church of Greece, the division to be found in Nikodemos Milas' *Ecclesiastical Law* is more apposite. This system was followed also by Professor Mouratidis of the University of Athens, with certain variations in regards to the naming of the individual sections, i.e.:

1. General part of Canon Law and its sources.
2. The form of government of the Church.
3. Authority and administration in the Church.

4. The life of the Church.

5. The relationship between Church and State.

We also have followed the spirit of this division, with certain variations.

That is to say, we have entered upon the following division below:

1. General Part of Canon Law. Here, general matters of Canon Law are examined in an introductory manner, as are its sources and their application.

2. The Form of Government of the Church. In this part, matters of Church organization are looked at and those aspects which are related to the organs of Church authority.

3. Authority or Administration in the Church. In this part, those things are examined which have to do with the administration of the Church in terms of its triple authority: i.e. the instructive, the sanctifying and the administrative, as also the administrative structure of the Orthodox Church today.

4. The Life of the Church. In this part, there is an examination of the sacraments and divine rites, which sanctify the various phases of people's lives, as well as time, matters concerning feasts, the honor paid to saints, etc.

5. The Relationship between Church and State. Finally, we set out the relationship between the Church, as a self-regulatory body and legal entity, with the state. Most Western canonists deal with this subject in their introduction. It is more to the point, however, to do so at the end, since it runs deeply through the canonical and legal life of the Church and so can be better understood when one has a broader spectrum of knowledge about the canonical organization of the Church.

An appendix sets out the institutions of the administration of the Ecumenical Patriarchate and the constitutional legislation of the Holy Archdiocese of America.

8 DISCIPLINES AUXILIARY TO CANON LAW. The discipline of Canon Law draws its subject matter from its own sources, though, because of its *sui generis* character as a theological discipline on the one hand but one which, in large measure, uses the methods of the science of the law. It also has recourse to certain other branches of knowledge as auxiliary to it. Of these, the most important are the following:

a) *From Theology*

1. Exegesis of the Old and New Testament. Holy Scripture is the fundamental source of Canon Law, and all the ecclesiastical ordinances are based on this.

2. Church History, which provides information on the conditions under which the institutions and the canons of Canon Law appeared, took shape and developed.

3. Dogmatics and the History of Dogma. All matters of Canon Law rest on dogmatic foundations, and, above all, the Church itself, whose organization and relations with its members and those outside it cover the whole breadth of Canon Law. This is a dogmatic concept and only in very small part a legal one.

4. Christian Ethics. As is well known, in the Christian Church, the rules of ethics and the canons of law constitute a single entity, through which the ethical order in the world is regulated.

5. Patrology and Church Literature.

6. Liturgics. The sacraments, the rituals and the liturgical life of the Church produce law and rest upon the canons of the Church.

7. Pastoral Theology (the relationship between the shepherd and the flock).

b) *From the Science of Law*

1. The Philosophy of Law, through which people are taught and made familiar with the elevated principles of the law.

2. Greco-Roman Law, with which Canon Law forms an unbroken entity in regards to its historical development. The influence of Greco-Roman Law on Canon Law and vice versa was very great. From as long ago as the first centuries of the Christian Church, when the Roman emperors were not Christian, the members of the Church, as Roman citizens, were required to obey relevant imperial ordinances, at least on some matters.

Roman Law was of even greater significance for the Church later, when the emperors were Christian. The Church followed ordinances of the civil law in all those legal matters where it had still not formed its own institutions and particularly in the formation of administrative institutions. Likewise, however, the influence of Canon Law on Roman was very great and mainly consisted of improvement in terms of ethical values and justice.

3. Hebrew Law was of great importance for the New Testament, since many ordinances of Mosaic legislation came into the Church, while Christ Himself, the founder of the Church, declared: "I have not come to abolish the law but to fulfill it" (Matt. 5:17).

4. The Law of every country or State where there is an Orthodox Church presence, because of the relations which are created between Church and State, as well as the specific characteristics created by these relations in the life of each local Church.

CHAPTER TWO

The Sources of Canon Law

1 **CONCEPT AND CLASSIFICATION OF THE SOURCES OF CANON LAW.** By the expression "sources of the law," both in the field of Canon Law and, indeed, in any other branch of the law, we mean two things: either the manner, the means, by which any existing legal system produces or applies law ("sources" in the essential, legislative meaning, *fontes juris essendi*); or we mean the monuments, the texts, through which we acquire knowledge of law as it was, or is, applied in a particular place and time ("sources" in the formal, diagnostic meaning, *fontes juris cognoscendi*).

To sources, in the first sense of the term, belong the ecclesiastical canons, law and custom; while to the second belong legal works, judicial verdicts and other documents, and information scattered throughout non-legal texts.[1]

In regards to the unity which must prevail in any society, there can only be one valid source of law, as the original from which others are or may be produced later. In the Christian Church, the original source of its law is the will of its Founder, from which all the other sources, ecclesiastical legislation and Church custom, take their shape and form. Since Canon Law, in its objective meaning, contains not only laws passed by the Church, but also those promulgated by the State (mainly Roman

---

[1] Cf. Anastasios Christophilopoulos, *Greek Ecclesiastical Law* (in Greek), Athens 1965, p. 24.

"Byzantine" ones) and recognized by the Church — laws which look to the external good estate of the Church and the consolidation of the relations between Church and State — civil laws are, therefore, also considered sources of law. Their significance and importance for Canon Law is auxiliary and historical.

The sources are presented in accordance with their degree of importance and their relationship to the initial source of Canon Law.

The fundamental laws of the Church are contained in Holy Scripture and Sacred Tradition. These laws do not include detailed ordinances concerning every individual part of Church life, so special work was required to produce these ordinances from the initial laws and to define precisely, through positive statutes: how the governance of the Church was to be established in accordance with the fundamental law expressed in Holy Scripture; how the administration of the Church should be organized in accordance with its purpose and its means; what were the rights and the duties of the members of the Church according to their various positions within it; and generally should the need arise, to promulgate its own laws and canons capable of consolidating order in the Church in all things in accordance with the spirit of the fundamental laws introduced into the Church at the time of its birth. The Church, exercising the authority which it received from its Founder, and on the basis of the precepts of Holy Scripture, had to supply this need. The authority of the Church is concentrated in the synod of the canonical ecclesiastical leaders (Matt. 18:17–20). Consequently, the synodal authority had to adopt and define what was necessary for the general organization of the Church. It was from this that Church legislation arose, the statutes of which, together with Holy Scripture and Sacred Tradition, constitute the basic source of Canon Law.

The highest legislative authority in the Church belongs to the Ecumenical Synods. Apart from these, provincial synods, convening in the various local Churches, either periodically or as circumstances dictate, also exercise legislative powers within precisely defined canonical bounds. Finally, the bishops also exercise legislative powers in the ecclesiastical areas entrusted to them, in the name of the synodal authority and within defined boundaries.

The laws and ordinances adopted by the legislative authority of the Church are given different names in the sources of law, depending on their principles and causes, or on the subject they deal with or according to the formulas in which they were published and so on. The usual name for the statutes dealing with the governance and life of the Church is "canon." The fundamental collections, apart from the canons adopted by the synods of the Church, also contain letters from certain Fathers of the Church, which, because of their content, are called "Canonical Epistles" (κανονικαὶ ἐπιστολαί). Those which provide answers to related questions are called "Canonical Responses" (κανονικαί ἀποκρίσεις), while a letter addressed to all the Churches and having weight and validity in all of them is called an "Encyclical Epistle" (ἐγκύκλιος ἐπιστολή). When the fundamental collection of canons was completed, the epistles which were published synodally under the supervision of the leaders of the Church and especially the Patriarch of Constantinople were given a variety of names in the volumes of law: i.e. tome (τόμος), synodal tome (συνοδικὸς τόμος), memorandum (ὑπόμνημα), synodal vote (συνοδικὴ ψῆφος), synodal note (συνοδικὸν σημείωμα), synodal decision (συνοδικὴ ἀπόφασις), synodal order (συνοδικὸν ἐπίσταλμα), synodal letter (συνοδικὸν γράμμα), patriarchal pittacium (πατριαρχικόν πιττάκιον), synodal response (συνοδικὴ ἀπόκρισις), synodal resolution (συνοδικὸν ψήφισμα), patriarchal sigillium (πατριαρχικὸν σιγίλλιον) and synodal act (συνοδικὴ πρᾶξις). The status and validity of the canons, canonical epistles and canonical responses depended on the status and canonicity of the publishing ecclesiastical authority and their ratification by the universal Church, while the status of the various synodal ordinances depended on their subject and dedication.

For practical reasons, it is possible to divide the sources into two groupings: 1) general sources which concern the whole Church; and 2) specific sources which, in parallel with the general, refer to the autocephalous Churches as they exist today. The specific sources will not concern us here, except those of the Church of Greece and the Ecumenical Patriarchate.

The general sources can be distinguished, according to the measure of their importance, as follows: 1) fundamental sources, to which category belong Holy Scripture, Sacred Tradition and the Sacred Canons; 2) supplementary sources, to which belong the ordinances of the synods and canonical epistles of the Shepherds of the Orthodox Church, which were published after the completion of the fundamental canonical collection and are considered supplementary to the fundamental sources and custom; 3) auxiliary sources, i.e. canonical opinions, studies and even the interpretations of outstanding canonists recognized by the Church, which were in use as a true hermeneutical resource in the application of Canon Law, and also the ancient ecclesiastical civil laws promulgated by the Roman ("Byzantine") emperors and which were included in the canonical collections.

2 THE FUNDAMENTAL SOURCES. a) *Holy Scripture.* Holy Scripture, and especially the New Testament, is not only historical and dogmatic, but also contains rules of law and, indeed, the basic ordinances concerning the Church, which were introduced by the Lord Himself.

The Christian Church was founded on the will of its divine Founder, who is ever active within it until the end of the ages (Matt. 28:20).

This will gives life to the Church both in terms of faith and law. Canon Law is based on it and through it acquires its validity and status. When Jesus Christ completed the Church on earth, He did not leave laws or rules to regulate its external life, but rather provided an indication and definition of the purpose of the Church, granting it the authority to use certain means for the achievement of its goal and promising it constant succor.

Christ's commandments are those principles on which the Church has been founded and has developed its life on earth. On these principles, as the original source, Canon Law has been based and has developed. These commandments of the Lord, contained in the New Testament, constitute divine law (*jus divinum*) and, as an expression of divine will, are eternal, unalterable and irreversible, they have status and validity for the whole Church; and they are the fundamental laws of the Christian Church. Such commandments, among others, are those referring to the service of the Apostles (Matt. 18:18; Jn. 20:23); to the relations of the Apostles among themselves (Mark 9:34ff); to baptism and the divine Eucharist (Mark 16:16; Matt. 28:19; Jn. 3:5; Luke 22:19; I Cor. 11:23 – 25); to marriage (Matt. 5:32; 19:3); to taking oaths (Matt. 5:33 – 36); to the Church's judicial jurisdiction (Matt.18:15 – 17); to recompense for spiritual ministries (Luke 10:7 – 12; Matt. 10:10 – 15; Jn. 12:5 – 6; 13:29); and to relations with the State (Matt. 22:17 – 22; Luke 22 – 26).

Subject to these commandments are many other ordinances concerning Canon Law, which were introduced by the Apostles on the strength of the Lord's command. Thus, the Apostle Paul in I Cor. 7:10 says: "… I enjoin, not I but the Lord" and then immediately afterwards "… I say, not the Lord." Among these Apostolic ordinances introduced on the strength of the Lord's command, it is possible to include those concerning ordination and the installation of presbyters in each place (Acts 14:23; Tit. 1:5); on tractability and obedience to the presbyters (Heb. 13:7, 17; I Peter 5:5); on the qualifications and duties of the Church leaders (I Tim. 3:1ff; 4:14, 5:22; II Tim 1:6; Tit. 1:5ff; I Pet. 5:1ff); on deacons (I Tim. 3:8ff); on maintenance of the clergy (I Cor. 9:6ff; I Tim. 5:16 – 17); on accusations against the clergy (I Tim. 5:19); on worship (I Cor. 11:4ff and 20; I Cor. 14:27ff and 16:2; James 5:16); on how to deal with the sacriligeous (I Cor. 5:9ff; 2 Thess. 3:6; I Tim. 5:20; James 5:16); on marriage (Rom. 7:1ff; I Cor. 5:1; 7:2, 10 and 39; 9:5; Eph. 5:22; Col. 3:18; I Pet. 3:1), on relations with the civil authority (Rom. 13:1 ff; I Cor. 6:1; I Pet. 2:13; I Tim. 2:1ff; Tit. 3:1); and on relations with non-Christians (I Cor. 5:9ff).

The Church as the authentic interpreter of Holy Scripture produces the principles of ecclesiastical legislation from it. The injunctions of Holy Scripture concerning the fundamental truths of the faith and of ecclesiastical governance have always been accepted by the Church, which has kept them as laws with absolute authority.

The Old Testament is also in use as a source of Canon Law. The legal ordinances of the Old Testament are valid only insofar as they have been repeated by Christian legal sources.[2] By the same token, provisions in Mosaic law concerning marriage are still applied today in Canon Law. The general prohibition in Deut. 23:19ff, on taking interest on loans applies only to the clergy.[3]

B) *Holy Tradition.* Another important source of Canon Law, after Holy Scripture, is Sacred Tradition. What we mean by Holy Tradition is not the simple, external event of the transmission of certain observances from one generation to another, or from one Church to another, but the successive, precise and irrevocable retention of fundamental principles in the universal Church, in both the teaching of the faith and in ecclesiastical administration, principles which were laid down and defined by the Founder of the Church Himself and, after Him, by those who first organized the Church and exercised the pastoral office within it,[4] the Holy Fathers.

Holy Scripture contains in general terms the fundamental bases of the system of governance, administration and life of the Church, but not the details thereof. These were defined by the Apostles, who, at the time that the Church was being organized, declared orally to those they had ordained how they should govern and have stewardship over the things concerning it. Thus, the Apostle Paul writes to Timothy that the latter should keep the example of the sound teaching which he had heard from him and that he should confide what he had heard to trustworthy people who would be able to teach others (II Tim 1:13 and 2:2). In their epistles to their flocks in the Church, the Apostles provide only general instructions on the administration of the Church, usually adding that they will deal with the rest in person when they come to visit the locality (I Cor.

---

[2] Canon 87 of Basil the Great.

[3] "Should a bishop or a presbyter or a deacon demand interest on loans, let him be suspended or defrocked" (44th Apostolic Canon). Cf. Canon 17 of the First Ecumenical Synod, Canon 10 of the Quinisext, etc.

[4] Nicodeme Milas, *The Ecclesiastical Law of the Eastern Orthodox Church...*, pp. 56–57 (in Greek translation, Athens 1906).

11:34). Either that or they permit the shepherds to run the administration on the basis of the verbal instructions which the Apostles have given to them (Tit. 1:5). It is entirely in keeping with the character of the Apostles that they considered their oral instructions to their shepherds to be more important than the epistles that they wrote to them (I Tim. 3:14 and 15): "I am writing these instructions to you so that, if I am delayed, you may know how to behave in the household of God, which is the Church of the living God, the pillar and bulwark of the truth."

In this way, the most important ordinances concerning the governance and life of the Church were already in place in the churches founded by the Apostles, even before they were explicitly defined by formal law, and have been observed by those who succeeded the Apostles in unbroken tradition.

This tradition is not merely the transmission of commandments and statutes, but the precise and unshakeable retention of the fundamental principles of the faith, of administration and the system of governance.

Tradition, as a source for the maintenance of ecclesiastical order, has always been accorded by the Church the same status as that of Holy Scripture.

Canon 21 of the Synod in Gangra declares that the Church must observe "that which has been handed down by divine Scriptures and the Apostolic traditions." The importance of this tradition is often extolled by the canons of the Ecumenical Synods as "the ancient customs to be kept" (Canon 6, First Ecumenical Synod), as "the ancient tradition" (Canon 7, First Ecumenical Synod), as "the old and canonical law" (Canon 13, First Ecumenical Synod).[5] Concerning these laws, it is declared that nothing new which is in opposition to the traditional teaching of the Church is to be introduced, so that the fundamental teaching may not be violated: "Should any bishop or presbyter not act in accordance with the order handed down by the Apostles ... let him be deposed, as ... making innovations to traditions" (canon 32, Quinisext Synod). Canon 7 of the Sev-

[5] Cf. Canon 18, First Ecumenical Synod; 2 and 7 of the Second; 7 and 8 of the Third; 1, 2, 13, 29 and 87 of the Quinisext et al.

enth Ecumenical Synod states that whatever has been overlooked and has gone uncared for should be renewed and reinstated in accordance with the written and unwritten institutions and should thus be defined. Anyone violating ecclesiastical traditions is to be deposed.

Canon 91 of Saint Basil contains the following noteworthy interpretation on the importance of tradition: "Of the dogmas and oral instruction (preachings) preserved in the Church, we possess some from written teaching and some from tradition handed down to us by the Apostles in mystery, both of which have the same validity in regards to piety (i.e. religion or faith); accordingly, no one gainsays these, at least no one who has any experience at all in ecclesiastical matters. For if we should undertake to disregard the unwritten tradition of customs on the basis that they have no great force, we should unwittingly damage the Gospel in vital parts and should rather be left with *kerygma* (preaching) confined to mere name."

This importance has always been accorded to tradition within the universal Church, particularly that obtaining in the most outstanding churches in regards to ecclesiastical life, so that in itself it already constitutes law and there is no need for it to be invested with a particular legal form.

c) *The So-called Apostolic Ecclesiastical Ordinances.* Before the formulation of the Sacred Canons by the Church in the first period of their history, certain anonymous works constituted a codification of the Apostolic tradition and of the customs that evolved at that time. The titles of these works hint at their immediate Apostolic provenance, or at a claim for the Apostolic spirit. Of these, the following can be considered sources of Canon Law:

i. *The Didache of the Lord through the Twelve Apostles to the Gentiles.* The *Didache* is a short work consisting of 16 chapters. It was probably composed in Syria or Palestine in the 2nd century. Many theories have been put forward concerning the dating of this text (1st – 4th centuries). *The Didache of the Lord* is a work of the Church. In it, the teaching of the two roads, the good and the bad, is developed; matters concerning worship are set out; and Church governance is dealt with, i.e. those questions pertaining to Apostles, Prophets, Teachers, bishops and deacons.

Finally, there is mention of the last things and the judgment to come.

ii. *The Didaskalia (Teaching) of the Apostles.* This is a text composed probably in Syria in the 3rd century. The Greek original has been lost, but a Syriac translation has survived, as has part of a Latin one.

iii. *The Constitutions through Clement and the Ecclesiastical Canons of the Holy Apostles.* This work consists of thirty chapters. The Twelve Apostles are presented, speaking in succession and initially giving commandments on Christian ethics and then on the organization of the Church, the qualifications of the clergy and of widows. It is a work dating from the 3rd or beginning of the 4th century. It was written in Syria or in Egypt. Apart from the Greek original, Coptic, Latin, Arabic, Syriac and Ethiopian translations have survived.

iv. *The Apostolic Constitutions.* The Constitutions or Ordinances of the holy, all-praised Apostles are a collection of ordinances which refer to matters of ecclesiastical law, good order and worship and were supposedly published by the Apostles, through Clement. Of course, they have no connection with Clement; they are a work produced probably in the second half of the 4th century in Syria. Some compiler, probably of semi-Arian persuasions, collected, supplemented and unified certain pre-existing texts and made this collection.

The Apostolic Constitutions consist of eight books and are a miscellany. The first six books deal with the duties of laymen and clergy and are an elaboration of *The Teaching of the Apostles* with variants. The first portion of the seventh book deals with the two ways (good and evil) and is an elaboration of the *Didache,* while the second is concerned with worship, especially baptism. The eighth book deals with charismatic gifts, ordinations and various matters of worship and ecclesiastical good order, while attached at the end are the eighty-five Apostolic Canons, there will be more about these later.

d) *The Sacred Canons.* The Sacred Canons, which are the fundamental source of the Canon Law of the Orthodox Church, are those of the Holy Apostles, of the Ecumenical and Local Synods and the canons of the Fathers of the Church, ratified by an Ecumenical Synod.

i. *The Apostolic Canons.* The collection bearing the title "Canons of the Holy and Most Venerable Apostles" has no connection with the Apostles. It was compiled later, with a pseudo-inscription, and contains eighty-five canons, pertaining, however, in an Orthodox spirit, matters concerned with ecclesiastical administration and order, as these had been formed toward the end of the 4th century.

These canons were the last (47th) chapter of the eighth book of the Apostolic Constitutions, but for a long time, it was believed, particularly in the East, that they were genuine canons of the Apostles, even though the supplementary (2nd) canon of the Quinisext Ecumenical Synod in Trullo clearly states that these canons were handed down "in the name of the holy and glorious Apostles," which means that this Ecumenical Synod was certain as to their inauthenticity.

In the West, these canons were the object of doubts concerning their authenticity from the beginning, while for a long time, no more than the first fifty were known there, contained in the collection of Dionysius the Lesser (Exiguus, circa 500 AD) with the observation "*qui dicuntur Apostolorum*," which does not differ from the "in the name of the holy… Apostles" of the Ecumenical Synod in Trullo. In any case, the authenticity of these canons became the object of scientific research mostly after the 16th century. Much coordinated research demonstrated that the matters with which these canons dealt testify to the fact that it is not possible to support the view that they derive directly from the Apostles. It may be that these canons come from the Apostolic tradition retained orally in the Church by the successors of the Apostles. There is nothing in them that contradicts the teaching of the Holy Apostles, and their contents are in accord with what the Apostles' successors expounded. It follows, then, that though these canons were not set out in written form by the Apostles, the name 'Apostolic' befits them, as does the importance accorded to them by the Church. The reasons for opposition to the authenticity of the Apostolic Canons are, firstly, that they were never included by the Church in the Canon of the New Testament; secondly, that until the First Ecumenical Synod, there is absolutely no mention of them anywhere, and thirdly, that their contents presuppose an organizational evolution of the Church much later than the Apostolic age.

On the basis of the different number of these canons mentioned in various manuscripts and collections, criticism has largely been concerned with ascertaining their number, which is sometimes put at fifty, sometimes at eighty-one, eighty-two or eighty-four and, finally, at eighty-five. The principal editors and critics of the canons express different views on their precise number, though among these opinions, the most prevalent is the number eighty-five, which agrees with that accepted by John Scholastikos (6th century).

Apart from the number of the canons, however, critics have also been concerned to establish the time and place of their composition. Many and varied views have been advanced by older and also by more modern critics, and according to these opinions, the canons were composed some time between the end of the 2nd and 4th centuries. Hefele considers these canons to be the sources for those of the First Ecumenical Synod, while Funk believes that they sprang from the canons of the synods in Antioch, Laodicea, Constantinople (381) and Constantinople (394).

In any case, these canons, which are regarded by some scholars as springing from earlier ones and by others as sources, have retained their absolute status in the Orthodox Church to this day. It is precisely their ratification by the Synod in Trullo, and the simultaneous rejection of the other Apostolic Constitutions as "spurious" and "foreign to piety" which proves that these contained nothing out of harmony with the Orthodox dogmas of the Church and that they were not written "erstwhile by the heterodox in order to affront the Church." The status of these canons is also demonstrated by their translation into the Coptic, Arabic and Latin languages.[6]

ii. *The Canons of the Ecumenical Synods.* Seven Ecumenical Synods, convening at various times between 325 and 787 AD, are recognized by

---

[6] A. Alivizatos, Ὁι Ἱεροί Κανόνες, Athens 1949.

the Orthodox Church. The convocation of these Ecumenical Synods as organs representing the whole Church was made possible by the cessation of the persecutions and by the recognition of the Christian Church, by the State, as the legal religion. The Ecumenical Synods were usually called on the occasion of dogmatic problems which were causing turbulence not only within the Church, but also within the State — hence the involvement of emperors, the aim of which was to ensure order and peace in the empire. The Ecumenical Synods are the highest Church body, in that they constitute the supreme ecclesiastical authority, exercising the highest administrative, judicial and legislative power. They are, however, "circumstantial" in the sense that they are not convened regularly. The particular task of the synods is the formulation of dogma as articles (ὅροι) and of matters of administration and order as canons (κανόνες).

Of the seven Ecumenical Synods, only five published canons, i.e. the First, Second, Third, Fourth and Seventh. The Fifth and Sixth Synods did not do so. The Fathers who took part in the Sixth Ecumenical Synod, however, were recalled to Constantinople, and in particular to the imperial hall known as the Trullos (Cupola), in the year 691 – 692 and published canons for the two Ecumenical Synods, the Fifth and Sixth. For this reason, these canons are known as the canons of the Quinisext Ecumenical Synod.

The first Ecumenical Synod was called in the year 325 in Nicea, Bithynia, by Constantine the Great, on the occasion of the heresy of Arius, who, as is well known, denied the divinity of the Lord and preached that "there was a time when He was not." The bishops who attended this synod were 318 in number. Initially, Eustathios of Antioch was chairman, since Alexander of Alexandria was Arius' accuser. Thereafter, the chair was taken by Hosios of Cordoba and others. The emperor himself was the honorary president. The First Ecumenical Synod was of great importance and constituted the basis for all the other Ecumenical Synods.

The First Ecumenical Synod condemned Arianism and adopted the term "*homoousion*" to refute him. It also settled the Novatian and Meletian schisms and ordained that the feast of Pascha was to be held on the first Sunday after the full moon of the vernal equinox. Matters of Church order and administration were arranged, such as those concerning ordination and so on, and the first articles of the Creed were formulated.

The First Ecumenical Synod published twenty canons. Apart from these, there are another eighty or eighty-four canons included in a variety of collections, but unlike the twenty, they are spurious and have no canonical validity. In all likelihood, they are of Western provenance and were used for the support of the views of the Church of Rome. Outstanding personalities at the First Ecumenical Synod were Alexander of Alexandria, Eustathios of Antioch, Makarios of Jerusalem, Nicholas of Myra, Spyridon of Trimythous, Hosios of Cordoba and others. Most outstanding of all, however, was the then archdeacon and later Archbishop of Alexandria, Athanasios the Great.

The Second Ecumenical Synod was called in the year 381 in Constantinople, in order to combat the budding heresy of Makedonios, Bishop of Constantinople, and his adherents — known as the *pneumatomachoi* (strivers against the Spirit) — who considered the Holy Spirit to be a creation of God. One hundred and fifty bishops from the Eastern part of the Empire took part in this Synod. Initially, the Second did not have the character of an Ecumenical Synod, but was recognized as such by the Fourth Ecumenical Synod in Chalcedon. This Second Synod was chaired by Meletios of Antioch until his death and then by Gregory the Theologian, who had at that time been elected Patriarch of Constantinople. After his resignation from the Patriarchate, he was replaced by Nektarios, his successor to the throne. The emperor himself was present at the beginning of the proceedings of the Synod. Seven canons are attributed to this Synod, of which, however, only the first four actually belong to it. Canons 5 and 6 properly belong to the synod which met the following year, also in Constantinople, and continued the work of the Second Ecumenical, while the 7th canon has nothing to do with either, and is, in fact, an "epistle" from Gennadios I, Patriarch of Constantinople (458 – 471), to Martyrios of Antioch "Concerning the manner in which heretics should be received into the Holy Catholic Church."

The following decisions were taken at the Second Synod: The dogma of the Holy Trinity was completed and defined that the Holy Spirit was the third Person thereof and equal to the Father. Thus, the Creed formulated in Nicea took its final form.

Canon 3 of this Synod is worthy of note, since it gives the priority of honor to the Patriarch of Constantinople, after Rome, "since it (Constantinople) is the New Rome."

The Third Ecumenical Synod met at Ephesus, in 431, on the occasion of the Nestorian heresy.

Two hundred bishops took part in it, mostly from the East. Cyril of Alexandria presided. The Synod accepted the twelve anathemas of Cyril against Nestorios and published eight canons, of which the first seven refer to the ecclesiastical turmoil which arose from the *kakodoxy* (false belief) of Nestorios. Canon 8 is concerned with the independence and autocephaly of the Church of Cyprus. Finally, there is a letter to the Synod in Pamphylia concerning its bishop Eustathios, who had resigned and then later retracted. This letter is important, since, for the first time, it defines the matter of the resignation of bishops.

The Fourth Ecumenical Synod was called in 451 in Chalcedon, during the reign of Emperor Markianos, in order to combat the new Christological heresy of Monophysitism.

This Synod defrocked Dioskouros, who, despite having been invited three times, did not attend to defend himself. It also anathematized Eutyches. Six hundred and fifty Fathers took part in this Synod. Thirty canons were published, which are contained in various collections. Important among them are the canons referring to the monastic life. Particularly worthy of mention is canon 28, which canonically ratifies the jurisdiction of Constantinople over Pontos, as well, and over Asia, Thrace and those living in barbarian lands. It also ratifies the rights of the Bishop of Constantinople and grants the same primacy of honor to him as to the Bishop of Rome. The ancient Church, through these canons, accorded the primacy of honor "to the throne of older Rome, because of the royalty of this city" on account of it being the imperial capital, and continues "and motivated by the same object and aim, the one hundred and fifty most God-beloved bishops (i.e. the Second Ecumenical Synod) accorded the like primacy to the most holy throne of New Rome, with good reason deeming that the city which is the seat of an emperor (king) and of a senate, and is equal to old royal (imperial) Rome in respect of other privileges and priorities, should be magnified also as she is in respect of ecclesiastical affairs, as being second after her ...".

It is quite clear from this that the ancient Church initially accorded the primacy of honor to the Bishop of Rome, mainly because of its geographical and political position as the capital of the Roman Empire. By the same token, it awarded the same primacy of honor to Constantinople, the successor of Rome as the capital of the empire. It follows, then, that the priority of Rome was not initially linked to the apostolic foundation of the see, nor to the capacity of the Bishop of Rome, who claimed to be the successor to the Apostle Peter.

The representatives of the Pope at the Fourth Ecumenical Synod (his Legates) did not accept canon 28, while the Pope himself wrote a letter to the emperor (May 22, 452) in which he protested against the equivalence established in canon 28 between the patriarchal throne of Constantinople and the throne of Rome.

The Quinisext Ecumenical Synod in Trullo convened in the year 691, in the reign of Justinian. It was called a continuation of the Sixth, and its purpose was to supplement the Fifth and Sixth Ecumenical Synods, in regards to the publication of canons, inasmuch as the former (Fifth and Sixth) were concerned exclusively with dogmatic matters and had not published any canons with legislative content. Besides, because of the turmoil and irregularities caused by the heresies mentioned above, Church discipline and good order had been prejudiced, so there was a need to restore this with canons which would have the validity of an Ecumenical Synod. Through canon 2, this Synod ratified the Apostolic Canons and those of local synods, as well as those of the most outstanding Fathers of the Church. In this way, these canons acquired universal validity.

This Synod published one hundred and two canons, that is more than any other synod which was held in the East. Not all its decisions were accepted by the Western Church, however, since some of them conflicted with the practices followed there. One such was canon 55, which condemned fasting on Saturdays during Lent, another was 13, which permitted the ordination of married priests and deacons, while the most outstanding instance is canon 36, which repeated the equivalence between the thrones of Constantinople and Rome, as adopted by canon 28 of the Fourth Ecumenical Synod.

There was no such conflict initially, however. The delegates of Rome participated in the Synod, while the signature of Basil, Archbishop of Gortyna, appears among the first in the minutes of the Synod, as having "also the place... of the whole Synod of the holy Church of Rome."[7] When, at the Seventh Ecumenical Synod, these canons were confirmed as canons of the Sixth, the representatives of Rome made no objection. Pope Hadrian, in his letter to Patriarch Tarasios and in another to the bishops of France, writing in defense of the Seventh Ecumenical Synod, declared that he recognized and accepted its canons.

Innocent III refers to canon 82 and calls it a canon of the Sixth Ecumenical Synod. Even the canonist Gratian considers these canons to be canons of the Sixth Ecumenical Synod. As time went by, however, some in the West began to doubt the validity of these canons for the reasons mentioned above, maintaining that those who accepted these canons erred.[8]

The Seventh Ecumenical Synod was convened in Nicea in 787, during the reign of Empress Irene and her son, Constantine VI, in order to settle the question of Iconoclasm, which it condemned. Tarasios of Constantinople presided. The whole Church, Eastern and Western, was represented at this Synod.

It published twenty-two canons of a generally administrative and legislative nature. To these was attached the letter on simony from Tar-

---

[7] Mansi, XI, p. 898.
[8] For the legislative work of the Quinisext Synod, see G. Gavardinas, *The Quinisext Ecumenical Synod and Its Legislative Work* (in Greek), ed. Epectasis, Katerini 1998.

asios, Patriarch of Constantinople, to Pope Hadrian, which was composed after the closure of the Synod and was therefore not included in its canons.

The Synods which are linked to the conflict between Patriarchs Ignatios and Photios are also of particular importance, as are those dealing with the dispute between the Eastern and Western Church.

The First/Second Synod of Constantinople, which met in the Church of the Holy Apostles (861), is called "First/Second" because it convened twice. That is, after the cancellation of the first session, because of a revolt by the heretic minority, it reconvened. The 9th century may be considered both as being a stormy one for the Church, and also as very sad because of its later effects on the unity of the Church.

The dethronement of Patriarch Ignatios and the elevation of Photios to the throne of Constantinople produced a great deal of unrest in the East and also provided the Pope with an excuse to meddle in the internal affairs of the Patriarchate of Constantinople.

A major contributory factor in the turmoil of this century was the upheaval produced by the iconoclast heresy.

Three hundred and eighteen Fathers, as well as the Emperor Michael III were present at the First/Second Synod. The Pope was represented by his own delegates. At this Synod, the condemnation of the iconoclasts was ratified, Ignatios was defrocked, and the election of Patriarch Photios was recognized as canonical. Seventeen canons were published, dealing with the organization of the monastic life and with Church discipline. These canons were included in the collections of canons and in *The Rudder* (*Pedalion*) are placed immediately after the canons of the Seventh Ecumenical Synod, as they are in Rallis and Potlis' collection. In the most important Slavonic collections, they are given the penultimate place in the series of the Sacred Canons.

The Synod of the year 879/880, which met in Constantinople, in the Church of Holy Wisdom (Hagia Sophia). Three hundred and eighty-three Fathers took part in this, while the Pope was represented by three delegates. Photios was recognized as the canonical patriarch by this synod, too, and peace between East and West was confirmed. It published three canons which referred to Church discipline. It characterized itself as ecumenical, and the canons published by it have never been challenged in the Orthodox Church. In the *Pedalion* and the collection by Rallis and Potlis, they appear after the canons of the First/Second Synod of Constantinople, while in the Slavonic collections, they occupy last place among the canons of the Ecclesiastical Synods.

iii. *The Canons of the Local Synods.* During the first period of Church history, when, for many reasons, but particularly the persecutions, the Church was unable to call Ecumenical Synods, local synods met in certain areas, following the example of the Apostolic Synod (Acts 15:6ff). In these, the bishops who took part in the synod discussed a variety of matters of general importance which had arisen in their own regions and also published their resolutions in the form of canons. These canons were compulsory for the above regions whose bishops participated in these local synods. We have many such local synods, but their canons have only historical importance today. Only the canons of the local synods referred to in the 2nd canon of the Quinisext Ecumenical Synod in Trullo and ratified by it acquired universal validity and are, therefore, incorporated in the collections of canons after the canons of the Ecumenical Synods. These are the following:

a) The Synod in Carthage, which convened in 256. Its sole canon refers to the validity of baptism performed by heretics. This synod rejected the baptism of heretics and required that heretics entering the Church be rebaptized.

b) The Synod of Ankara in Galatia, 314 AD. After the persecutions of Christians under Maximinus, when peace was reestablished in the Church, many Christians who had apostatized through fear or some other reason desired to return to the bosom of the Church. This synod aimed at regulating the matter of how the Church was to receive those who had fallen during the persecutions. Eighteen bishops met, under the chairmanship of Vitellios, Archbishop of Antioch. Twenty-five canons were published, of which the first nine define how presbyters and the laity who had fallen during the persecutions of Maximinus were to be received back into the Church. Canon 10 is worthy of note, since it allows deacons to marry after ordination, provided they had declared before ordination that it was their wish to do so. This canon was later deemed to have been occasioned by circumstances and was, therefore, revoked.

c) The Synod in Neocæsarea, Cappadocia, which met between the years 314 and 325. At this synod, twenty-four bishops met under the chairmanship of Vitellios, Bishop of Antioch, and published fifteen canons, which refer to matters of marriage, repentance and Church discipline.

d) The Synod of Gangra in Paphlagonia, which met, probably in 340, on the occasion of the exaggerated praise lavished upon the ascetic life by the Arianizing Bishop of Sebasteia, Eustathios, and his supporters. By their attitude, they had produced disorder in the Church and great confusion. Thirteen bishops took part in the synod, with Eusebios of Nicomedia in the chair, and twenty-one canons were published, of which twenty are aimed at Eustathios. Canon 21 is an epilogue to the other twenty.

e) The Synod in Antioch, 341. This synod convened on the occasion of the inauguration of the new church in Antioch, the so-called golden Basilica, the construction of which had been begun by Constantine the Great. One hundred bishops assembled and, when they had performed the inauguration, went on to convene a synod under the chairmanship of the Bishop of Antioch, Placetus. This synod dealt with dogmatic matters related to the Arian controversy and published twenty-five canons on Church order and discipline which enjoyed great respect in both the Eastern and Western Church.

f) The Synod in Laodicea, Phrygia, which convened between the years 342 and 381. This synod was attended by many bishops of Asia Minor and published 60 canons, most of which were of ethical or liturgical content, the prime source for which were the canons of the First Ecumenical Synod.

g) The Synod in Sardica (today's Sofia, Bulgaria) which was called in 343, on the occasion of the Arian controversies and the persecution of Saint Athanasios. Three hundred and seventy-six bishops took part, three hundred from the Western Church and seventy-six from the Eastern. They met under the chairmanship of Hosios of Cordoba. After the departure of the Arianizing bishops (about eighty), because the terms proposed by them were not accepted, those remaining reinstated the clergy persecuted by the heresy, among whom was Athanasios the Great, judging them innocent of the charges brought against them.

On the other hand, they condemned many of their opponents to defrocking and excommunication. They also published twenty-one canons. These were not, however, accepted immediately in the Church of the East, because they were published by a synod whose members were mostly bishops from the West, who, among other things, recognized the right of appeal to the Pope (canons 4 and 5).

h) The Synod in Constantinople in 394, which assembled under the chairmanship of Nektarios, Patriarch of Constantinople. Nineteen bishops took part and were concerned with the controversy between Bishops Agapios and Bagadios, both of whom wished to be bishop of the metropolitan throne of Bostra in Arabia. By a resolution of this synod, defrocking of a bishop was forbidden by two or three bishops. Instead, such a decision had to be submitted to the synod of bishops of the whole eparchy, and, after a resolution by the later synod of Carthage, not less than twelve (canon 12).

i) The Synod of Cartagena, in 419, which was called to examine the question of whether the Pope of Rome had the right to hear appeals against synodal resolutions of the Church in Africa. This synod convened under the chairmanship of Aurelius of Carthage, with two hundred and seventeen bishops participating, including delegates of the Pope, who put forward the argument that the right of the Pope derived from the canons of the First Ecumenical Synod.

This synod was constrained to have recourse to the Churches of Constantinople and Alexandria in order to discuss the real articles of faith of the First Ecumenical Synod and to promote these at the synod, which finally rejected the papal claim. This synod decided:

1) That the Pope did not have the right to hear appeals against decisions taken by the synod of bishops of the African Church.

2) It repeated and ratified one hundred and twenty-one canons of other synods convened in Africa between the years 348 and 418.

3) It published twelve new canons on Church order and discipline.

iv. *The Canons of the Holy Fathers.* In Canon 2 of the Quinisext Ecumenical Synod in Trullo, canons of twelve Holy Fathers are mentioned, while a canon by Cyprian is also presented. These canons, which were ratified by this synod, have universal status and validity throughout the Church.

Apart from these, universal status and validity were also granted by the Church to the epistle on simony from Patriarch Tarasios of Constantinople to Pope Hadrian.

The canons of the Holy Fathers were not initially published in the form of legislative ordinances, but either as an anthology from their various writings or, in the majority of cases, as epistles, which, because of their content, are called canonical epistles.

These epistles, with the passage of time and according to content, were divided up into individual canons and were then included in this form in the collections of canons, especially after their canonical importance had been confirmed by the synod in Trullo.

These canons are as follows:

a) By Dionysios of Alexandria († 265). These canons come from the canonical epistle which he sent in the year 260 to Basileides, Bishop of Libya, in response to four questions which the latter had submitted. The epistle was divided into four canons, in accordance with the answers to the four questions, which refer to matters of Church order and discipline.

b) By Gregory of Neocæsarea, the Wonderworker († 270). A number of canons survive under the name of Saint Gregory the Wonderworker. They derive from the epistle he sent in the year 258 to the Christians of Pontos (the Black Sea region), on account of their unworthy behavior during a barbarian raid. They encouraged the barbarians in their looting of cities, ate food sacrificed to idols and committed other serious transgressions. This epistle was divided into canons, the number of which varies in different collections of canons. In any case, the last canon in the collections does not belong to this epistle, but is a later addition taken from the canons of Saint Basil on the degrees of repentance.

c) By Saint Peter of Alexandria († 311). Peter, famous for his great learning, became head of the school of Alexandria in 295, and in 300 was elected Archbishop of Alexandria. The persecution of Diocletian began three years later, and during this, many Christians sacrificed to idols. When the persecution ceased, however, a large number of these repented and desired to return to the Church. Saint Peter, full of Christian love, was concerned both for them and for the manner in which they could be received into Church communion. He preached a homily on repentance in which he set out the way in which those who had abandoned the Church could come back to it. This homily provides the contents of the fourteen canons which survive under his name. To these was added a fifteenth, in the collections, concerning the Wednesday and Friday fast. This derived from a homily he preached during the feast of Pascha.

d) By Athanasios the Great († 373). Of the host of writings and epistles of Athanasios the Great, three epistles are of importance for Canon Law and have acquired the status of canons. The first, written in about the year 356, consists of an answer to the monk Ammoun, who had asked Athanasios about natural secretion. The second, from the year 367, deals with the canonical books of Holy Scripture and derives from the 39th festal epistle of the Saint. Finally, the third, written in 370, is addressed to Bishop Rufinianus, in response to a question posed by him as to how heretics coming into the Church were to be received.

e) By Basil the Great († 379). Of all the Fathers and Teachers of the Church, Basil the Great is of the greatest importance in regards to Canon Law and Church discipline as a whole. There are ninety-two canons of Saint Basil, garnered from his epistles and his thesis on the Holy Spirit.

The first eighty-six canons of Saint Basil derive from his epistles to Amphilochios of Iconium.

Canon 87 refers to matters of relationship and is addressed to Diodoros of Tarsus.

Canon 88 includes the order from Basil the Great to the Presbyter Gregory, in which he commands him to send away the nun he had living with him.

Canon 89 comes from one of his letters to *choroepiscopoi* (country bishops) who had overstepped the bounds of their jurisdiction.

Canon 90 comes from an epistle of his to bishops under him who had aroused suspicions that they were prompted by simony when ordaining.

Canons 91 and 92 were taken from the excellent dissertation of Basil the Great to Amphilochios *On the Holy Spirit*.

f) By Timothy of Alexandria († 385). Timothy was a disciple of Athanasios the Great and successor of his brother Peter to the archiepiscopal throne of Alexandria.

Eighteen of his answers to questions put to him by bishops have acquired the status of canons. These refer to matters of good order.

g) By Gregory the Theologian († 389). Of the writings of Saint Gregory the Theologian, the status of canons has been accorded only to thirty-four verses from his poem *On Which Books of the Old and New Testaments Should Be Read*, i.e. on the canonical books of the Old and New Testaments.

h) By Amphilochios of Iconium († 395). Amphilochios of Iconium also wrote on the same subject to Seleucus, enumerating the books of the Old and New Testaments in verse. From this poem, sixty-nine verses are included in almost all collections of canons.

i) By Gregory of Nyssa († 394). As is well known, Gregory of Nyssa was the younger brother of Basil the Great. He was famed for his strict mode of life, his learning, his zeal for the Orthodox faith and his great gifts of oratory.

Of his many writings, his canonical epistle to Letoios, Bishop of Melitine in Armenia, has been accorded canonical status. It was divided into eight canons, for the most part devoted to penances.

j) By Theophilos of Alexandria († 412). Theophilos of Alexandria was well known for his aversion to John Chrysostom. He wrote Paschal homilies, epistles and canons.

Fourteen canons by Theophilos are included in the collections, on his instructions on the Holy Epiphany and the Cathars[9] and to Ammon, Menas and Agathon. In Canon 1, he also talks about the ordination of the clergy, and in Canon 4 about regional synods.

k) By Cyril of Alexandria († 444). Although the nephew of Theophilos, he did not share the latter's views on John Chrysostom, toward whom, indeed, he showed great respect. He was an apologist for the genuine Orthodox faith.

Of his many epistles, two have been accorded canonical status, having been divided into five canons. One of these is addressed to Domnus, Archbishop of Antioch, on the occasion of accusations brought against him by Bishop Peter, who demanded that Domnus resign from the episcopal throne. From this letter, the first three canons were drawn. The second was addressed to the bishops of Libya and of Pentapolis, and referred to unlawfully performed ordinations.

l) By Gennadios of Constantinople († 471). Gennadios, Patriarch of Constantinople, was, as is well known, a faithful adherent to Orthodoxy and an opponent of Monophysitism. In the year 459, he convened a synod of eighty-one bishops, which published an encyclical letter against simony, addressed to all metropolitans and to the Pope of Rome. This encyclical was the work of Gennadios and having been ratified by Canon 2 of the Quinisext Synod was included in all the collections of canons of the Orthodox Catholic Church.

m) By Tarasios of Constantinople († 809). Tarasios became Archbishop of Constantinople in the year 786 and exercised great influence over Empress Irene, whom he persuaded to convene the Seventh Ecumenical Synod in Nicea, in order to combat Iconoclasm. Of Tarasios' many writings, the epistle on simony, which he sent to Pope Hadrian, is of importance to Canon Law and is included in almost all the collections of canons. In many of these, this epistle follows immediately after the canons of the Seventh Ecumenical Synod, since it was published immediately thereafter and appended to its proceedings.

---

[9] Καθαροί ("The Pure," Manicheans).

n) Canons concerning monks. To the canons of the Fathers also belong those referring to monks, the so-called "monastic canons," even though they concern only one category of person.

These canons are ordinances regulating the organization of the cenobitic monasteries, which had started to develop after the start of the 4th century, and the manner in which the monks were to live together. The most important of these were composed by Pachomios and Basil the Great.

It was Pachomios who introduced the cenobitic system. Until then, the prevalent mode of life for anchorites was that of the "lavra," that is a number of huts or cells, in which the hermits lived close to, but not with one another. Before 346, Pachomios composed canons for the use of those cenobia which he had founded in Egypt. Only fragments have survived of the Coptic original, as also of the Greek translation of it, though it seems that the Latin version, translated by Jerome in the year 404, in 194 chapters, was preserved intact.

A few decades later (before 379), Basil the Great devoted fifty-five *clauses in length* (ὅροι κατὰ πλάτος) to the regulation of monastic life (in Migne, *PG* 31, ll. 889 – 1052) and three hundred and thirteen more *in epitome* (ὅροι κατ᾽ ἐπιτομήν) in the form of questions and answers (in Migne, *PG* 31, ll. 1052 – 1306). Relevant to these, though of a much vaguer character, are the *Ascetica*, also by Basil the Great. The canons of Pachomios and Basil the Great were never ratified by any synod, but the prestige of their authors and their widespread use has given them, in practice at least if not in law, an authority which is hardly less than those canons mentioned above which have been officially recognized by the Church as sources of Law.

o) Pseudepigraphal canons of the Fathers. The canons supposedly composed by Patriarch Nikephoros I of Constantinople (806 – 815) were never ratified by a synod, though they are contained in many collections. For the most part, if not as a whole, they are wrongly attributed to Nikephoros.

Similarly, collections of "penances," corresponding to the *Libri Poenitentiales* of the Western Church, were wrongly attributed to outstanding figures in the Church, such as the Patriarchs Athanasios the Great of Alexandria († 374) and John Chrysostom of Constantinople († 407) and John the Faster (582 – 595). These contained ordinances on how the mystery of repentance was to be dealt with by spiritual fathers, and also referred to the spiritual penalties imposed by confessors.

3 THE SUPPLEMENTARY SOURCES. A) *The Canonical Ordinances of the Patriarchal Synods. The Synod of Constantinople — The Endemousa Synod.* In the Orthodox Catholic Church, the task of legislating is performed by Synods. After the Ecumenical Synods, legislative authority in the Church is exercised, within canonically defined borders, by the synods, i.e. by the synod of bishops of each local Church. If we except the Synods of Lyon (1274) and Ferrara-Florence (1438), the decisions of which, as is well known, were rejected by the Orthodox Church,[10] then since the 9th century no Ecumenical Synod has been convened.

After the era of the Ecumenical Synods, the most important legislative activity of universal validity was undertaken by the Patriarch of Constantinople and the Patriarchal Synod meeting with him. The reason for the continuance of the legislative authority of the Patriarch of Constantinople, in effect exercised over the whole Church, may be summarized as follows:

1. The Patriarchal Throne of Constantinople holds the seniority of honor over all the others in the Orthodox Church.[11]

2. For many centuries, this throne maintained its political independence, while the other patriarchal thrones in the East were oppressed by the infidels.

---

[10] They were also explicitly overturned by the Synod of Constantinople (1482).

[11] "Renewing the laws made by the one hundred and fifty Holy Fathers who assembled in this God-guarded imperial capital city, and by the six hundred and thirty of those who assembled in Chalcedon, we declare that the throne of Constantinople shall have equal seniority with the throne of Older Rome, and in ecclesiastical matters shall be magnified as the latter, and shall be second after it; after which shall be ranked the throne of the great city of Alexandria, then that of Antioch, and afterwards that of the city of Jerusalem" (Canon 36 of the Quinisext Ecumenical Synod). Cf. Canons 28 of the Fourth and 3 of the Second.

3. Because of this position of Constantinople toward the other Church centers in the East, the Patriarchal Synod of Constantinople also decided on matters not principally of concern to the Patriarchate of Constantinople, but also to other autocephalous Churches, which were not in a position to deal with them as they were of great importance for the Church as a whole. Hence, these decisions by the Patriarchal Synod of Constantinople had a universal and authentic character throughout the Orthodox Church.

4. The canonical resolutions of the Patriarchal Synod of Constantinople are of great importance because this Church is the mother Church of all those peoples who were converted to Christianity by its missionaries. A natural consequence of this was that the Churches of these peoples and nations turned to the Mother Church for guidance in the ordering of their internal life and sought instructions from it.

These instructions given by the Patriarchate of Constantinople had status and validity not only in the Church which sought them, but, based on fundamental Church institutions, had a universal and authentic character throughout the Eastern Church and were a rule and measure for the whole Church. Viewed and examined in this light, therefore, the canonical ordinances of the Patriarchal Synod of Constantinople bear the character of a canonical source, which supplements the fundamental source of the Canon Law of the Orthodox Catholic Church and sets out the development and application of the fundamental canonical ordinances. Examples of such decisions are the "Tome of Unity" (920), published under Patriarch Nicholas I (901 – 907 and 921 – 925), on the occasion of the fourth marriage of Leo VI, the Wise. Through this tome, peace was restored between Church and State and a fourth marriage was absolutely forbidden, though a third might be contracted under certain restrictions; the Tome published under Sisinios II, through which new impediments to marriage were introduced; the memorandum of Patriarch Alexios I, in the year 1027, "on those receiving monasteries through donations"; the tome of Patriarch John VIII Xiphilinos, equating engagement with wedding in regards to impediments to marriage; and decisions by Patriarchs John IX Agapitos (1115) and Luke I Chrysoberges (1156 – 1169).

During the latter's term as Patriarch, the legislative work of the Patriarchal Synod of Constantinople was particularly fruitful. A host of ordinances and decisions were published on matters of the Patriarchate and on marriage, as well as on other matters of general importance, of which the following may be mentioned here:

1. The ordinance through which it was forbidden for clergy to engage in tasks and professions unbecoming to their office.[12]

2. The decision by which at least twelve bishops are required to act in the defrocking of a bishop.[13]

3. The decision by which it is forbidden for the clergy to have recourse to civil courts.[14]

4. The decision on the punishment imposed on a bishop for celebrating in a Church which has not been inaugurated, i.e. "unenthroned,"[15] etc.

During Patriarch Manuel II's term (1244 – 1255), three synodal ordinances were published, which were answers to six questions posed by the Bishop of Vella concerning Church order and discipline, the transfer of bishops and the law pertaining to the right of building and occupying a monastery or a church.

Endemousae Synods. During the time of Turkish rule, and even long before this, it was not possible, because of the conditions prevailing, to call Ecumenical Synods, or, often enough, regional ones either. Consequently, the patriarchal synod was made up of the Patriarch, those metropolitans

---

[12] Gedeon, *Κανονικαὶ διατάξεις Β'.* 13 – 16. *Σύνταγμα Ἱ. Κανόνων,* Rallis and Potlis III, 344. Cf. Canon 16 of the Synod in Carthage and commentaries on it by Zonaras, Balsamon and Aristenos. *Σύνταγμα III,* 342 – 351.

[13] Gedeon, *Πατρ. διατ. Β'.* 17, *Σύνταγμα III,* 324. Cf. Canon 12 of the Synod in Cartagena and commentaries by Zonaras, Balsamon and Aristenos. *Σύνταγμα III,* 322 – 25.

[14] Gedeon, *Πατρ. διατ. Β'.* 18, *Σύνταγμα III,* 345. Cf. Canon 16 of the Synod in Cartagena and commentaries on it. *Σύνταγμα III.*

[15] Gedeon, *Πατρ. διατ. Β'.* 18, *Σύνταγμα III,* 345. Cf. Canon 16 of the Synod in Cartagena and commentaries on it. *Σύνταγμα III.*

whose sees are close to Constantinople, and those metropolitans of the East who were residing as visitors in the capital. Of all of these, almost always present at these synods were the metropolitans of places close to Constantinople, i.e. Heracleia, Kyzikos, Nicomedia, Nicea, Chalcedon, and, later, Derka, while those of Cæsarea and Ephesus were invited for their position of honor. These metropolitans were also called "Γέροντες (Gerontes)" and, in effect, administered the Church of Constantinople.

These synods were known as "endemousæ" (from ἐνδημέω "to reside"), because those bishops who were residing temporarily in the capital also took part. Indeed, when the Church was dealing with great and weighty matters, representatives of the other ancient Patriarchates of the East usually attended also, so that any decisions taken would acquire greater status and validity.

In this, their broader form, the endemousæ synods consisted of:

a) The bishops of the synod of the Church of Constantinople, under the Ecumenical Patriarch.

b) The Gerontes of the throne, i.e. the Metropolitans of Caesarea, Ephesus, Heracleia, Kyzikos, Nicomedia, Nicea, Chalcedon and Derka.

c) The bishops residing in Constantinople on the business of their eparchies.

d) The Patriarchs of the East, i.e. Alexandria, Antioch and Jerusalem, or their representatives.

Endemousæ synods, in their narrower form, were those in which the Patriarchs of the East or their representatives did not take part.

Important decisions taken by endemousæ synods during this period were the following:

a) During the period between the years 1572 – 1579, the question of Protestant Confessions was discussed, since these had hoped to be granted recognition by the Orthodox Church.

b) During the period 1580 – 1584, the Gregorian calendar was discussed and rejected.

c) Between the years 1589 – 1593, the Church of Russia was declared autocephalous and raised to the rank of Patriarchate.

d) During the term of Dionysios III (1660 – 1665), ordinances were published by him in common with Patriarchs Paisios of Alexandria, Makarios of Antioch and Nektarios of Jerusalem, on twenty-five matters of Church order and discipline.

e) During the term of Anthimos IV (1850), the Church of Greece was declared autocephalous and, as a result of this, autocephaly was established generally in the Orthodox Church as a system of administration, largely imposed on it by the then Great Powers.

f) Under Joacheim III (1879), through a Patriarchal and Synodal Tome, the Church of Serbia was declared autocephalous, while in 1920, it was raised to the rank of Patriarchate.

g) Under Joacheim IV (1885), through a Patriarchal and Synodal Tome, the Church of Romania was declared autocephalous, while in 1925, it was raised to the rank of Patriarchate.

h) Under Meletios IV (1923), a Patriarchal and Synodal decision was taken, by which the Churches of Estonia and Lithuania were declared autonomous under the Ecumenical Patriarchate.

i) Under Gregory VII (1924), the Church of Poland was declared autocephalous by the publication of a Patriarchal and Synodal Tome.

j) Under Benjamin I (1937), the Church of Albania was declared autocephalous.

k) Also under Benjamin I (1945), the Bulgarian Schism was eradicated through a synodal decision.

Certain ones of these decisions, especially the last ones, were taken by the Patriarchal Synod of Constantinople, without any representation from other Patriarchates of the East.

B) *Custom.* Another source of law, different from the canons and the State law on ecclesiastical matters is custom (*consuetudo*), which is closely linked and related to tradition, but at the same time differs from it. They coincide inasmuch as both tradition and custom constitute unwritten law.

The source of custom is the immediate conviction of the members of a society concerning a subject considered entirely necessary for it, which much be retained and kept active. Tradition, on the other hand, depends on the authority from which it springs. The source of Church custom is the conviction of the Church community that an action which is repeated over a long period and in the same way constitutes a law. In civil law, it is possible for custom, founded on the immediate conviction of society, to exist of itself. In Ecclesiastical and Canon Law, however, it depends on a certain tradition, or presupposes such, and is the traditional truth as expressed in practice.

It follows, then, that a custom must be followed for an extended period of continuous usage, the length of which, however, is not possible to define *a priori* and must be accompanied by the common conviction of those adopting it that they are observing an unwritten rule of law (*opinio necessitatis*). Many things in Canon Law, which for a variety of reasons were never defined as canons, were legitimized and established in the Church through habit, which through long usage eventually also became a source of Canon Law itself. For custom to constitute a source for Canon Law, however, it must not conflict with any dogma or teaching of the Orthodox Faith and must find itself in complete agreement with Holy Scripture and Sacred Tradition. If the custom in question is local or particular, it must not be opposed to the whole spirit of Canon Law and Christian ethics. Moreover, for custom to have status and validity in the Church, it must also contain some truth. The case of Church custom must be of a purely ecclesiastical nature, and its purpose must be in harmony with the main aim of the Church. If these prerequisites are absent, if custom is not founded on some truth, then it can have no validity and status, whether or not it is ancient.[16] Custom must be accepted and ratified by the Church, or else refuted.

Due to the lack of official codification of Canon Law, customs are of great practical importance in meeting any gaps appearing in Church legislation as a whole. They are divided into universal, that is, customs which have grown wherever the Orthodox Church is predominant, and

---

[16] Cyprian, *Ad Pompejus Ep.* 74, Clement the Alexandrian, *Stromata (Miscellanies)*, book 7, chap. 16.

local, that is those which apply only to a particular region. Universal and local customs may, moreover, be general, as having to do with all members of the Church, or particular, being limited to one specific category of class of persons such as monks, for example. Local traditions prevail over universal ones and particular over general.

The force of custom was also recognized by the Ecumenical Synods and the Fathers of the Church. The proclamation of the First Ecumenical Synod that the privileges of the leading bishops were law was based upon the usages prevailing at the time, i.e. on custom: "Let the ancient customs in Egypt, Libya and Pentapolis prevail, that the Bishop of Alexandria have authority in all these, since this is customary for the Bishop of Rome also" (Canon 6); and "since custom and ancient tradition have prevailed that the Bishop of Aelia should be honored" ... (Canon 7).

This same synod condemned the usage prevailing in some places of deacons administering communion to priests, because this had not been transmitted either by the canons or by habit (Canon 18). In this way, it equates the importance of custom with that of the canons.

The Third Ecumenical Synod, in Ephesus, in upholding the privileges of the Church of Cyprus, rejected the claim of the Bishop of Antioch that he should consecrate the Bishops of Cyprus "so as not to conflict with the habit obtaining" (Canon 8). Basil the Great, in his epistle to Diodoros, Bishop of Tarsus, commends the importance of habit in the most positive way, declaring specifically that "custom has of itself the force of law" (Canon 87).

In Title I, chap. 3 of the *Nomocanon in fourteen titles*, it is particularly urged that "... unwritten Church custom be kept as law," while the canons relating to this are also mentioned.

From what has been said, the importance of custom as a source of Canon Law has been made clear, as also when and under which circumstances it is valid in law. In the first years of the Church, when there were only a few written canons, custom was entirely considered to be law and was regarded as the confirmation of the teaching handed down by the Church. In regards to this, there is the classic testimony of Tertullian, an author who, as is well known, flourished around the end of the 2nd and beginning of the 3rd centuries. His testimony is important, because Tertullian was well versed in law and his theories were included in the Digests of Justinian. Tertullian says: "If what is not written is observed everywhere, then assuredly custom, based on tradition, has confirmed it and made it prevail. If anyone claims that, even concerning tradition, written authority is required, we are able to present many ordinances, which, though unwritten, are yet observed by the power of tradition and custom." After giving examples, he concludes with: "If, for these and other such ordinances, you require written law, you will find none. For in these, tradition acts as the base, custom as confirmation, and faith as guardian."[17]

Ecclesiastical tradition, established through custom and preserved through faith, had the validity of law in the ancient Church. In cases of doubt or uncertainty, it is the ecclesiastical authority which decides on the legal validity of a custom which has not been confirmed or established by the canons, i.e. the law of the Church. On the basis of this verdict, the custom either becomes law or is proscribed.

4 AUXILIARY SOURCES. A) *Interpretations by Official Canonists.* The interpretive opinions of canonists recognized by the Church on matters of ecclesiastical life for which no Church ordinances have explicitly been published must also be numbered among the sources of Canon Law.

These interpretations by the canonists do not, of course, have the same status as the Sacred Canons and Church ordinances, but having been included in the collections of canons of the Church, they have, over the years, acquired their own considerable status.

These opinions have been given in the form of question and answer, or canonical studies and memoranda and, occasionally, as canons.

Thus, among the interpreters of Canon Law, Patriarch Photios was outstanding in the 9th century, then, in the 11th, Metropolitan Niketas of Herakleia, Peter the Chartophylax (Archivist), Nikephoros the Char-

---

[17] *De Corona Militis*, chap. 3.

tophylax, Metropolitan Elias of Crete and Nicholaos III Grammatikos, Patriarch of Constantinople. In the 12th century came Patriarch Luke Chrysoberges, Niketas, Chartophylax of the Great Church and later Metropolitan of Thessaloniki, and John of Chalcedon; in the 13th, Archbishop Demetrios Chomatenos of First Justiniane; in the 14th or 15th, Metropolitan Prochoros of Stravroupolis and Presiding Bishop of Crete (πρόεδρος); and in the 15th century, Archbishop Symeon of Thessaloniki.

Important studies on Canon Law were published by: Metropolitan Arethas of Cæsarea (beginning of the 10th century), a pupil of Photios, on the transfer of bishops; Demetrios of Kyzikos (11th century) on degrees of kinship, Demetrios Chomatenos on a variety of subjects, Neilos Cabasilas, Archbishop of Thessaloniki († 1364), on the interpretation of Canon 12 of Antioch, et al.

The most outstanding canonists of the Byzantine period, however, flourished in the 12th century and were the following:

1. Alexios Aristenos († after 1166), Deacon, Hieromnemon, Nomophylax, Protekdikos, Orphanotrophos and, finally, Grand Oikonomos of the Patriarchate of Constantinople. On the orders of Emperor John II Comnenos, he wrote an interpretation on the canons in their concise form, as presented in the collection of Stephen the Ephesian and Symeon Metaphrastes.

2. John Zonaras (end of the 11th, beginning of the 12th centuries) rose to the highest state offices of Grand Drugarios of the Vigla and Protoasekretes. He later became a monk in the Monastery of Saint Glykeria. He wrote an exegesis on the full text of the canons, which was finished after 1159.

In the collection of Zonaras, the canons are set out in accordance with the importance of the sources, i.e. in the following order: first the canons of the Apostles, then those of the Ecumenical Synods, those of the local synods and, finally, those of the Holy Fathers, and especially those contained in the collection of canons appended to the *Nomocanon in fourteen titles*. Zonaras does not restrict himself merely to the letter of the Sacred Canons, but attempts to discover their true meaning. His interpretations are a source of Canon Law for the Orthodox Church, while for Canon Law itself, they are of great importance.

The most outstanding canonist of his time, Theodore Balsamon, follows the interpretation of Zonaras almost to the letter and calls him "most prodigious." Vlastares also refers to the interpretation of Zonaras. In general, the honor in which his work is held is so great that good collections of canons are called simply "Zonaras."

3. Theodore Balsamon (†after 1195), was deacon of the Great Church, Nomophylax, Chartophylax and First of Vlachernae. Between the years 1185 and 1189, he became Patriarch of Antioch, though he was unable to travel to his see because it was under occupation by the Latins. He was the most distinguished canonist of his time and wrote the most exhaustive interpretative memorandum on the Sacred Canons and the *Nomocanon in fourteen titles.* The main aim of Balsamon in his work was to harmonize the regulations of the canons with the ordinances of civil law and to declare what was legally included in the Basilica (legal ordinances) from civil law and which, on this basis, had status and validity for all. Balsamon, as has been said, followed the interpretation of Zonaras in everything, merely adding to it slightly and presenting the ordinances of the Patriarchal Synod of Constantinople for interpretation by means of one or another of the canons. The second part of the Nomocanon is dealt with freely.

B) *"Appellations of Metropolitans"* (*Notitiæ Episcopatuum*). The "Appellations of Metropolitans" are catalogues of metropolises, archbishoprics and bishoprics subject to the metropolises. Archbishoprics were autonomous vis-à-vis the metropolises and were subject directly to the Patriarchs. In essence, these lists are catalogues of bishops, which is why they are known in the bibliography by the Latin term of *notitiæ episcopatuum.* They provide information about the organizational structure of the Church and first appear toward the end of the 4th century. These catalogues, which were employed to affirm the hierarchical order of the members of synods and other ecclesiastical conventions which, however, altered over the years. It became necessary, therefore, to revise them in order to ratify the administrative changes that had taken place (e.g. changes in seniority, the foundation of new metropolises or bishoprics, the dissolution of others and so on). Today, therefore, we have many "appellations of metropolitans" which date from a variety of historical periods.[18]

   c) *Roman Civil Laws on Ecclesiastical Matters.* From the time of Constantine the Great and the First Ecumenical Synod, apart from the Sacred Canons, we have a new factor as source of Canon Law: the law of the State. Through the recognition of Christianity as the permitted religion of the Roman State, there began a new period for the whole of the organization of the Church. The Church, then, received officially its position in the world of law which had been the dominant principle in the Roman Empire. As the most important organization in the Roman State, one whose jurisdiction and extent surpassed the boundaries of the Empire, the Church naturally was the object of the most lively interest on the part of the State. Whereas in the period preceding this, the Church had had to face the wrath of the emperors, at this time it was more endangered by their excessive interest in it. The interest of the Christian Roman emperors sometimes tended to overstep the bounds of protection of the Church and to take the form of its complete subjugation to the authority of the State. In this critical period of fundamental importance for the future shaping of the relations between Church and State, an inestimable contribution was made to the harmonization of Church/State authority by the teaching and efforts of especially Athanasios the Great, Basil the Great and John Chrysostom in the East, and Ambrose and Augustine in the West, all of whom labored mightily on the Church's behalf. What must be said here, however, from the point of view of Canon Law, and especially of the great Church leaders of the 4th century, is that the fundamental principle which should govern relations between Church and State is that of cooperation and mutual respect, with each party having its own primary authority.

---

[18] Critical edition: J. Darrouzès, *Notitiae episcopatuum Ecclesiae Constantinopolitanae*, (Géographie ecclesiastique de l'Empire Byzantin, I), Paris 1981. Also, H. Gelzer, *Texte der Notitiae episcopatuum*, Munich 1900. Rallis and Potlis, *Syntagma*, vol. V, et al.

During the Christian period of the Roman Empire, most matters were arranged by the State, with the explicit tacit tolerance of the Church, which had not been foreseen by the canons. And so, from the time of Constantine the Great until the fall of Constantinople, State laws were published on Church matters.

The laws of the Christian emperors were incorporated into the collection of canons, particularly those known as Nomocanons. This makes it clear that these laws (laws, usages, civil ordinances) ought to be considered as sources of Canon Law.

In the 6th century, John Scholastikos composed a systematic collection of canons, to which he later attached an appendix consisting of an overview of the *Novellae* of Justinian related to ecclesiastical matters. In the introduction to this collection, it says that these laws of the emperors were in accordance with the spirit of the canons of the Church and that they impart to the canons special importance, since "the royal power gives authenticity with the addition of what is legal and God-pleasing..." In other words, they give them the force of the law of the land.

The Church accorded this importance to the laws of the Christian emperors from the time when the first Roman emperor proclaimed the legal existence of the Church within the state. Later, when the Christian religion was recognized as the religion of the State, the Church was proclaimed to be the basis of legitimate order, while policy on certain matters depended on belonging to the Church or not, and each person's civil position and capability toward the law. The Church, then, voluntarily ceded to the civil authority the power to legislate in common with the ecclesiastical authority, usually on matters of an ecclesiastical nature. These laws, which, as Scholastikos says, were imbued with the spirit of the canons of the Church, were accorded full status and validity. The Church accepted them as a source of Canon Law. It was able to do so because the Roman emperors also gave the canons of the Church the same status and validity as the laws of the land. By a law of the year 530, Justinian laid down that what was forbidden by the canons should also be forbidden by the State laws.[19] He also promulgated, in his sixth *Novella*, that the canons ought to have, in the state, the same validity as its laws. In particular, in *Novella* 131, he orders that all canons published or ratified by the four Ecumenical Synods had universal status and validity, that the dogmas of faith had the same validity as the Holy Scriptures and the canons the same as the laws of the State. At the same time, he declared invalid any state law which contradicted the canons.[20] This relationship toward the Roman laws held well not only in the Eastern Church, but also in the West, until the 13th century, and, indeed, in part until the 16th.

The Church's recognition of the laws of the land as a source of Canon Law caused no dissension. Doubts might have arisen only in a case where canons and civil laws clashed, despite the Justinian legislation mentioned above regarding the relationship between laws and canons. Balsamon, certainly, in his comments on the Nomocanon judges the question with great clarity. When two laws were published by Emperor Alexios Komnenos which seemed to be in conflict with the canons, the question was raised as to whether in matters of Church administration greater weight ought to be given to the canons or to the laws.

Balsamon concluded "… canons have greater validity than laws. For the canons, having been promulgated and supported by emperors and holy Fathers, are accepted as the holy Scriptures, while the laws have been introduced or composed only by emperors and for this reason do not outweigh either holy Scriptures or the canons."[21]

This interpretation prevailed completely in the Eastern Church, as it did in the West, and was expressed even more positively in the collection of the Sacred Canons, i.e. the *Syntagma* of Matthew Vlastares[22] (14th century).

The main sources from which Canon Law draws the relative legal ordinances from civil legislation are the following:

---

[19] *Codex Justinianus*, Lib. I Tit. III, Const. 45.
[20] Chap. II of Title I of the *Nomocanon in Fourteen Titles*.
[21] *Nomocanon in Fourteen Titles*, title I, chap 3.
[22] *Ibid.*

1. The Theodosian Codex (*Codex Theodosianus*), compiled under Theodosios II and Valentinian III in 438. It was published with the stipulation that from January 1, 439 AD, it was to serve as the only source, "*Juris Principalis*," i.e. the laws of the State concerning the Church published from the time of Constantine the Great to 438. This codex contains many laws distributed among sixteen books (*Libri*), each of which is subdivided into many titles. The last book (the sixteenth) contains laws exclusively concerned with ecclesiastical matters and is divided into eleven titles, which refer to the catholic faith, bishops and clergy in general, monks, heretics, baptism, apostates, Jews, etc.

2. During the reign of Justinian (527 – 565), all the sources of Roman law then in existence were revised and examined critically and collated into special collections. Collections which contain ordinances of interest to Ecclesiastical Law are the following:

a) The Justinian Codex (*Codex Iustinianus*). This *Codex* contains imperial edicts and was published in the year 529. After revision, it was published again in the year 534. This *New Codex* contains imperial edicts from Hadrian (117) to the last law of Justinian, published in the year 534. The *Codex* consists of twelve books, which are divided into titles. The first thirteen titles of the first book deal with ecclesiastical matters (the Holy Trinity, bishops and clergy in general, monks, commissioners for orphans, ascetics, etc.).

b) The second collection of laws of Justinian: the *Digesta se Pandectæ* (Πανδέκται), which are divided into fifty books. These were published in 533. They contain ordinances from ancient Roman Law, garnered in various writings by earlier jurists, which were useful during the Justinian era. The *Pandectæ* contain very few ordinances related to Church law.

c) The *Institutions* (Εἰσηγήσεις). These were published to be used as a methodical introduction and guide to the study of the law contained in the *Codex* and *Pandectae*. They were published at the same time as the *Pandectae*. They consist of four books, divided into titles. Each title is further divided into paragraphs. They also include ecclesiastical laws.

d) The *Novellæ Constitutiones* (Νεαραὶ Διατάξεις). These are laws published by Justinian after the publication of his *Codex* (534). They are known as "New Laws," because they are of later provenance than those contained in the Justinian *Codex*. It follows that these laws are not contained therein. The text of the *Novellæ* was, for the most part, written in Greek. Each *Novella* is headed by an inscription stating to whom it is addressed. This official was charged with its execution and application. The greater part of the *Novellæ* is directed to the *Præfectus prætorio*, except for the ecclesiastical ones, which are usually addressed to the Patriarch of Constantinople, although it is certain that they were also relevant to the other patriarchs, who were obliged to forward them to metropolitans, and they in their turn to the bishops. Many of the *Novellæ* of Justinian regulate matters of ecclesiastical law and certain of them, such as numbers 5 (from the year 535), 6 (535), 120 (544), 131 (545), 133 (539), 137 (565) and, especially the most extensive of all, 123 (546) divided into forty chapters, form, in a way, a small codex of ecclesiastical law.

3. Another collection is that from the time of Emperor Leo III, the Isaurian, and Constantine Copronymos and is known as the *Ecloga* (741 AD). This contains relatively few ordinances of direct interest to the Church, such as, e.g., XVII 4, which provides that anyone striking a clergyman be punished. Leo's purpose was to gather into one collection the most important laws of the four collections of Justinian. In the original, the *Ecloga* consists of eighteen titles and an introduction.

4. The *Procheiros Nomos* (Manual) of Basil I, probably published between the years 870 and 879 and containing ordinances referring to Church matters, particularly in titles 24 and 28.

5. The *Epanagoge*, composed by the same emperor between the years 879 and 886. The *Epanagoge* was never accorded legal status but remained a draft bill. It contains a good number of Church ordinances, more than the *Procheiros Nomos*, especially in titles III, VIII, IX and X.

6. The *Basilica* (Royal) of Leo the Wise. The *Basilica* is a most important work in regards to Ecclesiastical Law. It is the well-known, great codifying work of Leo VI, the Wise (886–912), which contained in a

unified whole the material of the Justinian legislation, which until then had been spread over four sections. The *Basilica* are a most important source from the point of view of State law and also a continuous source of the Canon Law of the Orthodox Church. They were published toward the end of the 9th century. This collection consists of sixty books, each of which is divided into titles, the titles being divided into chapters and the chapters further divided into paragraphs (subjects). Balsamon made a critical comparison of the canons contained in the *Basilica*.

The *Basilica* also served as the main source for the last important work on civil law published in the East in the Middle Ages, i.e. the *Hexabiblos* of Constantine Armenopoulos.

This *Hexabiblos* was composed around the year 1345 by Armeno-poulos, who was a *nomophylax* (lit. Keeper of the Law) and judge in Thessaloniki. The work was in the form of a handbook, which is why it was called *Procheiron*, and was divided into six books. It also contained ordinances related to Church Law.

7. The *Novellæ* (Νεαραὶ or New Laws) published post-Justinian. The emperors who came after Justinian published many other *Novellæ* which were directed toward Church matters.

Emperor Leo the Wise alone published one hundred and eighteeen *Novellæ*, of which more than half were concerned with Church discipline, good Church order and marriage. All the *Novellæ* from Emperor Justinus until Constantine Palaiologos, i.e. from the year 566 to 1451, were published in a special tome by S. E. Zachariae and A. Lingenthal in Leipzig, in 1857, thereafter being republished by the Zepos brothers. The most important *Novellæ* were also included in Rallis and Potlis' *Syntagma*.

D) *The Church and the Sources of Its Law under the Ottoman Occupation*. After the Fall of Constantinople and the enslavement of the Roman (Greek, Orthodox) nation by the Ottomans, new conditions were created for the Church, too. Initially, the conquerors behaved with tolerance toward the Church, for the following two basic reasons:

i. The Koran was, for the Ottomans, not only a religious but also a legal code. It was not possible, therefore, to apply it to non-Muslims.

Consequently, the Ottoman State tolerated the existence of non-Muslim subjects (*reaya*), who were obliged to pay a poll-tax (*harac*) (to keep their heads), and it recognized them as a separate religious and ethnic community (*millet*), having as its head the Ecumenical Patriarch and the metropolitans and bishops under him and subject in large part, and particularly in regards to family relations and inheritance, to Roman Law.

ii. In order to thwart cooperation between Romans (Greeks) and the West and any prospect of joint action against him, Mehmet II (1453 onwards) strengthened the hand of the anti-Union party.

Thus, in 1454, one of the leaders of the anti-Union movement, Gennadios Scholarios, was made Ecumenical Patriarch. Mehmet bestowed many privileges on the Church and its leaders. He recognized the communities of Romans (Rum) as a special religious and, in many ways, political entity, at the head of which was the Ecumenical Patriarch, who became Ethnarch of the Romans (i.e. Orthodox). Besides this, their family law and inheritance rights were fixed on the basis of Roman Law.

The privileges of the Church consisted mainly of the following: a) the free and undisturbed conduct of divine worship; b) its internal self-administration and exemption from taxation; c) the freedom to administer ecclesiastical property, with the empowerment of the Church to impose obligatory contributions on its members; d) the administration of charitable and educational institutions and of the local communities in general; e) the exercise of jurisdiction over family and inheritance law, enabling the Church (through its higher clergy) to act very often as arbitrator in all kinds of other matters. Not infrequently, Christians, and even Muslims, voluntarily submitted to the judgment of the ecclesiastical courts, which inspired greater confidence in their impartiality than did the Turkish *kadi*; f) bishops were tried exclusively (for civil or penal matters) before the Sultan's *divan* (Council of State). Moreover, the election of the Patriarch was ratified by the Sultan. However, the consent of the Sublime Porte was required for the execution of any decision which was not of an ecclesiastical nature.

These privileges were recorded in a Sultan's *berat* (edict), which was published every time a Patriarch or metropolitan was elected. Despite this official and constantly repeated recognition of the privileges, they were not always respected by the Ottoman authorities. The various forms which their oppression of the Church and its ministers took are well known, ranging from the imprisonment and murder of hierarchs — even Patriarchs — submitting them especially to economic extortion through the enforced payment of large sums of money under various names and guises (*peşkeş*, a present, *harac*, poll-tax, and *moukareti*).

These privileges were retained until the 19th century, when, under pressure from the liberal spirit which was dominant then in Europe and from the Christian States, the relatively favorable position of the Church within the Ottoman State was further strengthened, at least theoretically. Thus, under Sultan Abdul Mecit, the royal decree known as the *Hatti-Şerif* was published in 1839, followed by another, the *Hatti-Hümayun* in 1856. Both of these were protective measures for the religious minorities living in the Ottoman State. Attempts were made by the Ottoman government, in the years 1883/84 and 1890/91, to restrict the Church's privileges, but they failed, due to the courageous resistance of Patriarchs Joacheim III and Dionysios V.

The *Hatti-Hümayun* stated the following, regarding Church organization: 1) it recognized the spiritual privileges of tax exemption for the Christian communities; 2) it guaranteed complete freedom for all religions; 3) it granted the right to build churches, schools and charitable institutions; 4) it rejected any change of religion effected by force and declared the full equality of all subjects; 5) it granted to all subjects the right to hold administrative office; 6) it imposed the setting up of mixed courts, allowed a sum of money to be paid instead of military service and granted the right to own foreign property; 7) it imposed total religious tolerance.

On the basis of this, in 1857, the Sublime Porte assigned to the Patriarch the task of drawing up the Regulations which would govern the organization and administration of the Patriarchate of Constantinople in general.

In 1858, the National Council was established, consisting of seven hierarchs and 21 lay members under the chairmanship of the Ecumenical Patriarch. After very troubled proceedings, this body drew up the National Regulations of the Ecumenical Patriarchate, between the years 1858 – 60. These were then ratified by the Turkish government in the years 1861 and 1862 and became the law of the land.

Through the Treaty of Sèvres (1920), by which the war between Turkey and the Allies (1914 – 18) was brought to an end, the position of the Church was restored as was that of the *Rum*, i.e. Orthodox minority in general. Unfortunately, this treaty was never applied, because of the revolution by Kemal Attatürk and the Asia Minor disaster. This treaty was replaced by that signed in Lausanne (1923). With this treaty, the Patriarchate was deprived of most of its flock, and its authority was limited to the purely ecclesiastical sector.[23]

During the time of Ottoman rule, apart from customs as they developed over the course of this period, the decisions of the Patriarchal Synod of Constantinople were the sources of Canon and Ecclesiastical Law. As during the previous era, these were of a legislative, not merely administrative and judicial, nature. The "General Regulations" mentioned above shoud also be included among the sources, since they contained the basic regulations for the organization and administration of the Patriarchate from 1862 to 1923. These were, however, shaped and formed under the influence and pressure of external factors and political powers, and not on the basis of the sacred Canons of the Church.

Of the numerous documents which survived the fall of Constantinople, special importance is attached to the so-called "codices" of metropolitans and bishops, i.e. books in which are recorded the most important administrative and judicial acts published by individual bishops over the course of time.

During this period, research into Canon and Church Law was mainly restricted to collected works.

---

[23] Christophilopoulos, *op. cit.*, p. 62.

5 **COLLECTIONS.** The codification of the sources of Canon Law occurred gradually, as new sources made their appearance. Ordinances issued were valid as canons from the time of their publication. Every member of the Church was expected to know the ordinances in force. Much more so, the leaders of the Church had not only to know these ordinances, but also to see that they were scrupulously applied. No sooner was a new law of universal force and validity issued by the authority responsible than they took care to attach it to the earlier laws, so that they could supervise and be aware of all the laws. These works of codification were initially private, i.e. they were undertaken by individuals for practical purposes. Later, when the competent authority scrutinized and studied these works, and found them both useful and beneficial, the works acquired an official character and became collections of universal force and validity.

The history of the codification of Canon and Ecclesiastical Law may be divided into three periods. The first includes the time from the beginning of the Church until the recognition of its legal status by the Edict of Milan (313). During this period, the Church drew on Holy Scripture and living Apostolic tradition for the laws necessary for its administration. The second period includes the time of the Ecumenical Synods and those local synods whose Canons have status and validity throughout the Church. During this period, the codification of the sources of the Law of the Church evolved, and this development reached its peak with the publication of the fundamental collection of Canons, i.e. *Nomocanon in Fourteen Titles* (833), through which necessary additions were made to the fundamental law of the Church. The third period begins after the publication of the Nomocanon. During this time, the legislative organs of the local Churches, on the basis of general Church legislation, dealt with the regulation of Church life and only special matters were resolved in accordance with local relations. The task of the canonists in this period was, on the one hand, to make the fundamental laws of the Church accessible to everyone, and, on the other, to harmonize all the other sources of Church Law with these laws, whether these sources derived from political legislation or from local Churches. The canonical collections of the first two periods enjoyed the respect of the whole Church, as sources for the undivided Church. During the third period, the schism was introduced into the Church, and since then, different law has existed in the Orthodox Catholic Church from that of the Church of Rome. In this present chapter, in regards to the third period, we shall restrict ourselves solely to the compilation of canonical collection in the Orthodox Church.

In regards to content, these collections may be divided into those which are purely canonical/ecclesiastical, those which are civil/ecclesiastical and Nomocanons.

The first group contains ordinances of Church legislation exclusively, the second legal ordinances of civil legislation on ecclesiastical matters, and the third ordinances of ecclesiastical and civil origin. These collections are also divided into general, if they are aimed at the whole Church, or specific, if they refer to some local Church. Moreover, these collections differ among themselves in regards to the manner in which the text of the laws is laid out. The text may be set out in full, as in the original, or synoptically, or periphrastically, either with or without short or extensive interpretations.

A) *The First Period, until the Edict of Milan (313).* The collections of this first period, known as Apostolic, were treated above (pp. 38ff), while in the same period, there was no collection of official, formal, legal ordinances.

B) *The Second Period, from 313 until the Publication of the Fundamental Canonical Collection of the Church (883).*

i. *Collections of Sacred Canons.* After the publication of the Edict of Milan, by which freedom was granted to the Church within the Roman Empire, its legislative activity developed with a view to its organization and to a definition of the needs of Church order and discipline. As the legislative work of the Church evolved, the codification of the ecclesiastical ordinances kept pace with it, and so, this period affords us a series of such collections.

In regards to the first collections of canons from this period, little evidence has survived. Reference is made to a canonical collection for the first time in the Acts of the Fourth Ecumenical Synod. Certain indications, however, point to the existence of canonical collections even before the time of this Synod. Between the years 314 and 325, there was a Greek collection containing the canons of the synods in Ankara and Neocæsarea, and this was translated into Latin.[24] Because of the time of these synods, these collections may be considered the basis of all the canonical collections which followed. According to E. Schwarz and W. Plöchl, the first collections took shape as follows: the oldest nucleus was formed, as mentioned above, from the canons of the Synods of Ankara (314) and Neocæsarea (between 314 and 325). The canons of the First Ecumenical Synod and of the Synod of Gangra (341 – 342) were added later. Before the year 381, the collection was extended through the addition of the canons of the Synods of Antioch (341) and Laodicea (between 343 and 380). It is believed that it was Bishop Meletios of Antioch[25] who made these additions. After the completion of the proceedings of the Fourth Ecumenical Synod in Chalcedon (451) and at many sessions thereof, the canons of previous synods were read from a special book (codex), which included all the canons of the Church synods which were called before that of Chalcedon. E. Schwarz tried to restore the collection which had taken shape between the years 342 and 381. Thereafter in this book, the canons of the Synod of Chalcedon are added.

The first complete collection of canons which has come down to us, and which was compiled probably in the 6th century, is attributed to Stephen Ephesios, under the name *Canonical Synopsis*. It contains a digest or overview of the Apostolic Canons, as well as those of the Synods of Nicea (First Ecumenical), Ankara, Neocæsarea, Gangra, Antioch, Laodicea, Constantinople (Second Ecumenical) and Ephesus (Third Ecumenical). This collection increased in regards to the number of canons with the publication of newer or later canons which were added to its original form.

The first printed edition was published as the *Synodikon* of Beveridge, and thereafter in Rallis and Potlis' *Syntagma*, in its expanded form, as

---

[24] Maussen, *Geschichte des Kanonischen Rechts*; W. Plöchl, *Geschichte des Kirchenrechts*, I, p. 274.
[25] Plöchl, *op. cit.* p. 274

completed in the 12th century. Aristenos wrote an interpretation of this augmented Synopsis in the 12th century.

This collection was supplemented by a certain Symeon "Magister and Logothete" by the addition of later canons. He called his collection "An Overview of the Canons." It contains a digest of the canons of the Apostles, of the first five Ecumenical Synods and of the first seven local synods, as well as the canons of St. Basil the Great. They are set out according to the importance of their sources, i.e. first those of the Apostles, then those of the Ecumenical Synods, the local synods and, finally, the Holy Fathers. This order was followed in all collections of canons published thereafter.

The first systematic collection of canons is that referred to in the prologue of the collection of John Scholastikos and belonging chronologically to the first half of the 6th century (535).[26] The author is unknown. This collection is divided into sixty titles and contained the Canons of the Apostles, those of the first four Ecumenical Synods and of the local ones, those of Sardica also being included.

A second systematic canonical collection was made in about 550 by John Scholastikos (= Lawyer): "A Concordance of Ecclesiastical Canons, Divided into Fifty Titles," while he was still a presbyter in Antioch. He later became a presbyter and representative (*apokrisarios*) of the Church of Antioch in Constantinople and, later still, Patriarch of Constantinople (565–577). This collection contained, in fifty titles, the canons in sixty titles of the collection referred to above. These fifty titles were arranged according to the model of Justinian's *Pandectæ*. In addition, sixty-eight canons of St. Basil the Great were appended to the collection, i.e. those drawn from his second and third letters to Amphilochios.

In the West, in the first centuries, the life of the Church lacked that development which occurred in the Church in the East, and there were consequently fewer sources of Ecclesiastical Law than in the East. For many centuries, there were no collections of canons in the Church of the West from its independent sources. The first collections of canons in the

---

[26] Plöchl, *op. cit.* p. 274.

West were translations of the canons by which the Church in the East was governed. These canons, which were also ratified by the Pope, had status and validity throughout the Western Church until the appearance, in the mid-9th century, of the Pseudo-Isidorean collection. As time went by, the canonical ordinances of the Western Church's synods, and particularly the decretals of the Popes, were added to the translated collections.

Of the large number of collections of canons translated from Greek into Latin, we would mention here that of Dionysios Exiguus, the *Codex Canonum ecclesiasticorum Dionysii exiqui*. This collection occupies pride of place among all the collections of canons in the West which were published in the first nine centuries.

Dionysios Exiguus was the head of a monastery in Rome and lived in the first half of the 6th century. He also included in his collection a translation of certain Greek collections: fifty canons of the Apostles, the canons of the first four Ecumenical Synods and those of seven local synods, i.e. those of Ankara, Neocæsarea, Gangra, Antioch, Laodicea, Sardica and Cartagena, in other words, the canons in force in the East at the time of the translation.

Proof of the value and importance accorded in the West to this collection of Dionysios is the order by Pope Hormisdas (514–523) that an official edition be prepared, in which the Greek text of the canons should be set out in parallel with the Latin translation.

Thereafter, Dionysios went on to make another collection, the *Collectio decretorum pontificum romanorum*, in which were contained the Decretals of eight Popes, from Siricius (384–399) to Anastasios II (496–498). These two collections were afterwards combined into a common collection, under the title *Collectio Dionysio Hadriana*, and, when certain new Decretals had been added, was given by Pope Hadrian I (774) to Charlemagne as a gift. This last collection had the validity of the official collection of canons in the Frankish state.[27]

Through the publication in the 9th century in the west of the Pseudo-Isidorean ordinances *Collectio canonum Isidori mercatoris*, a radical

---

[27] Milas, *op. cit.*, pp. 239–240.

change came about in the Canon Law of the Western Church. This collection is divided into three parts. The first contains the Apostolic Canons, sixty decretals of thirty Popes, from Clement (1st century) until Melchiades (first years of the 4th century). The second consists of four different articles, one of which is the letter concerning the Donation of Constantine the Great to Pope Sylvester, the canons of ten synods in the East and certain others in Africa, Spain and Gaul. Apart from certain small articles, the third consists of papal decretals from Sylvester, the successor of Melchiades, until Gregory II (†731). Most of the papal decretals in this collection are not genuine. The purpose behind the production of this collection was to strengthen papal power and authority and, thus, to combat the limitless extension of the power of civil leaders, especially in the Frankish state, where Church authority had all but vanished. Opposed to the power of the civil leaders was that of the Church, reinforced by the augmentation and deployment of the authority of the Pope.[28] No one now accepts the authenticity and authority of this collection, which is generally referred to as the *Psuedo-Isidoriana collectio* or *Collectio falsarum decretalium Isidori mercatoris* (or *The False Decretals*).

Because of the trust which was accorded to this collection in the 9th century and the protection afforded to it by Pope Nicholas I, it played a decisive role in the formation of new ecclesiastical law in the Western Church. In this new law, the sources of Canon and Ecclesiastical Law changed places, in regards to importance and authority. In the West, ecclesiastical authority was now concentrated in one person, the Bishop and Pope of Rome, while various canonical questions were now dealt with mainly through papal decretals.[29] Due to the fresh appraisal of the sources of Canon Law in the West from the 9th century, Western collections since that time are of no further importance for the Law of the Eastern Church.

---

[28] *Ibid.*, pp. 240–242.

[29] The general sources of Canon Law in the West are arranged in the following order: Holy Scripture and Sacred Tradition, Decretals and other ordinances of the Pope of Rome, decisions and ordinances of the Ecumenical and local synods (Phillips in Milas, *op. cit.*) Cf. Klaus Mörsdorf, *Kirchenrecht*, 1964, vol. I, p. 26.

ii. *Collections of Civil Laws on Church Matters.* The legal ordinances of Roman civil legislation which refer to Church matters are contained in three collections:

1. *The Collection of Eighty-Seven Chapters (Collectio LXXXVII capitulorum).* This collection is attributed to John Scholastikos, having been drawn up during the time of his term as Patriarch (565–578) and attached as an appendix to his work *Synagoge of Ecclesiastical Canons*... This collection, divided into eighty-seven chapters, contains fragments of Justinian's *Novellae* of concerned with Church matters.

2. *The Collection of Twenty-Five Chapters (Collectio XXV capitulorum).* The editor of this collection is not known. In any case, he proceeded with this edition during the years between the death of Justinian and before Herakleios (610–641). The collection contains twenty-five chapters from the Justinian Codex and four from the *Novellae* of Justinian.

3. *Collection of Ecclesiastical Ordinances or Tripartite Collection or Paratitla (Collectio constitutionum ecclesiasticorum or Collectio Tripartita or Paratitla).* This collection contains all the civil laws concerning ecclesiastical matters which are contained in the legal collections of Justinian. As can be deduced from the title, this collection is divided into three parts. The first part contains the first thirteen titles of the Justinian Codex, in summary, together with parallel passages (*Paratitla*) from the other titles of the Codex and of the *Novellae*. The second part contains six titles without parallel passages, which are summaries of the Pandectæ and Introductions referring to spiritual matters. The third part, divided into three titles, contains three *Novellae*. At the end of the whole work, four *Novellae* of Herakleios are added. The editor of the work is not known. The date of its composition must have been the final years of the reign of Herakleios,[30] or in any case before the middle of the 7th century.[31] This collection was in general use in the East, and it would appear to have been the main source for the composition of the Nomocanon in fourteen titles.

---

[30] Biener, Heimbach, Milas
[31] Christophilopoulos, *op. cit.*, p. 50.

c) *Nomocanons*. In order to assist those charged with the administration of the Church and because of the great importance of the canons
and the relative civil laws on ecclesiastical matters, the need arose for
canons, ecclesiastical laws and civil laws to be combined in a single collection. These mixed collections were called Nomocanons.[32]

1. The first such collection to have survived until today is the Nomocanon in fifty titles, or the Nomocanon of Ioannes Scholastikos. This
collection was put together from the collection of canons by Ioannes
Scholastikos, the *Synagoge of Ecclesiastical Canons Divided into Fifty Titles* and another, attributed to the same author, in eighty-seven chapters.
Each title is displayed and under it the relevant canons and civil laws.
This Nomocanon was composed after the death of Justinian and was
later (9th century) translated into Slavonic.

2. Far greater significance was accorded to the Nomocanon in fourteen titles once attributed to Patriarch Photios, for whom it is named
the Nomocanon of Photios. In fact, however, it was composed in the
first half of the 7th century, by the author of another work, "On Apparent Contradictions" (Ἐναντιοφανείων) to which the writer of the Nomocanon refers (4, 10) as his own. According to some, this person was
Stephen, the interpreter of the *Pandectae*; according to others, it was
someone known as Anonymous. Be that as it may, the author remains
unknown. A second edition of the Nomocanon was prepared in the time
of Photios, in 883, by an unknown person, and this supplemented the
Nomocanon with canons published after the 7th century.

The subject matter of the Nomocanon is divided into fourteen titles, and each title is subdivided into chapters. Each chapter first has
the number of canons, of which the contents and purpose are uniform,
and thereafter the relevant Roman laws. The canons of the Apostles, of
the first four Ecumenical Synods, of the first eight local synods and the

---

[32] This term was later used also for collections which did not include civil laws, but only
canons, as well as canons which contained only canons of penances, e.g. the Canons of
John the Faster et al.

canons of the twelve Holy Fathers (except Tarasios) are presented in the part related to the canons in this first edition of the Nomocanon.

The second edition of this Nomocanon (883) agrees with the first in regards to content and external form. The difference lies in the fact that in the second edition, an addition was made of the canons of the Quinisext Synod in Trullo, as well as those of the Seventh Ecumenical Synod in Nicea, those of the synods held in Constantinople in the years 861 and 879 and the epistle of Patriarch Tarasios of Constantinople on simony. In this way, the second edition of the Nomocanon in fourteen titles contained all the canons then in force in the Church, the same as are in force to this day in the Orthodox Catholic Church. The second part of the Nomocanon, which included the relevant civil laws, was preserved intact, except for certain minor changes. Immediately after the Nomocanon, which had the form of a systematic table of contents of all the material on the canons, there followed the full text of the canons themselves. As time went by, because of its systematic layout and its usefulness, and after the collection of the canons had been appended to it, this Nomocanon displaced all the other collections of canons. In 920, it was officially ratified by a great synod in Constantinople, attended by representatives from the whole Church, and it was declared to have status and validity throughout the whole of the Christian Church. Since the attachment to it of the collection of canons containing the full text of the canons, the Nomocanon is today the fundamental collection of canons of the Orthodox Catholic Church.

c) *Third Period, from the Publication of the Nomocanon (883) — Ottoman Period*. After the publication of the Nomocanon, the fundamental collection of canons and ecclesiastical laws, the system of government and administration of the Church was established, and, through this, its canonical life. The legislative authority of the Church now had to apply all the fundamental laws published in the above second period and to ensure their observance in the spirit in which they were published. As time passed, because of changed relationships within the Church and the various ways in which the ecclesiastical laws were being interpreted, the need arose for the publication of new collections to meet the practical requirements of the conditions of the time. These were meant to interpret the true spirit of the fundamental laws of the Church, as well as those ecclesiastical ordinances which were in essence contained in those laws, in order that in each time the aim of the Church should be achieved: that is the salvation of Man in Christ.

During this period and for this purpose, a variety of collections of canons were published, of which the most important are those containing interpretations of the canons. This made a major contribution to the evolution of Canon Law.

During the same period, elementary collections were also published, in which the canons are presented in brief, as well as collections with interpretations and systematic collections.

To the brief collections belongs the short *Synopsis of the Nomocanon* by a certain Michael Psellos (11ᵗʰ century), which was meant for practical use, and the *Nomocanon* of Gregory Doxapatris (first half of the 12ᵗʰ century).

In about 1060, an attempt was made by Nikon, a monk of the Monastery of Roidios, on the Black Mountain, and thereafter by Symeon the New in the Wonderful Mountain in Syria to undertake a broader collection of 63 chapters, with a partial legal character, which was called Pandectæ. This work is, for the most part, still unpublished.

Interpretations of brief collections, of the full text of the canons and of the Nomocanons were written:

1. By the Deacon and Nomophylax of the Great Church of Christ, Alexios Aristenos (1130) on the Canonical Synopsis of Stephen the Ephesian, as this was later augmented. The title of Aristenos' interpretative collection is: "The Nomocanon, Interpreted, by God's Grace, by the Right Reverend Nomophylax, Lord Alexios Aristenos."

2. By John Zonaras, at the beginning of the 12ᵗʰ century, who wrote an exegesis on the full text of the canons, as these are included in the collection of canons attached to the Nomocanon in Fourteen Titles. This collection, which includes Zonaras' interpretation, bears the title: "Ex-

egesis of the Holy and Divine Canons, Those of the Holy and August Apostles and of the Sacred Ecumenical Synods, but also Those of the Local Synods and the other Holy Fathers, Made by the Monk John Zonaras, who Became the Grand Drugarios of the Vigla and Protoaskretes."

3. By Theodore Balsamon (12th century), on the Nomocanon in Fourteen Titles, by order of Emperor Manuel Komnenos and Michael Anchialos, Patriarch of Constantinople.

The title of this collection is "Exegesis of the Sacred and Divine Canons of the Holy and All-Praised Apostles and of the Sacred Ecumenical Synods, and also of the Local Synods, i.e. Some of Them, and of the Other Holy Fathers, and a Declaration of the Laws in Force and Those not in Force which Were Included in the Initial Fourteen Titles of the Texts of the Canons, Made by the Command of the King and of the Patriarch to Theodore Balsamon, the Humble Deacon of the Most Holy Great Church of God, Nomophylax, Chartophylax, and First of Vlachernae, who after some Years Became the Patriarch of the Theoupolis, Antioch the Great, and all the East."

Systematic collections were also written by:

1. Arsenios the Athonite (13th century), who composed the Synopsis of the canons in one hundred and forty-one chapters.

2. The monk Matthew Vlastares, who composed the most famous systematic work of this period (1335), the "*Syntagma* (Constitution) according to the Alphabet," divided into twenty-four parts. Under each "letter," the most important themes are included, which begin with the relevant letters of the Greek alphabet. This work consists, in all, of three hundred and three titles, each of which contains, on the one hand, the canons and, on the other, the civil laws, both in the form of a summary.

3. Constantine Armenopoulos, as a complement to his *Hexabiblos*, composed a collection of canons (14th century), which is divided into six parts, further subdivided into titles. This material formed the *Pedalion* (*Rudder*) which is in use today. With this work of Armenopoulos, the earlier history of collections of canons comes to a close.

The later era begins with the publication, in the second half of the 16th century, of the Nomocanon of Manuel Malaxos, which was the most widely-known canonical work in the Orthodox Church during the time of Ottoman rule. Also included in this Nomocanon are matters unrelated to Canon Law, i.e. philosophical, geographical and so on. Also worthy of mention is the Nomocanon in two hundred and twenty-eight chapters (beginning of the 15th century) which, in translation, forms the end of the Slavonic Great Book of Prayer (*Euchologion*). The Nomocanon of Manuel Malaxos mentioned above was composed in archaic language and survives only in four manuscripts.[33] A paraphrase was made of it in simpler language, of which many manuscripts survive, which, however, differ among themselves in regards to number of chapters and also content, because the copyists and adapters of this Nomocanon were seeking, on the one hand, to enrich it with sources other than the ones used by Malaxos, and, on the other, to adapt it to customs, as these had been formed, and also to the law as it was generally applied in practice. The greater part of Malaxos' original text remains unpublished.[34]

A certain Archimandrite Iakovos, "Chancellor (Ἐπίτροπος) of Ioannina" (1645), compiled a collection in the language of the common people, under the title "The Pastoral Staff," which was further elaborated by Neophytos, a monk on Lesvos.

Bishop Theophilos of Kampania (1749–1795) compiled a collection of laws under the title "Nomikon" or "Ecclesiastical and Civil Law" (between the years 1780–1790), in which, apart from the introduction concerning the sources of law, matters of ecclesiastical and civil law are also presented.

The collection funded by John Ispanaios from the Peloponnese, and the "New Synopsis of the Book of Laws and On Confession in Eight Books" (1753) by Demetrios Georgiou from Ioannina, the two-volume "New and Most Lavish Compilation ... of the Holy Synods" (1761), published by the

---

[33] See Christophilopoulos, *op. cit.*, p. 64.
[34] In his doctoral thesis, submitted to the Theological School of the University of Thessaloniki, Theodore Yiangou published on the canonical work of the monk Nikon.

cleric Spyridon Melias, who came from Corfu and lived in Venice, as well as the "Collection of All the Sacred and Divine Canons" (Venice 1787) by the hieromonk and preacher Agapios Leonardos from Demetsana, may be considered the most important collections published thereafter.

Of all the collections from this period, however, the most important and useful is *The Pedalion (The Rudder)*.

The Pedalion was composed in the year 1793 by the Athonite hieromonks Agapios and Nikodemos. This collection was published first in 1800, but because of the interpolation of personal views on the part of the publisher, was condemned by the author and by the Patriarchal Synod. It was then published a second time, with the approval of the Patriarchal Synod, in 1841. This second edition was used as the basis for later editions. After a long prologue, this collection contains the canons of the Apostles, of the Ecumenical and Local Synods, and, finally, the canons of the Holy Fathers, all of which are to be found in the fundamental collections of canons. Alongside the text of each canon are displayed the corresponding canons and a lengthy, detailed interpretation of the relevant canon. Finally, as an appendix, instructions and teachings are added concerning: a) the degrees of kinship and b) types of different letters and epistles of an ecclesiastical nature.

As was mentioned above, during the period of Ottoman rule, the main source of Church Law was, in essence, the decisions of the Patriarchal Synod of Constantinople, which, as in the previous period, were of a legislative, as well as administrative and judicial nature. Also of importance are the archives of the metropolises and bishoprics in which were recorded the administrative and judicial acts published by each hierarch.

The most important of all the writings concerning the sources of the collections of the Canon Law of the Orthodox Church in recent times is the collection approved by the Patriarch of Constantinople and the most important Autocephalous Churches, which thus have validity and authority over all and bears the title:

"*Syntagma* of the Divine and Sacred Canons of the Holy and All-Praised Apostles, and of the Holy Ecumenical and Local Synods and of

Certain Holy Fathers, Published with Many Other Ordinances which Condition the Existing Situation of the Church, with the Ancient Exegetes and Various Readings, G. A. Rallis and M. Potlis, with the Approval of the Holy and Great Church of Christ."

The "*Syntagma*" was published in Athens between the years 1852 – 1859, in six volumes, by Rallis, the President of the *Areios Pagos* (Supreme Court) and Potlis, Professor at the University of Athens. The first volume contains the *Nomocanon* of "Photios," while the second the canons of the Holy Apostles and of the Ecumenical Synods, as well as the final two synods in Constantinople, with the full text of the canons and the interpretations of Zonaras and Balsamon, plus the summarized version of the text of the canons with the interpretation of Aristenos.

The third volume contains the canons of the other local synods, presented in the same way as those in the second volume. The fourth contains the canons of the Holy Fathers, with the text and interpretation, as in the previous volumes. Then come those canons which were not officially approved by the Ecumenical Synods, but were nevertheless recognized by the Church as having universal validity. Also included are the "canonical responses" of Balsamon, eight (8) of his studies on the canons, four (4) studies on fasting and, finally, two (2) studies on the canons by Zonaras. The fifth volume contains canonical ordinances by the Patriarchal Synod of Constantinople from the year 911 until 1835, the laws of the Roman ("Byzantine") emperors from Justinian to Andronikos (1226), certain studies of the canons on a variety of subjects, a table of the episcopal thrones of the Orthodox Church, an essay on ecclesiastical offices, forms of ecclesiastical letters on the installation to Church offices and various other matters. The sixth volume contains the *Syntagma* according to the Alphabet by Matthew Vlastares. The *Syntagma* by Rallis and Potlis is the best work ever published on the sources of the Church Law of the Orthodox Catholic Church.

The Holy Canons and current Ecclesiastical Laws of the Greek State were published some time ago (twice, in 1923 and 1949) by the late Professor of the University of Athens and Academician, A. Alivizatos, with introductory notes on the Synods and the Holy Fathers by whom canons were issued.

The late Metropolitan Barnabas of Kitros published the Constitutional Legislation of the Church of Greece in a collection (1967) and, in another volume, the Constitutional Legislation of the Orthodox Patriarchates (1971). Metropolitan Panteleimon of Corinth wrote the Key "Of the Sacred Canons" (1971), the Key "Of the Orthodox Canonical Ordinances" (1979) and the Key "Of the Proceedings and Texts of the Local and Ecumenical Synods of the Undivided Church" (1986).

6 LATER CONSTITUTIONAL LEGISLATION OF THE LOCAL AUTOCEPHALOUS ORTHODOX CHURCHES. All the individual autocephalous Orthodox Churches, which are in communion of faith, mysteries and ecclesiastical administration and order, together constitute one Church, the "one Holy, Catholic and Apostolic Church." It follows, therefore, that the administration of all the Orthodox Churches is uniform, common to all and unalterable, given that the Church always showed great concern to ensure that, in parallel with the confession of the faith, there should also be preserved "ecclesiastical order, with the wisdom of each (bishop) and all" (2nd canon of the Synod in Cartagena). This concern was shown also in the decisions of the Ecumenical Synods which refer to matters of faith but also of order, both through the whole tradition of the Church. All the local Orthodox Churches are in agreement on this principle. This is, of course, true for the general and fundamental principles, while individual institutional ordinances vary in the local Churches. These are altered from time to time, depending on the relationship between Church and State achieved in the country and on specific occurrences or local conditions, which have often disturbed the position of certain local Churches in regards to the canonical exactitude and tradition of the Church.

The late Metropolitan of Kitros, Barnabas Tzortzatos, as mentioned above, published the basic administrative institutions of the Orthodox Patriarchates (in Athens, 1972), and also the Constitutional Legislation of the Church of Greece (in Athens, 1967), the basic administrative institutions of the Orthodox Church of Greece (in Athens, 1977) as well as the basic administrative institutions of other autocephalous Orthodox Churches (Cyprus, Poland and Albania). More recently, the Church of Cyprus has itself published its new Constitutional Charter (in the periodical *Apostolos Barnabas*, 1979).

Since the Church within the realm of Greece belongs canonically either to the Ecumenical Patriarchate or the Autocephalous Church of Greece, we refer only to the constitutional laws of these two Churches in the Greek text of this book.[35] In this English translation, we have not published the Patriarchal and Synodical Tomes and Acts which refer to the Church of Greece. In their place, the Charters of the Holy Archdiocese of America, which have been granted by the Ecumenical Patriarchate from the founding of the Holy Archdiocese until today, have been included.

1. The Ecumenical Patriarchate, first throne of Orthodoxy and as such designated by decisions of the Second, Fourth and Sixth Ecumenical Synods and by long historical tradition, has from the first been administered on the basis of the Sacred Canons and the State ordinances of Roman law. Its administrative institutions, then, should be sought in those ordinances, as well as in various sigillia, tomes, memoranda, en-

---

[35] Subject to the Ecumenical Patriarchate are: the semi-autonomous Church of Crete, the metropolises of the Dodecanese and those of the so-called Neae Chorae, i.e. Epirus (except Arta), Macedonia, Thrace, the eastern islands of the Aegean and, in Thessaly, the Metropolis of Elasson. Also the monastic Community of the Holy Mountain and the stavropegic monasteries of Patmos, Vlatadon in Thessaloniki and St. Anastasia in Halkidiki. To the Autocephalous Church of Greece belong the metropolises of Terra Firma Greece or Rumeli and the Cyclades islands, the Peloponnese, Thessaly (except Elasson), the Ionian islands and Arta from Epirus. By a Patriarchal and Synodal Act (1928), the Metropolitans of the New Lands (Ecumenical Patriarchate) take part in the synods of the Hierarchy of the Autocephalous Church of Greece and also, in equal numbers with those of the eparchies of the Autocephalous Church of Greece, in the Permanent Holy Synod of the Church of Greece. Thus, while "the highest canonical right of the Most Holy Patriarchal Ecumenical Throne is retained, the administration in these individual eparchies is conducted" by the Church of Greece "as steward" and has been since 1928.

cyclicals and decisions of the Ecumenical Patriarch and the Synod under his presidency, in customs and traditions. In the year 1635, hierarchs and other officials, clerics and laymen attempted without success to draw up regulations for the administration of the Patriarchate. During the term in office of Patriarch Sophronios II (1774 – 80), another attempt was made to compose regulations, drawn up in 1775 and ratified by the *Hatti Şerif* of the Sultan Selim III. These regulations envisaged the setting up of an Economic Committee of the Patriarchate, to consist of four hierarchs and sixteen lay members. Due to fierce opposition, largely on the part of the hierarchical clergy, these regulations were watered down before being implemented. Another attempt was made to draw up regulations in 1847, but without success.

Following the publication of the first *Hatti Şerif* (Edict) by Sultan Abdul Meçit (1839), by which religious freedom was guaranteed to all subjects of the Ottoman Empire, this was confirmed by another, the *Hatti Hümayun*, 1856, which more precisely defined the relations between the Government and the various religions, in particular toward the Orthodox Church. After the provisions of the Treaty of Paris (1856), a provisional National Council was formed in 1858, consisting of seven hierarchs and twenty-one lay members, under the chairmanship of the Ecumenical Patriarch or the next hierarch in seniority. Patriarch Kallinikos of Alexandria, who was living in Constantinople at that time, also took part. Between the years 1858 – 1860, and after much wrangling, this Council drew up the General or National Regulations of the Ecumenical Patriarchate, which were ratified by the Ottoman Government (1858 – 1862). As such, they became laws of the State and remained in force until 1923.[36]

After the Asia Minor catastrophe and the signing of the Treaty of Lausanne (1923), the Ecumenical Patriarchate was restricted to its religious mission, and its administrative jurisdiction was located within its eccle-

---

[36] *General Regulations for the Settlement of the Ecclesiastical and National Matters of the Orthodox Christian Subjects of His Majesty the Sultan in Constantinople who are under the Jurisdiction of the Ecumenical Throne*. From the Patriarchal Press 1888. See in Bas. Stavridis, *The Ecumenical Patriarchs 1860 – Today*, Thessaloniki, 1978.

siastical responsibilities, which the Ecumenical Throne has acquired over centuries through tradition and on the basis of unalterable ordinances.[37]

2. After the liberation of Greece from Turkish occupation, and within the framework of the politics of the great powers of the day concerning the dismemberment of the Ottoman Empire, a number of small states were created in the Balkan region, each with a local national and spiritual consciousness. This policy was implemented in preference to the reestablishment of the earlier Roman state ("Byzantium"), the religious, spiritual and cultural heritage of which Orthodoxy, through the Ecumenical Patriarchate, had retained during the Ottoman occupation throughout the whole extent of the Ottoman state. Thus, in 1833, the Church of Greece was declared autocephalous by the Vice-Regent in a wholly uncanonical and unacceptable move. In this declaration, which was made uncanonically and without the prior consent of the Ecumenical Patriarchate, the hierarchs of free Greece who had assembled in Nafplion agreed to nominate the Permanent Holy Synod as the highest administrative body of the Church of Greece, which at the time was, in essence, schismatic. This declaration naturally provoked a strong reaction, but nevertheless, the Constitution of 1844 "of the National Assembly of the Greeks on September 3rd, in Athens" (1844), contained an article concerning the autocephalous Church of Greece. This article has since been included verbatim in all succeeding constitutions. Following petitions by the Church in Greece and the Greek Government, the Ecumenical Patriarchate declared the Church of Greece autocephalous in the year 1850, through the publication of a Patriarchal and Synodal Tome, which was accompanied by a Patriarchal Encyclical to the Hierarchy of Greece and to the Orthodox laity in Greece.

---

[37] In the appendix (p. 213 ff), we have set out the situation as it exists today in the Ecumenical Patriarchate, as contained in the work *The Ecumenical Patriarchate* (Athens 1967, pp. 95–107 in Greek) by Prof. Bas. Stavridis and as they were properly ordered by the late Metropolitan of Kitros, Barnabas Tzortzatos, in his work *The Basic Administrative Institutions of the Orthodox Patriarchates* (Athens 1972, pp. 31–37, in Greek) and as set out in the *Hemerologion* (Diary-Diptychs) of the Ecumenical Patriarchate for the year 1998.

Later, through other Patriarchal and Synodal Acts, the ecclesiastical eparchies of the Ionian islands were ceded to the Church of Greece, after their own integration into Greece (1866), as were the eparchies of Arta in Epirus and Thessaly[38] after their incorporation into the Greek state. In 1928, the eparchies of the Neae Chorae (i.e. Macedonia, Epirus, Thrace, and the islands of the Eastern Aegean except for the Dodecanese) were assigned to the stewardship, so that the ecclesiastical administrative organization of the Orthodox Church of Greece today is as described above.

We find the first official faltering steps toward an administrative organization for the Church in Greece, of which the invaluable contribution to the Greek nation, both during the time of enslavement and also during the liberation struggle had attracted deserved recognition and gratitude,[39] in the *Hegemonikon*, or *Royal Constitution*, of 1832, which never came into force. Articles 6 – 12 of this document refer to religion in general and especially to the administration of the Church. The following year, 1833, a Royal Ordinance was published under the title "Declaration concerning the Independence of the Greek Church," which was the Constitutional Charter of the Greek Church, which, as was said above, had arbitrarily broken away. This ordinance, expressing the absolutist ideas of the age and also the Protestant outlook of Mauer, the member of the triumvirate Vice-Regency responsible for Church affairs, was a copy of foreign models, especially that of the Bavarian Consistory, and contained regulations which were fundamentally uncanonical. Thus, it overturned the mutual cooperation which had existed for centuries since, indeed, the time of Constantine the Great in relations between Church and State, and made the Church, in essence, a servant of the State. The uncanonical

---

[38] "…the most Holy Metropolis of Larissa, with the most holy Bishoprics of Trikka, Stagoi, Thavmakos and Gardikion under it and the most holy Metropolises of Arta, Demetriada and Phanariapharsala and the most holy Bishopric of Platamon, subject to the most holy Metropolis of Thessaloniki, as also twenty villages of the most holy Metropolis of Ioannina from the department of Tsoumerka and three others of the same Metropolis from the department of Malakasi…" (Patriarchal and Synodal Act of 1882).
[39] Cf. Metropolitan Barnabas of Kitros, *The Constitutional Legislation of the Church of Greece* … (in Greek, p. 71ff).

regulations contained in this Ordinance were, unfortunately, retained for a long time, were included in later legislation, and affected the whole of ecclesiastical legislation, as, indeed, they do to this day.

After the declaration of the autocephaly of the Church of Greece by the Ecumenical Patriarchate in 1850, Laws 200, "concerning Bishoprics and Bishops and the clergy serving under Bishops," and 201, "concerning the Charter of the Holy Synod of the Church of Greece," were published in 1852. These laws, despite the clear instruction in the Patriarchal Tome regarding non-interference by the State in the internal affairs of the Church, basically legislated on these matters in the spirit of Mauer's law of 1833, retaining the uncanonical, centralized system of administration (Permanent Holy Synod) and especially the absolute State authority in Church/State relations, making the Royal Commissioner in the Synod all-powerful. Any decisions of the Synod which were not signed by the Commissioner were invalid.

These laws remained in force until the end of 1923, when they were replaced by the Charter of December 31, 1923, published following a resolution by the Plastiras Revolutionary Government. This law brought an improvement in the administration of the Church and a partial restoration of canonical order. It attempted to end the centralized system of administration, abolished the Permanent Holy Synod and restored the canonical institution of the Holy Synod of the Hierarchy as the highest administrative authority of the Church of Greece. Bishops were now to be elected by this body, the power of the Royal Commissioner was reduced to a minimum, and interventions by the State in the affairs of the Church, on the pretext of legality, were restricted.

This law, unfortunately, did not survive long, but was modified after two years (1925), during the Pangalos dictatorship, by means of a Legislative Ordinance which brought back into force many of the provisions of Laws 200 and 201. There followed numerous modifications through the publication of new laws concerning the administration of the Church — 5187/1931, 5438/1932, P. D. 25-5/178.1932. This last Presidential Decree also underwent many modifications through a series of Compulsory Laws. In 1940, following advice from the Holy Synod, there was published a Charter of the Church of Greece, no. 2170/1940. None of these laws added anything of substance to the administration of the Church, nor did they allow it to be run in accordance with its own, centuries-old canonical tradition, but rather continued, in their essentials, the ecclesiastical policy imported from abroad and imposed on the Church by Mauer.

During the time of Archbishop Damaskinos, the Charter 671/1943 was published which was ratified by Cabinet Act 184/26.3.46. Through this law, ecclesiastical administration was improved, and an attempt was made to gain separation for the Church from the State, particularly in regards to the election of the Archbishop and Metropolitans. A series of amendments again followed, without the consent of the Church, principally from the year 1959 and thereafter, when tension arose in Church/State relations.

Intervention by the State in Church affairs also occurred in 1967 by the dictatorship, and without consultation with the Church, Compulsory Law 3/1967 was published, by which the Holy Synod of the Hierarchy was essentially disbanded and a nine-member Permanent Holy Synod instituted (comprising four hierarchs from the Church of Greece, four of the Metropolitans of the Ecumenical Patriarchate from the Neae Chorae and the Archbishop of Athens. In a departure from all the sacred canons, a Holy Synod *"according to superior merit"* (ἀριστίνδην) was temporarily appointed (until September 30, 1967) with the possibility of extending its term (it was extended until March 10, 1969). Law 3/1967 stated a) that the election of the Archbishop of Athens and of metropolitans was henceforth to pass from the Synod of the Hierarchy (671/1943) to the Permanent Holy Synod and b) that the King was to choose them, from three candidates to be submitted to him by the Permanent Holy Synod, as had occurred under Laws 200 and 201 (of 1850).

In 1969, a Charter of the Church of Greece was published (Law 126) which provided for three central bodies of administration for the Church: the Holy Synod of the Hierarchy, the Permanent Holy Synod and the General Church Assembly plus two executive bodies — entirely new from the point of view of Canon Law — the Central Ecclesiastical Council and the Synodal Administration. The Archbishop of Athens was appointed chairman of all these central administrative and executive organs.

In 1977, after the reestablishment of democracy, the present Constitution of the Church of Greece (Law 590) was passed by the Parliament. This provides for two central bodies of the Church of Greece, i.e. the canonical institution of the Holy Synod of the Hierarchy and the Permanent Holy Synod, as the Permanent administrative organ of the Holy Synod of the Hierarchy. Both bodies have their headquarters in Athens and are headed by the Archbishop at the time. This Constitution also provides, as did the previous one, for the operation of twelve (12) Synodal Committees attached to the Synod. These are to report to the Holy Synod on particular matters arising, on which the Synod itself will then decide. It is important that through the present Constitutional Charter, there is laid down (as there was in the previous Charter) the right of the Holy Synod of the Hierarchy to publish canonical regulations on the organization and internal administration of the Church, published in *Ecclesia*, the official organ of the Church of Greece, and through the *Journal of the Government*. This law also enshrined the generally accepted right, based on decisions of the Ecumenical Synods, of appeal to the Ecumenical Patriarchate for all the hierarchs of the Church of Greece and not only those of the Neae Chorae. The present Constitutional Charter is a positive feature in the relationship between the Church and State and, to a great extent, restores the canonical administration of the Church of Greece.

7 **THE APPLICATION OF THE SOURCES OF CANON LAW. A)** *The Status and Implementation of the Holy Canons.* In this chapter, the canons issued by the Church and their status are examined on the basis of its authority.

The canons differ from one another in regards to their subject. Canons which refer to dogmas and faith are called "*terms*" (ὅροι). The Church does not create new dogmas, but invests truths already revealed in a clear and precisely formulated written model. Terms are absolutely unalterable.

The other institutions of good order and discipline which regulate the external life of the faithful are necessary for the maintenance of ecclesiastical order and for the accomplishment of the aim which is the very *raison d'être* of the existence of the Church. These are the disciplinary and administrative canons, which, despite the fact that they also have a theological and dogmatic basis, may be modified and altered in accordance with the needs of the Church and the changes wrought by social conditions and by the times. These alterations may be made, as they always have been in the life of the Church provided that they safeguard the fundamental institutions of ecclesiastical governance and that they are observed with due deference to earlier canons. Any alterations must be made after proper attention and reflection and without haste, so as not to represent a stumbling-block to the faithful.

The 12th canon of the Synod in Trullo, for example, states that a married clergyman who becomes a bishop may not live together with his wife. This canon was a reversal of the fifth Apostolic Canon, which threatened a bishop with defrocking if he put away his wife. This alteration was imposed by the conditions of the age, and the synod in question justified its decision by stating that this custom, i.e. of a bishop living together with his wife, had, at that time, become a stumbling-block for the people. And it concludes: "Since, therefore, it is our particular care that all things should be effected for the benefit of the flock in our hand, it has seemed good that henceforth nothing of the kind shall in any way occur. And we say this not to abolish and overthrow legislation passed with Apostolic authority, but for the salvation of the peoples and their advancement to better things, and lest any reproach be directed at hieratic prestige. For the divine Apostle says: 'Do all to the glory of God, give none offense, neither to the Jews, nor to the Greeks, nor to the Church of God, even as I please all men in all things, not seeking mine own profit but the profit of many, that they may be saved. Be imitators of me, as I am of Christ.'"

The canons may also be divided into general and particular, according to the sphere of their validity and status.

General canons are those in force throughout the Church and having to do with the fundamental matters of the administration and form of government of the Church, while the particular ones are those which have validity in this or that geographical ecclesiastical area, this or that branch of Church administration, this or that Church institution and so on. These are the two essential differences between the canons according to their subject, i.e. the sphere of authority and force of each.

Due to this difference between the canons, their status and implementation is different. For a canon to enjoy the necessary status and force for its implementation, certain basic terms have to be observed, some of which are concerned with the internal character of the canon and others with the external.

In regards to the internal character of the canon, this must have been issued by the Church authority responsible, within the bounds of its circle of activity, the subject matter of the canon must be of an ecclesiastical nature, its substance must agree with the basic principles of the Church and, finally, it must have in view the interest and the benefit of the faithful.

With regard to the external character of the canon, to become valid it must be published or ratified by the competent ecclesiastical authority ("*promulgatio*"), as has been enjoined.[40]

All the institutions of the Church issued on the basis of the authority given to it are obligatory for all its members.

The idea of this power to compel was expressed in the second canon of the Ecumenical Synod in Trullo, which having numbered all the canons issued by the Church until that time, which the whole Church is obliged to accept and recognize, declares: "No one shall be permitted to countermand or set aside the canons previously laid down, or to recognize and accept any canons, other than the ones herein specified, that

---

[40] Cf. Holy Scripture: Exod. 20:1 – 22, Matt. 5:17ff, John 10:34.

have been composed under a false inscription by certain persons who have undertaken to barter the truth. If, nevertheless, anyone be caught innovating with regard to any of the said canons, or attempting to subvert it, he shall be responsible in respect to that canon and shall receive the penance which it prescribes and be chastized by that canon which he has offended."

In the first of their canons, the Fathers of the Seventh Ecumenical Synod affirm, in regards to the canon of the Quinisext quoted above: "We welcome and embrace the divine canons, and we corroborate the entire and rigid fiat of them that have been set forth by the renowned Apostles, who were and are trumpets of the Spirit and those both of the six holy Ecumenical Synods and of the ones which assembled regionally for the purpose of setting forth such edicts, and of those of our Holy Fathers. For all those men, having been guided by the light dawning out of the same Spirit, prescribed rules that are in our best interest."

These canons clearly affirm the obligatory force and authority of all the canons issued by the Church for all those who belong to it.

According to the synods mentioned, the canons issued by synods up to that time have obligatory force and authority. The legislative task of the Church did not end there, however. It continues to be performed and will be so forever by the Church, and its canons will have obligatory force and authority, always provided that this legislative task is carried out canonically, on the basis of the fundamental institutions of the Church.

The institutions of faith and ethics have absolute force and authority over all the members of the Church, at all places and all times.

The Church institutions which define the external relations of the Church also have absolute validity. However, the legislative authority of the Church has and always will have the right, while keeping faithfully to the fundamental principles of the Gospel, to revoke earlier institutions and adopt new ones, according to circumstances. This also happened in the past. Later synods did away with institutions from earlier ones or invested them in a different manner. Any synod convoked today would also have the right to employ this right.

It follows, then, that the ordinances of the two synods mentioned do not forbid the legislative authority of the Church to alter older institutions, but allow it to modify the canons enumerated by them in their substance and in a manner which does not conflict with the basic institutions and spirit of the Church. They curb arbitrariness on the part of individuals, no matter what rank they hold in the hierarchy, and they also set limits on local Churches to prevent them from altering institutions which have been accepted by the Church as a whole, in such a way as would be at variance with the general Canon Law. They do not, however, prevent the responsible Church authority, should new needs of the Church dictate, from publishing new canons, nor from investing existing ones in a new formula, while keeping faithfully to the predominant spirit of the canonical and legal institutions of the Church. The Holy Spirit, who enlightened the Fathers, has never ceased — nor will He ever do so — to act in the Church, when its Fathers come together in one place in the name of Christ to meet the needs of the Church by altering existing institutions or publishing new ones.

The validity and status of the canons referred to by the Quinisext and Seventh Ecumenical Synods should not be understood as absolute, but rather as relative, i.e. of such duration as the time until a new legislative body emerges equipped with the same authority to publish canons and institutions as these two synods enjoyed.

The Quinisext Synod in Trullo, which in this way proclaimed the universal force and authority of the canons and institutions accepted by the whole Church for all its members allowed local Churches, through canon 39, to have their own ecclesiastical law for the administration of their external life. This specific law, however, should, in its fundamentals, agree with the general basic institutions of the Church, be imbued with the spirit of the general Canon Law and in its special form continue to seek the same final goal as that pursued by general Canon Law.

Moreover, the canonical and legal ordinances of the individual Churches have status and validity only in those Churches themselves, so long as they are not revoked by the responsible authority or have been replaced by other canons. For the sake of mutual relations between the individual Churches, of order and for unity in the faith, the institutions in force in the individual Churches ought to enjoy the respect of the other Churches too and, above all, to be consistent with the Holy Canons, ecclesiology and the general canonical tradition of the Church.

Every member of the Church without exception is subject to its institutions, but above all, those who hold ecclesiastical authority, the Church leaders, the bishops, who may not extend their authority over the Church teachings accepted and confirmed as proper to be held and preached,[41] nor over the ordinances concerning the fundamental institutions of the Church, nor over the liturgical ordinances adopted by it. Not only are they themselves are bound to observe these, but they must provide for their observance by all others too.[42]

Also subject to the institutions of the Church are those leaders and political authorities who desire to have a share in the spiritual benefits of the Church. Emperor Markianos, speaking concerning a disciplinary matter on which the Fourth Ecumenical Synod was about to decide, expressed the following view: "Whatever the Holy Synod decides is a law unto me; I follow it and believe in it."[43]

This he said because political authority does not have unlimited force in the Church, nor may it address ecclesiastical matters and issues directly, but only, when there is a need, through the Church authority and with its express consent.[44]

---

[41] "For those who have been allotted a sacerdotal dignity, the representations of canonical ordinances amount to testimonies and directions ... Seeing that these things are so and are attested to us and rejoicing at them 'as one who finds great spoils' (Ps. 118:162) we welcome and embrace the divine canons, and we corroborate the entire and rigid fiat of them that have been set forth by the renowned Apostles, who were and are trumpets of the Spirit and those both of the six holy Ecumenical Synods and of the ones which assembled regionally for the purpose of setting forth such edicts, and of those of our Holy Fathers. For all those men, having been guided by the light dawning our of the same Spirit, prescribed rules that are to our best interest" (Canon 1 of the Seventh Ecumenical Synod). See also Canons 7 of the Third, 1 and 19 of the Quinisext.

[42] Canons 29, 32 and 81 of the Quinisext Ecumenical Synod.

[43] J. Harduin, *Conciliorum Collectio Regia Maxima*, Concil B 432–434, Paris 1715.

[44] "If any bishop, or presbyter, or anyone at all of the Canon (clergy), without the consent and letters of the bishops in the province, and especially of the bishop having

The Church permits exemption from observance of ecclesiastical ordinances only when physical or moral powers have failed. It, thus, applies economy, while preserving the validity of the canons.

B) *Interpretation of the Sacred Canons.* Like every other law, in its implementation, an ecclesiastical canon also must clearly define the content of a certain canonical relationship, i.e. it must clearly express the meaning of the canon which guarantees the authenticity of this canonical relationship against any arbitrariness and error. For the interpretation of the canons of the Church, the method generally employed is rather more

---

charge of the metropolis, should presume to betake himself to the King, let him be outlawed and made to be an outcast not only from communion, but also from the dignity which he happens to have, on the grounds that he has been guilty of daring to trouble the ears of our most God-beloved King, contrary to the law of the Church. But, if any urgent need should require any one to go to the King, he must do so after reflection and with the consent and approval of bishop in charge of the metropolis of the province, or of those therein, and be furnished with letters from them" (Canon 11 of the Synod in Antioch).

"If any clergyman has a dispute with another clergyman, let him not forsake his own bishop and resort to secular courts, but let him first submit the matter to his own bishop or let it be tried by referees chosen by both parties and approved by the bishop. Let anyone who acts contrary hereto be liable to canonical penalties. If, on the other hand, a clergyman has a dispute with his own bishop, or with some other bishop, let it be tried by the Synod of the Province (eparchy). But if any bishop or clergyman has a dispute with the metropolitan of the same province, let him apply either to the exarch of the diocese or to the throne of the royal capital, Constantinople, and let it be tried before him" (Canon 9 of the Fourth Ecumenical Synod).

"Any election of a bishop, priest or deacon by temporal rulers shall be invalid, in accordance with the canon which states: 'If any bishop comes into possession of a church by the aid of the secular rulers, let him be deposed from office and excommunicated, and all those who communicate with him, too'". Canon 30 of the Apostolic Canons. "For he who is to be promoted to a bishopric must be voted for by bishops, as was decreed by the holy fathers of Nicea ..." (Canon 3 of the Seventh Ecumenical Synod).

"Since there actually is a canon which says that twice a year in each eparchy, canonical matters shall be discussed in an assembly (synod) of bishops; but because of the inconvenience and lack of means faced by those called upon to assemble, the holy Fathers of the Sixth Synod decreed that one assembly be held each year, without any regard to means or excuse, and that things which are amiss be corrected. This canon we now renew. And if any temporal ruler be found to be forestalling this, let him be excommunicated ..." (Canon 6 of the Seventh Ecumenical Synod). Cf. also canons 5 and 12 of Antioch, 8 and 9 of Sardica and others.

free than that of interpretation of the provisions of civil law, the aim being to disclose the true meaning, beneath its linguistic integument, of the ordinance being interpreted: "Moved by the Holy Spirit, holy men of God spoke" (2 Peter 1:21). It is not, therefore, possible to interpret the Sacred Canons, which are the expression of the Holy Spirit dwelling in the Church, in accordance with the dry letter, but rather through the same Spirit through whom they were written. "Who (God) has made us worthy to be servants of the New Testament. Not of the letter, but of the spirit. For the letter kills but the spirit gives life" (2 Cor. 3:5 – 6). This spirit of freedom allows us to seek the true meaning of the ordinance being interpreted. The individual ordinances of Canon Law are not the products of a single legislative will, but are of different ages and historical provenance, and therefore, the proper method for their interpretation is historical, with due regard to the special features mentioned above. It is required in particular that the canons be interpreted in relation to the legal and canonical climate to which the sources of each are linked in terms of time and place, their ecclesiological basis and their validity within today's legislative system, a task which is not always straightforward.

In the implementation of Canon Law, particular importance is attached to the institution of economy, which makes it more flexible and subtle than any other branch of the law. Ecclesiastical economy is "the permitted temporary or permanent divergence from exactitude, either from need or for the sake of the greater benefit of certain members or of the Church as a whole, officially, under certain preconditions, and providing that respect remains unsullied and dogma intact." This non-implementation of otherwise applicable Canon Law may be exercised with a view to the future or retrospectively, so that in the first case, the consequences provided for by law would not be implemented from then on, and, in the second, that those already applied would be moderated.

There is no limitation in regards to the exercise of the most ancient institution of economy, provided, as has already been said, that no harm is done to the dogma of the Orthodox faith. Since ecclesiastical economy is an expression of unfettered Church freedom, it should not be exercised in advance since it would then be no more than mere casuistry, bereft of any spark of the spirit and unable to balance the attachment of the Orthodox Church to the precision of tradition. This institution is, as has been mentioned, very ancient and has been applied unceasingly by the Church, but there is no actual canon which regulates it *ex professo*, it being indirectly recognized in certain canons.

c) *Abrogation of the Sacred Canons.* The *dogmas* (terms of the faith, ὅροι), as was mentioned earlier, are unalterable and unchangeable, while those concerning ecclesiastical good order (τάξις) and discipline are subject to alteration in accordance with the needs of the Church and the changes in life which social conditions and circumstances create over the centuries.

A canon, properly introduced, has power and authority for as long as it is not altered in the canonically accepted way. Every alteration is either general or partial.

In the first case, the force of the law ceases entirely (*abrogatio*), and it loses its power either as the result of a direct decision from the competent legislative authority or because the law has passed into disuse (*desuetudo*) since no one observes it. "Just as the form of the law is written or unwritten, so its rescinding occurs either by a written law or through unwritten, i.e. disuse."[45] In the second case, only a part of a particular law or canon may be rescinded through a new addition or it may be replaced, or not replaced, in its entirety. It is, however, possible for a law to be in force and for only certain individuals to be exempt from its observance. This occurs either by reason of privilege (*privilegium*) or by economy and consent (*despensatio*).

1. Abrogation (rescinding) of a law may occur:

a) When the competent legislative authority, for justifiable reasons, publishes a new law in its place, in which case the new law comes into force in place of the preceding one. Any law, however, can be rescinded only by an authority either of equal and like standing to the one which

---

[45] Commentary by Balsamon on chap. III of the *Nomocanon in Fourteen Titles.*

published it, or superior to it. The Ecumenical Synods, as the highest legislative authorities in the Church, were empowered to exercise that right over all those laws adopted before them which, because of the needs of the Church, had to be replaced.

We mentioned earlier that canon 12 of the Quinisext Ecumenical Synod rescinded the 5th Apostolic Canon. The ruling, in canons 37 of the Apostles, 5 of the First Ecumenical Synod and 19 of the Fourth Ecumenical Synod, according to which episcopal Synods were required to meet twice a year in each metropolitan area, was also rescinded by canons 8 of the Quinisext and 6 of the Seventh Ecumenical Synod, because of the circumstances of the Church. These canons ordained that in the future such synods might also meet once a year and not twice.

b) A canon published for a specific length of time and because of particular circumstances ceases to have the force and action of law after this time has expired, and especially when the particular cases no longer exist.[46]

c) The force and action of a canon cease if the subject addressed by it no longer exists, or no longer exists in the same way as envisaged in the canon, or if the canonical or legal need which brought forth the canon no longer exists. For example, in the early years of the Church, the jurisdiction of the ecclesiastical authorities was extended not only to transgressions of Christians, of an ecclesiastical nature, but also to violations of a political character. "If anyone insults the king or temporal lord, contrary to what is right and just, let him pay the penalty: if he be a clergyman let him be defrocked, if a layman, excommunicated" (84th Apostolic Canon).

This action of the Church was justified by the fact that it was governed entirely separately from pagan political society. When the Church became linked to the state, however, and the latter began to protect the Church and provide for the maintenance of order within it, all legal matters concerning Christians which were not of a purely ecclesiastical

---

[46] Cf. Canon 102 of the Synod in Cartagena: "The contents of the present canon, being earlier by far, have been set aside." Commentary by Balsamon on this canon. Cf. canon 3 of the Quinisext, 8 of Neocæsarea et al.

nature passed into the civil courts and so the canons relating to those courts ceased to be functional.

d) A canon ceases to be in effect if it no longer corresponds to the changed circumstances in which the Church finds itself and the ecclesiastical authority deems it necessary to rescind it because of these new relations, or if Church legislation, because of these changed relations, adopts new canons on a subject, which differ from those already in existence on the same subject. Without it being expressly stated, the previous canons are rescinded.[47]

e) If a new canon or law does not state its meaning explicitly and absolutely, it must then be accepted that the legislator aimed at the rescinding of such content as would be out of concord with the conditions of the times, while that which was not included would remain in force and valid as before. In the *Basilica*, this law is expressed as follows: "The specific prevails over the general" (Book 2, title III, 80).

The 2nd canon of the Synod in Constantinople (879), for example, declares that a bishop who embraces the monastic life of repentance and asceticism should not lay claim to the office of bishop. Through this canon, the custom which had been introduced into the Church whereby certain bishops neglected their ecclesiastical affairs and devoted themselves to the monastic life was abolished. Despite this, the practice and custom of a hieromonk being elevated to the office of bishop is in no way repealed.[48]

A law may also cease to be in force through not being applied or through the introduction of a custom different from that law. In his commentary on the *Nomocanon in Fourteen Titles*, Balsamon mentions the proposal of Vulpianus, that a law may cease to be in force if it is not applied. Therefore, this canon of Roman legislation also acquired immediate significance for ecclesiastical legislation. Desuetude, however, must be entirely justified, and the custom prevailing against the positive canon be based on truth and be in harmony with the general spirit of the law. "That which is not introduced with reason but has prevailed

---

[47] Cf. the 5th Apostolic Canon in relation to canon 12 of the Quinisext Synod et al.
[48] See the interpretations of Zonaras and Balsamon on the above canon.

through error and custom should not be retained in similar cases. The authority of habit and use is not so great as to overcome reason and the law" (Basilica Book II, title I 47, 51).

According to the decision of the Synod which met in Constantinople in 861 (AB) "nothing introduced against order and the law can revoke what has been canonically decreed." It follows that only reasons and relations arising from the internal life of the Church are able to bring about the rescinding of an existing law. That is, this can only happen if the absolute need has been recognized for the use and application of things which are different from those which have been in force so far; if it is a matter of guaranteeing the security of the internal canonical life and the external peace of the Church; and if, in the pursuit of this, there is no suggestion of political or other aims and efforts foreign to the spirit and interests of the Church. In addition, the validity of a canon can be rescinded only by the competent authority and must fall within the bounds set by the general legislation of the Church, taking into account all the factors arguing in favor of the need for rescinding the canon. The new canon must be better and more complete than the one rescinded, truly sufficient for the needs of the Church. Finally, it must be based on the immutable fundamental canons and institutions of the Church and depend entirely upon them.

2. It may be possible for a canon still to be in force but for certain people to be excused from observing it for the sake of economy, the result of this being that someone is given exceptional exemption, by the competent authority, from the observation of the ordinances of the canon in question. Economy or acquiescence does not have the sense of necessity, *per se*, but is rather permission and concession toward human weakness, justified by the attempt to rebuff or prevent some wrong. Either that, or it is applied for a certain time for the general benefit within the Church.

In all legal ordinances which are issued by people, the rule applies that it is possible to grant permission and exemption from their observance when the general good demands this or if, the need for concession and forgiveness should arise for the sake of particular persons.

This principle is also valid for the canons and ordinances published by the ecclesiastical authority. The canons permit those entrusted with ecclesiastical authority to allow concessions and to be lenient toward certain people in regards to the strictness of the application of the canons in question, especially in exceptional circumstances, provided the general good of the Church is promoted by this or that order is guaranteed within it. "And change of the law occurs out of need," said Patriarch Sophronios in a letter of his (August 1864). Basil the Great, in his first letter to Bishop Amphilochios (canon 1), states that heretics returning to the Church must be accepted, though he permits this canon to be breached "if it were to prove an obstacle to general economy." In his letters to Maximos of Antioch and Archimandrite Gennadios, Cyril of Alexandria also mentions acquiescence and concession toward the strict observance of the canons in certain cases.[49]

This leniency within the Church is in no way dependent on the free will of the leaders of the Church. Rather, there are clearly defined limits within which they are to act, these being the protection of the dogma of the Church and of the institutions which the whole Church has invested with general force and validity.

As was noted above, only the law has the right to grant concessions or to implement economy, and those in authority may act only within certain boundaries and on the authorization explicitly given to them by the legislative power. For example, canon 2 of the Synod in Ankara states: "As for deacons who likewise sacrificed to idols, but thereafter succeeded in recovering their senses, they are to enjoy the other marks of honor, but are to cease all sacred services, including both that of the bread and that of offering the cup and that of teaching. But should some of the bishops, however, sympathize with their toil and meek humility, and wish to give them something further or to take away anything, the power rests with them."

Economy or concession ends when the cause which occasioned it is removed.

---

[49] Cf. Canons 12 of the First Ecumenical Synod, 102 of the Quinisext, 10 of Peter of Alexandria. 4, 5, 7, and 8 of Gregory of Nyssa, et al.

D) *Holy Canons and Civil Laws on Ecclesiastical Matters.* It was said above that the sources of Canon and Ecclesiastical Law are, on the one hand, ecclesiastical legislation (Holy Scripture, Sacred Canons, patriarchal and synodal acts, custom, traditions, etc.), with the Church as legislative source, and, on the other, civil legislation (laws of the Roman emperors on ecclesiastical matters, and in the modern Greek State, the Constitution, the constitutional acts a variety of laws and in general every act of the State related to the arrangement of Church matters), with the State as legislative source.

Ecclesiastical legislation, particularly the Apostolic Canons, the Canons of the Ecumenical Synods, the canons of local synods and of the Fathers, ratified by Ecumenical Synods, as well as many patriarchal and synodal decisions, based on Orthodox ecclesiology, i.e. the Orthodox dogmatic teaching concerning the Church, is legislation of the whole Orthodox Church everywhere on earth and is binding on all Orthodox. As an expression of ecclesiology in practical affairs of administration and order, as well as of the religious life, this legislation also constitutes a common possession of all the individual Orthodox Churches and a powerful bond between them.

It is well known that the teaching of the Ecumenical Synods forms part of Holy Tradition, as a source alongside Holy Scripture, of Divine Revelation and of equal authority with it. It follows, therefore, that the Sacred Canons published and ratified by an Ecumenical Synod are also part of Holy Tradition, a common source of Divine Revelation, of all the individual Churches. It is true, as was said above, that the canons are not unalterable, unlike the *"terms"* (ὅροι) of the faith. They are, indeed, altered, amended and rescinded. This, however, is performed by the competent ecclesiastical legislative authority equal or superior to that which promulgated those canons. In the case of canons promulgated by or ratified by an Ecumenical Synod, indeed, only such an Ecumenical Synod has the power to amend or alter them, and certainly no State legislative authority.[50]

---

[50] "… and no one shall be permitted to countermand or set aside the canons previously laid down, or to recognize and accept any canons, other than the ones herein specified,

This holds true also for the canons which have fallen into disuse. This disuse is finally ratified by the competent ecclesiastical authority, either explicitly or through the publication of other canons which supercede the contents of the canons which have fallen into disuse.

From the above, it is clear that the canons have status for the whole Church, independently of whether they are ratified by the State. Recognition by the State, any State, or legislative fortification of the Sacred Canons has the sense that the Sacred Canons also enjoy civil legal status. From the point of view of the Church, however, they are in force even if they have not been legally reinforced by the State.

The Christian Roman emperors recognized the Sacred Canons and accorded them the status and validity of civil laws. Justinian, in distinguishing two authorities, the hieratic and the royal,[51] considered that the Sacred Canons had the same validity as the laws of the state: "We declare, therefore, that the holy ecclesiastical canons published or ratified by the Holy Synods should have the same status as laws."[52] When legislating, he took care to ensure that the laws of the State did not conflict with the Sacred Canons.[53] Not only this, but it was often stressed that the Sacred Canons prevail over the laws of the State.[54]

---

that have been composed under a false inscription by certain persons who have taken in hand to barter the truth. If, nevertheless, anyone be caught innovating with regard to any of the said canons or attempting to subvert it, he shall be responsible in respect of that canon and shall receive the penance which it prescribes and be chastised by that canon which he has offended" (Canon 2 of the Quinisext Synod).

"… we welcome and embrace the divine canons, and we corroborate the entire and rigid fiat of them that have been set forth by the renowned Apostles, who were and are trumpets of the Spirit and those both of the six holy Ecumenical Synods and of the ones which assembled regionally for the purpose of setting forth such edicts, and of those of our Holt Fathers. For all those men, having been guided by the light dawning of the same Spirit, prescribed rules that are to our best interest" (Canon 1 of the Seventh Ecumenical Synod).

[51] *Novella* 6.

[52] *Novella* 131, chap 70.

[53] Introduction to *Novella* 6. Cf. *The Justinian Code*, book 1, title 3, chap. 42, *Novellae* 5 and 133.

[54] In Rallis and Potlis, Σύνταγμα…, vol. 6, p. 317.

In his commentary on chapter 23 of title I of the *Nomocanon*, Balsamon also observes: "The canons are to be preferred above the laws."

With regard to this matter, the remark of Emperor Leo the Wise in one of his *Novellae* is worth mentioning. This is in relation to the Justinian law precluding the elevation to episcopal office of anyone who had a wife and children. Since, as Leo noted, the canons derive from inspiration of the Holy Spirit, they are excellent, and it is, therefore, a wonder that anyone should publish other laws to revoke the canons, as if they were imperfect. In general, the Christian Roman State considered the Sacred Canons as having status and validity independent of their ratification by the emperor. "And the synodal decrees are published with the same privileges as the royal decrees..."[55] Interference by certain emperors in Church affairs, even dogmatic questions, should be seen as arbitrary intervention and as a departure from the proper mutual relationship between Church and State.

The perceptions concerning the Sacred Canons and State laws are the faith of the whole of the Orthodox Church, and after the fall of Constantinople, the Church retained its internal integrity, being administered on the basis of its canonical tradition. This integrity was disturbed in the Greek territories, after the liberation, by the legislation of the Viceroy Mauer, under King Otto, which was foreign to the Greek Orthodox tradition and was inspired by Bavarian notions and practice. This created a Statist outlook and a tradition of arbitrary legislation and other state interventions in the internal affairs of the Church. This also happened in the other new Balkan states and in the local and now national Churches, at the inspiration and instigation of the great powers of the day.

Mention was made above in the chapter on modern charters of the local Orthodox Autocephalous Churches of the history of the relations between Church and State since the foundation of the Greek State and of recent ecclesiastical State legislation. It must be said that, nevertheless, all the Constitutions of the Greek State have enshrined the Sacred Can-

---

[55] Interpretation of Balsamon on Canon 12 of Antioch, cf. *Novella* 6 of Justinian, chap. 1, *Nomocanon* title I, chap. 2.

ons from the point of view of constitutional State legislation and that, therefore, any civil legislation on ecclesiastical matters must comply with them, or else be unconstitutional.

The present Constitution (1975), as the others before it, continues the constitutional and spiritual tradition of the country and ensures that the Sacred Canons and the independence of the Church of Greece from the State are firmly enshrined. The Orthodox Church of Greece "is indissolubly united with the Great Church of Christ in Constantinople and all other Churches of Christ of the same faith, unfalteringly observing, as they do, the holy apostolic and synodal canons and sacred traditions. It is autocephalous and administered by the Holy Synod of active hierarchs and the Permanent Holy Synod which derives from this, constituted as decreed by the Charter of the Church, in observance of the ordinances of the Patriarchal Tome of June 29, of the year 1850, and the Synodal Act of September 4, 1928" (Article 3, § 1).

It is worthy of note that the present Constitution refers not only to the Sacred Canons but also to the Patriarchal Tome of 1850 and the Synodal Act of 1928, thus enshrining all this ecclesiastical legislation.

The Constitution of the Greek Republic (1975), therefore, recognizes the Eastern Orthodox Church of Christ as the dominant religion in Greece and constitutionally enshrines the dogmatic and canonical communion and union of the Orthodox Church of Greece with the Ecumenical Patriarchate and all other Churches of Christ of the same faith and the unfaltering observance by it, together with them, of the Sacred Canons and holy traditions. It also decrees that the Church of Greece is autocephalous, under terms contained in the Patriarchal Tome of June 29, of the year 1850, through which the Church of Greece was declared autocephalous. It also confirms, as a supplement to the above, the Patriarchal and Synodal Act of September 4, 1928, by which the administration and canonical order of the Metropolises of the Neae Chorae has been arranged, by placing them "under the stewardship" of the autocephalous Church of Greece. It, thus, enshrines the observance of the ordinances of the Patriarchal Tome and the Synodal Act.

PART TWO

THE CHURCH'S SYSTEM
OF GOVERNMENT

CHAPTER THREE

Church Organization

1 **CLERGY AND LAITY.** In the introductory chapters, we referred to the concept of the Church. From what we said, it is clear that the Church is an organization and communion created by God, founded by the Lord for the salvation and sanctification of the human race. Thereafter, it was shown that the Church is also a communion of people linked through the same faith and through communion in the same mysteries. The people, as the Church, constitute one body, with the Lord as the head. This body is governed by the clergy, instituted by the Lord in unbroken succession from the Apostles. In this body, the redemptive work of the Lord is taken upon themselves by the people.

The whole system of government of the Church is constructed on the fundamental principle of the unity of the divine and human elements in the Church and on the unity of the members of the Church in one body.

In accordance with the fundamental system of government of the Church, its members are divided into two orders, clergy and laity, to which, during the evolution of the life of the Church, was later added a third, that of the monastics, which, as has been said, lies between clergy and laity. It is not, however, an intermediary order, but a third one. Monastics are not clergy, nor are they lay people. They are monastics. The basis for this division of the members of the Church into clergy and laity was laid by the Divine Founder of the Church, Christ Himself, who established a special order of believers dedicated to the exclusive service of the mysteries of God and of the whole congregation of the Church. The specific distinction between clergy and laity is "ordination," i.e. "the ceremony instituted by God in which, through prayer and the laying on of the hands of the bishop, Divine Grace flows and assigns the candidate to one of the three degrees of the priesthood." The higher clergy make up the hierarchy of the Church, through which the Lord governs it. The hierarchy, which has been constituted by divine right, is also the most important institution in the organization of the Church and defines and characterizes the system of government as hierarchical. The hierarchical organization of the Church consists of the fact that the Church, as a visible institution, is not shaped fundamentally or in the main by the will of the faithful, but by the will of God. The hierarchy is called upon, as having been authorized by God, to apply faithfully and with exactitude the Divine Law within the Church, since it is precisely through this that the will of God is expressed. Although the organization of the Church is hierarchical, it is based on principles which are entirely democratic, though this, again, is not to be understood in the usual sense. The Orthodox Church accepts that there is not one but many who govern the Church, in whom its highest authority is concentrated. As for the whole Church (visible and invisible), it accepts the monarchic principle, i.e. it accepts that the Church as a whole has Our Lord Jesus Christ as guide and sole head. This monarchic principle, however, is not applied to the visible Church. And although the bishop is in some sense a monarch in his eparchy, the organization and administration of the whole of the visible Church is based on democratic principles. The order of the clergy, apart from the right of governing the Church and acting as shepherds to the faithful, a right belonging to them by virtue of their priesthood, has no other privilege or right over and above those of the laity. In regards to the ranks of the bishops, nowhere is there any recognition of any higher office being accorded to any one of its members. Just as all the Apostles without exception had the same authority and none of them (including Peter) claimed a superior position as against the other Apostles (Matt.

23:8 and Mark 10:36 – 38, 42 – 45), by the same token, all their successors, the bishops, have without exception the same authority within the Church. This position was the cause of the acute conflict between the Orthodox Church and the Latin in relation to the supreme authority of the Bishop of Rome, which is based on the supremacy of the Apostle Peter, which never existed.

As mentioned above, Church organization consists of two parts, of the order of the clergy and that of the laity. This distinction does not carry the sense of division or opposition between the faithful, nor that of the formation of privileged classes, in the sense of greater rights or fewer responsibilities, nor that of a difference in worth or quality being created among the faithful. Naturally, the laity does not have the special property of the priesthood, even though they participate through baptism in the triple office of the Lord. Everyone, however, clergy and laity, partakes of one and the same Spirit. The distinction is external and in no way eliminates the fundamental principle of equality of all the faithful toward the gifts of the grace of the spirit. As the late Professor Alivizatos so aptly observes: "The order of the clergy is the governing order of the Church. This administration of government, however, apart from the rights of honor and respect due to the governing order, does not provide any privileges over the order of those governed (the laity), just as, in the State, the members of the government do not have greater privileges before the existing legal order than any other citizens. Moreover, the order of the laity is the governed order in the Church, that is, it does not occupy an inferior position as opposed to the clergy. The duty of the governing order to govern is at the same time an absolute right." The order of the clergy has, by divine law, the duty and right to govern the laity spiritually, while the order of the laity also has by divine law the duty and right to be governed by the clergy. In order to achieve the success of His pastoral mission in the world, Christ established the Apostles beyond all doubt, as they did the bishops, who, together with the presbyters and deacons, are duty bound to govern the laity, the people, spiritually. The position of both orders in the Church organization, as governing and governed, is justified on the basis of rights and, at the same time, duties. The bishops and the rest of the clergy do not merely have a right but, primarily, a duty to govern the laity spiritually, while the latter are not governed merely as their duty, but mainly as their right. The faithful, for instance, have the right to be baptized, married, buried and entirely sanctified by the Church, while it is the duty of the clergy to conduct these ceremonies in the Church, according to the law, as servants of Christ and instruments of the Church, having no say in the matter themselves on a personal level.

The bishops, precisely as were the Apostles, have always been equal among themselves, without exception, although naturally enough the secular position of the city, and especially the capital of the (Roman) eparchy, the *metropolis* (= *mother city*) conferred upon its bishop — even in regards to the name, *metropolitan* — a more prominent position in regards to the other bishops of the eparchy. This position in no way affected in depth the essence of the clerical rank, but was limited in meaning to the recognition of the honor naturally due to the first in order. The metropolitan, the bishop of the capital of the eparchy (the metropolis), and later the bishop of the capital of the *theme* (θέμα), i.e. a larger administrative region, and then even more so the bishop of the capital of the empire (of Rome), i.e. the Patriarch and Pope, as he came to be called, and thereafter the bishop of the new capital (New Rome/Constantinople), the Ecumenical Patriarch, were recognized as *primi* in order. That is to say that they held the prominent position of first brother among the bishops of the eparchy, *theme* or empire, though this position did not confer upon them any superior rights or essential privileges over the rest of their brother bishops.

The hieratic authority of the Church is based upon divine law, in that the Apostles and their successors have the right and the duty to teach, to celebrate the Divine Mysteries, to sanctify and to administer.

The exercise of the authority of teaching (*potestas màgisterii*) within the Church is the task and right of the hierarchy, while lay persons who show disrespect for the bishop or his representative by arbitrarily taking upon themselves this authority are condemned.[1] Arbitrary assumption of the authority to teach is to be condemned even more when it occurs in the case of a cleric who wishes to teach in Church without the permission of his own bishop. It is, however, possible for a layman to assist the hierarchy in its task of instruction, in theology, in preaching, in catechizing and so on.

The hieratic or sanctifying authority (*potestas ordinis*), however, is the exclusive prerogative of the clergy. The laity support and assist the clergy in this. During the divine offices, they also participate in the holy mysteries through their prayers in the service of the altar, and indeed, during the Divine Liturgy, they unite their prayers with those of the celebrant and as one body, clergy and laity, invoke the Holy Spirit upon the proffered gifts, etc.

The laity also takes part in the administrative authority in the wider sense (*potestas jurisdictionis*), which has also been entrusted to the clergy, insofar as this is permitted by the relationship between shepherd and flock laid down in the canonical tradition of the Orthodox Church.

The position of clergy and laity in the Church is defined by the fundamental system of government of the Church, in which the relations of the rights of the clergy and laity are also set out. The clergy, the bishops, received their authority in the Church by divine law, and so, it is not possible for the Church to exist without this authority.[2] Since that authority has been conferred upon the hierarchy for the sake of the Church, which is made up of the faithful laity as well as the hierarchy, and since the laity also has a duty to be vigorous and energetic members of the Church and to contribute according to their powers and gifts toward the well-being of the Church, the hierarchy is obliged to recognize these rights. Because of the character of necessity which the hierarchical authority *per se* bears

---

[1] "It does not befit a layman to dispute or teach publicly, thus claiming for himself authority to teach, but he should yield to the order appointed by the Lord, and to open his ears to those who have received the grace to teach, and be taught by them the things divine..." (Canon 64 of the Quinisext Ecumenical Synod).

[2] Cf. Term 10 of the Confession of Dositheos.

within the Church, the rights of the laity must be regulated in accordance with those of the hierarchy. The hierarchical authority is called upon to administer all ecclesiastical matters, while the laity is invited to assist in this.

"Only the common action within the Church of the hierarchy and the laity in their precisely defined limits is appropriate to the spirit of the Orthodox Church. A fundamental truth of the Orthodox Church was highlighted by what was stated in the encyclical of the Patriarchs of the Orthodox Church of May 6, 1848, addressed to all Orthodox Christians, i.e. that 'the body of the Church, i.e. the people themselves, is the guardian of Orthodoxy, the body of the Church.' From this arises a fundamental truth of the Orthodox Church which defines the significance of all the rights of the laity within the Church" (Milas).

This recognition of the significance and importance of the laity within the Church does not, however, affect the authority of the hierarchy, nor may the conclusion be drawn that the exercise of hierarchical authority depends on the position occupied by the faithful within the Church. The vehicle and agent of ecclesiastical authority is the synod of bishops which exercises this authority. Over the whole world it exercises its authority as an ecumenical synod, while over local Churches as a local ecclesiastical synod.

The synod of bishops transfers ecclesiastical authority to each of the bishops, to their particular eparchy, by consecration. It follows, then, that the bishops are the agents of ecclesiastical authority, and as canonical successors of the Apostles, they alone have the right to teach the people, to sanctify them through the mysteries and to guide their flock spiritually.

The laity is also bound by divine command to take heed of the teaching of their shepherds, to enjoy the benefits of the mysteries and to submit to their spiritual direction.

According to this, the rights of the hierarchy in the Church bear the character of absolute necessity, while the character of the rights of the laity in the Church is relative and defined by the overall aim of the Church.

For the sake of this aim, the laity is called upon to work and to act with all its spiritual powers, and they have the right and authority to reap the benefits of all their labors, through which they become participants in the blessing of God.

Since the blessing of God is transmitted through the pastors of the Church, i.e. the bishops, the Canon Law of the Church teaches that the laity are duty bound to be obedient to their shepherds, in spiritual, pastoral matters and to submit to all the ordinances of the hierarchy made law within the boundaries drawn by the Lord. Jesus Christ says: "Let he who refuses to listen even to the Church be unto you as a Gentile or a tax-collector" (Matt. 18:17), while the Apostle Paul writes: "Obey your leaders and submit to them, for they are keeping watch over your souls" (Heb. 13:17). The same is repeated by the Fathers of the Church, such as Clement of Rome (*To the Corinthians*, 42, 44) Irenaios (*Against Heresies*, 4, 26), Cyprian (*Ep.* 25 and 27) and others. Ignatios the God-bearer writes to the Trallians: "When you are subject to the bishop, it seems to me that you are subject to Jesus Christ ... Thus, it is necessary that you do nothing without the bishop ..." (chap. 11). This is also taught by the later Fathers and by recent books of the faith of the Orthodox Church.

This teaching of the Holy Scripture and of the Fathers and Teachers of the Church was formulated in greater detail by the ecclesiastical synods as canons. Almost all the canons recognize in the bishop the supreme authority in matters concerning the Church and its life, so that without the bishop, it is not possible to do anything in any branch of ecclesiastical life and administration. It follows, then, that all the rights belonging to the laity and the Church depend on episcopal authority. All of this is confirmed by the canons, in regards to the threefold office of the bishops.

From as early as Apostolic times, lay persons were permitted to take part in ecclesiastical synods. Many such took part in the First Ecumenical Synod. The Church in the West records the participation of the people particularly in the ecclesiastical synods of ancient times (Carthage, etc.). It was only the bishops taking part in the synod who were able to vote, however. The canons affirm that the bishops call ecclesiastical synods in order to deliberate matters concerning the needs of the Church.[3]

In regards to the laity, they affirm that it is permissible for them to participate in synods and to listen only to what is discussed and decided. It is also legitimate for specially trained and God-fearing lay persons, if urged by the synod, to express their opinions on certain matters and, thus, to enlighten the members, though the resolutions of the synod may be signed only by the bishops or by their delegated priests and deacons. The ecclesiastical synods are characterized in history specifically and solely as synods of bishops and are named by the number of bishops taking part. The right of decision (*jus decisivum*), which in Ecumenical Synods only the bishops have, and which in local synods is also exercised solely by them, is likewise conferred upon each of them in regards to matters of his episcopal eparchy, on the basis of the authority given by the synod of bishops and, mainly, through their consecration as bishops.

The laity also has the right to be consulted over certain matters of ecclesiastical property, in the form of consultation, though this should not be taken to extremes, as will be noted in the proper place. There is also a distinction between the administration of the property of the Church and its disposal and use. The canons make provision for the administration of ecclesiastical property and regulate it in accordance with its subject (i.e. owner). Since the subject (owner) of Church property is the Church itself, however, it follows that the administration thereof lies purely with the ecclesiastical authority, i.e. the bishop of each episcopal eparchy. The 38th Apostolic Canon affirms: "Let the bishop have the care of all Church things and let him manage them," while the 41st Apostolic Canon is even clearer: "We command that the bishop have authority over the property of the Church. For if the precious souls of human beings ought to be entrusted to him, there is little need of any special injunction concerning

---

[3] "Let there be a synod of the bishops twice a year, and let them examine among themselves the decrees concerning faith and settle the ecclesiastical controversies which may have occurred…" (Apostolic Canon 37). Cf. Canons 5 of the First Ecumenical Synod, 19 of the Fourth and 8 of the Quinisext.

money; so that everything may be entrusted to be governed in accordance with his authority, and he may grant to those in need through the presbyters and deacons with fear of God and all reverence." According to this, the right to administer and manage Church property rests with the bishop. Since it was not possible for the bishop alone to take care of the administration and management of this and to use the revenues for the purposes of the Church, the canons also refer to presbyters and deacons, who were to be assistants to the bishop in these matters.[4] It was later ordained that the bishop should have his own ecclesiastical steward (οἰκονόμος), who was to be selected by him from his own clergy to administer Church property in accordance with the mind of his bishop.[5] Administration of the property of the parishes is conducted by their priests, with the authorization of the bishop, and the priests are answerable to the bishop for this. Although the canons nowhere mention any participation by the laity in this administration nor the disposition and use by the laity of revenues accruing from this property, such disposition and use by the laity were employed in the practice of the Church and were recognized by it, provided they were likely to bring benefits, and always under the inspection of the bishop and with his approval. This custom was agreed upon from as early as the time of the Apostles, when certain communities appointed God-fearing men as assistants to the Apostles in this task. The men were called elders and, on the instructions of the Apostles and presbyters, conducted the philanthropic work of the Church, especially during the time of the persecutions. When the Church achieved its independence and autonomy in the Roman state, it did not reject the partici-

---

[4] 41st Apostolic Canon et al.

[5] "Since in some Churches, as we have been informed, the bishops are administering ecclesiastical affairs without the services of a steward, it has seemed most reasonable and right that each and every Church that has a bishop should also have a steward selected from its own clergy to manage the ecclesiastical affairs of that particular Church in accordance with the views and ideas of its own Bishop, so that the administration of the same Church should be witnessed and that the property of the same Church should not be squandered as a result of such stewardless administration and to prevent any obloquy from being attached to holy orders."

pation of the God-fearing laity in matters pertaining to Church property, under the guidance of the shepherds of the flock. It was from these that parish councilors later derived. When the Roman ("Byzantine") Empire was dissolved and the hierarchy was deprived of political protection in the East, the leading members of the Church assisted the bishops in the disposition and use of the revenues accruing from parish Church property and, even more so, in ecclesiastical areas larger than parishes.

2 **CLERGY.** The clergy are distinguished from the laity, being the bearers of spiritual authority in the Church, i.e. of teaching, sanctifying and administrating. The clergy itself is divided into two classes: a) that of the higher clergy, i.e. bishops, priests and deacons, and b) that of the lower orders, i.e. subdeacons, readers, chanters, doorkeepers, sextons and so on.

The criterion for this distinction has to do with the manner in which these orders are installed: for the higher clergy, this is by ordination within the sanctuary, with the invocation of the Holy Spirit on the person being ordained, while for the others this ordination takes place outside the sanctuary. Ordination is a holy mystery.

Church authority, which is acquired through ordination, is distinguished into: a) sanctificatory or teleturgic or high priestly authority (*potestas ordinis*); b) prophetic authority, i.e. to teach (*potestas magisterii*); and c) royal, i.e. administrative authority (*potestas jurisdictionis*), which includes legislative and judicial authority as well as "administrative" in the narrow sense.

Priestly authority, which is enjoined upon the person who bears it, can only be increased by ordination or consecration to a higher order, while it is lost in its entirety through the person being sentenced to the punishment of being defrocked. Resignation from the priestly office is not permitted. Administrative authority is subject to alterations, and as a concession, resignation from an administrative position may be allowed, though, even then, this would not detract from the essential administrative authority of the priesthood.

A) *Acquisition of the Capacity of Clergyman.* A clergyman may only become so through ordination. Repetition of such ordination to the same order is not permitted.

Ordination is the sole prerogative of the bishops who constitute the instrument through which authority in Church is transmitted. The exercise of this prerogative is defined by the Sacred Canons and by ecclesiastical ordinances, and non-compliance with these would entail the invalidation of the ordination. If the ordination is to be valid, certain requirements must be met in regards to the qualifications of both parties: the person ordaining and the person being ordained.

B) *Qualification for the Person Ordaining.* The ordaining bishop must: a) be a bishop of the Orthodox Church, and thus enjoy Apostolic succession; b) be canonically consecrated and canonically installed in his see; c) be personally competent and be the local bishop; d) not be defrocked; e) not be a heretic or schismatic; f) not have resigned; and g) not be self-consecrated.

Depending on the status of the person ordaining, the ordination may be:

1. Canonical, sound and valid, if the person officiating has the above qualifications.

2. Uncanonical and unsound, if the person officiating does not have the above qualifications, or any of them.

3. If the person ordains a cleric or tonsures a monk "beyond the parish," i.e. outside his own district or subject to another bishop, this flaw may be remedied either by later ratification by the competent bishop or by prior agreement.

The abbot of a monastery may, with permission of the bishop and if he is a hieromonk, proceed to the laying on of hands for readers and subdeacons, but only in his own monastery.[6]

Ordination to any rank of the clergy should not take place "ἀπολελυμένως," i.e. in an open-ended fashion, but must always be to

---

[6] "A person having the position of abbot, being a priest, ordains readers and subdeacons in his own monastery" (Canon VI of Nikephoros the Confessor).

a specific position in the ecclesiastical organization (Canon 6, Fourth Ecumenical Synod).

Any ordination which results from simony or from the intervention of secular leaders is uncanonical (Canons 29 and 30 of the Apostolic Canons, *Novella* 6 — year 535 — chap. 1, Canon 22 of the Quinisext Synod, Canons 3 and 5 of the Seventh Ecumenical Synod et al.).

Moreover, for the ordination to be valid, the free consent of the candidate is required. This must neither be forced nor due to sickness of the mind or any other disturbance of his mental faculties which would interfere with his awareness of his actions.

c) *Qualifications for Ordination.* For the ordination to be canonical and valid:

1. The candidate must be an Orthodox Christian.

2. He must be male.

3. He must be of canonical and legal age (in his 30th year for the priesthood, and 25th for the diaconate).[7]

4. He must be firm in the Orthodox faith and, therefore, not a recent convert.

5. He must have the necessary spiritual qualities to succeed in his mission, especially the theological training required.

6. He must be free of any bodily impediments which would hinder the performance of his priestly duties and must not be suffering from mental illness.

7. The marital status of the candidate is also important for the ordination, i.e. whether he is married or single. As things stand at present, only unmarried clergy may be consecrated as bishops. Married and single men may be ordained priests and deacons without distinction. Marriage is forbidden to all clergy after they have been ordained. In the

---

[7] "Let the canon of our holy God-bearing Fathers be confirmed in this also, that a presbyter shall not be ordained before he is thirty years of age, even if he be a very worthy man, but let him be held back. For our Lord Jesus Christ was baptized and began to teach when he was thirty. Likewise, let no deacon be ordained before he is twenty-five..." (Canon 14 of the Quinisext Ecumenical Synod). See also Canons 11 of the Synod of Neocæsarea and 16 of Carthage.

Church of Rome, as is well known, clergy in general have been forbidden to marry, while in the Protestant persuasions, clergy of all ranks are permitted to marry after ordination.

The following are barred from ordination:

1. Anyone who has contracted an illegal marriage.[8]

2. A bigamist.[9]

3. Anyone who marries a widow or divorcee.[10]

4. Anyone who marries an adulteress.[11]

5. Anyone who abandons his fiancée and marries the fiancée of another, provided the betrothal was consecrated by a religious ceremony. In such as case, the couple is considered bigamists.

6. The prospective cleric must be distinguished for the decorum of his life and his irreproachable behavior.[12]

Precisely which transgressions make the behavior of the candidate reprehensible is not clarified in detail by the Sacred Canons, but rather is indicated in general terms, thus leaving the person ordaining with

---

[8] "...the canon does not permit anyone who has wed two sisters, or aunt and niece to become a clergyman, even if such a marriage is broken. And you should know that not only a man who does things such as these, but also one who contracts another marriage impeded by ties of blood or kinship is not to be ordained, but rather to be given a penance..." (Comment of Balsamon on the 19th Apostolic Canon). Cf. Canons 3 and 26 of the Quinisext Ecumenical Synod and 27 of Basil the Great.

[9] "He who has been twice married after baptism, or who has had a concubine, cannot become a bishop, presbyter, or deacon, or any other of the sacerdotal list" (17th Apostolic Canon). Cf. Canon 3 of the Quinisext Synod, 7 of the Synod in Neocæsarea and 12 of Basil the Great.

[10] "He who has taken a widow, or a divorced woman, or a harlot, or a servant-maid, or an actress, cannot be a bishop, presbyter, or deacon, or any other of the sacerdotal list" (18th Apostolic Canon). Cf. Canon 3 of the Quinisext Ecumenical Synod.

[11] 18th Apostolic Canon, as above.

[12] "Bishops are to be appointed to the ecclesiastical government by the judgment of the metropolitans and neighboring bishops, after having been long proved both in the foundation of their faith and in their conduct of a upright life" (Canon 12 of the Synod in Laodicea).

"If anyone is to be ordained, let his life be investigated as to whether he has a wife and, if so, when and where. Also whether he has been cast out either by a clergyman or a monastery. Should he be found beyond reproach, let him be ordained" (Synopsis of Canon 4 of Cyril of Alexandria). Cf. Canon 89 of Basil the Great.

the responsibility of deciding whether there is a question of the candidate leading "of an upright life," bearing in mind the promotion of the Church's mission.

7. The candidate cleric must not have committed an offense which precludes ordination, according to the Sacred Canons or which is punishable by the laws of the State by the withdrawal of civil rights (relevant articles of the Greek Penal Code).

D) *Results of Ordination.* 1. The Ineradicable Nature of the Priesthood. According to this theory, ordination is ineradicable, and should a defrocked priest be restored, his ordination is not repeated. The Orthodox Church has not declared officially on this matter. The Church of Rome established this doctrine at the Council of Trent (1545 – 1563). Only some Orthodox theologians, influenced by Roman Catholic teaching, have accepted this theory. The long-standing practice of the Church, however, as well as its teaching on grace, reject the theory of the ineradicable nature of the priesthood. Priests who are defrocked return to the ranks of the laity or monks.

2. Once ordained, no one can contract a legal marriage.

3. A cleric is not permitted to involve himself in matters which conflict with his priestly status and mission.

4. He does not swear an oath, but gives confirmation, invoking his priestly office.

5. A man who is canonically ordained may not resign and, therefore, may not set aside voluntarily his priestly status.

6. Clerics have the right to be maintained by the church at which they work.

7. As was said above, the status of a cleric cannot be set aside by resignation, but the loss of the priestly office comes about by defrocking, which is the most serious punishment awarded to clerics and through which the cleric returns to the ranks of the laity or monks.

Holy mysteries and offices celebrated by defrocked clergy are null and void. Anyone conducting such ceremonies commits the offense of impersonating authority,[13] while in Church terms he is liable to the punishment of excommunication or being anathematized.

3 MONASTICS. Monastics constitute the third class in the ecclesiastical organization. This class is differentiated from those of the clergy and the laity and did not originally exist in the Church, but rather appeared as an organized ecclesiastical institution (cenobitic monasteries) at the turn of the 4th century.

The monastic life, which is not confined to Christianity, experienced three periods within the Church.

1. During the first period, the ascetics, who embodied the monastic ideal, lived within the bosom of the Christian community.

2. Monastics, in the form of anchorites, made their appearance in the middle of the 3rd century. It was then that the ascetics left the residential areas and went out into the desert, far from the temptations of the world, where they struggled for their spiritual perfection either alone or in groups. In this form, monasticism has neither strict organization nor centralized authority. Each hermit or anchorite regulates his asceticism according to his own inclination. Those who flee to the desert seek experienced ascetics in order to learn from them.

From the circles of monks who gathered near renowned ascetics, there came into being the *lavra*, which is an organization somewhere between that of independent anchoretism and the institution of the cenobium. The monks who make up a lavra are under a central administration, but live in their own individual cells and retain their freedom in regards to the degree and intensity of their asceticism.

3. The cenobium system. The cenobium system is the historical and organic development of anchoretism. The new element in this form of

---

[13] "Whosoever deliberately simulates the exercise of a governmental, municipal or local service is to be punished with one year's imprisonment or with a fine. This regulation also applies to the pretense of being a lawyer and to the pretense of being a cleric of the Eastern Orthodox Church of Christ, or of any other religion known in Greece" (*Greek Penal Code*, art. 175).

monasticism is the common life, i.e. strict organization on the basis of the *typikon* or rule of the monastery, under a unified administration and the supervision of the abbot, who is in charge of all the expressions of monastic life, of worship and of abode, of the timetable, of labor, of spiritual effort and so on.

The inspirer and founder of the cenobitic institution was Pachomios (4th century). His work was complemented by Saint Basil the Great, through his famous *Ascetics* and especially the *clauses in length* (ὅροι κατὰ πλάτος), consisting of 55 "terms" and three hundred and thirteen more *in epitome* (ὅροι κατ᾽ ἐπιτομήν).

Monasticism, which emerged from the bosom of the Church, was initially in parallel to the ecclesiastical organization. Some have chosen to see the monastic ideal as a protest against the secularization of the Church and a renunciation of the Church hierarchy. This view, however, is in conflict with the sources. Saint Anthony the Great did not protest against the hierarchy of the Church, but submitted to it. The same was true of Pachomios. The anchorites and monks were most closely bound to the Church through their participation in its sacramental life and worship. Indeed, the creative contact, from the very beginning, between monastic organization and that of the Church and its administration led to the *de facto* full admission of monasticism into the ecclesiastical organization. By resolutions of the Fourth Ecumenical Synod, the whole of the monastic organization became subject to that of the Church, and in particular to the immediate and total jurisdiction of the local bishops.[14]

---

[14] "Let those who truly and sincerely lead the monastic life be counted worthy of becoming honor; but, since certain persons use the pretext of monasticism to bring confusion both upon the churches and into civil affairs by going about indiscriminately in the cities, while at the same time seeking to establish monasteries for themselves, it is decreed that no one anywhere build or found a monastery or oratory contrary to the will of the bishop of the city, and that the monks in every city or village shall be subject to the bishop, and embrace the life of quiet, and concern themselves only with fasting and prayer, abiding patiently in the places to which they were sent. And they shall meddle neither in ecclesiastical nor in secular affairs, nor communicate, nor leave their own monasteries to take part in such, unless, indeed, they should be allowed to do so at any time through necessity by the bishop of the city ... And if any one shall transgress

The State also gave the force of law to the monastic life under the Church organization through Justinian's *Novellae* 5, 123 and 133.

A monk becomes so through the monastic tonsure, which is a sacred rite through which the candidate monk is officially inducted into the monastic brotherhood, of which he is a canonical member.

During the course of the monastic tonsure, the candidate monk gives the monastic confession, through which he is dedicated to God and promises to observe poverty, chastity and obedience to the orders of the abbot and the brotherhood as long as he shall live. The ceremony of donning the monastic habit may not be repeated, unless it was invalid in the first place.

Before the tonsure, the candidate must be inducted into the monastery for a time as a novice. The novitiate usually lasts three years. Exceptionally, the bishop may reduce the time of the novitiate and release the candidate from it entirely, provided the latter is properly trained and spiritually mature. The time of the novitiate must be spent entirely in the same monastery. The old monastic practice did not lay down a specific age for entering the novitiate in a monastery. Basil the Great, in accordance with the spirit of the Gospels, considered that it was possible to present oneself for the novitiate at any age.[15] The Quinisext Ecumenical Synod in Trullo, following the spirit of the teaching of Basil the Great, condones the entry of a novice into a monastery at the age of ten, but devolves the right to prolong the novitiate in such a case upon the bishop — "if he is moved to increase the time for him for his benefit" — thus counteracting the excessive zeal which led to the dedication of children to the monastic life at an earlier age. On the Holy Mountain, where it was always forbidden for eunuchs, pre-adolescents and those without beards to be admitted into the novitiate, the age limit is set at around

---

this our judgment, we have decreed that he shall be outside communion, that the name of God be not blasphemed. The bishop of the city, however, must make the whatever provision is necessary for the monasteries" (Canon 4 of the Fourth Ecumenical Synod). See also canons 7, 8, 16, 18, 23 and 24 of the same Synod.

[15] "… any time, even of the earliest age, is appropriate for the reception of those presenting themselves for the novitiate" (*Longer Rule*, 15).

adolescence, as may be concluded from article ninety-three of the Constitutional Charter of the Holy Mountain.

For someone to be accepted as a novice, he must be proposed by one of the monks, under whose supervision he is to pass his novitiate, and the proposal must be agreed by the Abbot's council and the bishop.

For the tonsure, it is required: 1) that an empty place be available in the monastery for which the tonsure is taking place; 2) that the candidate monk have reached the legal age of consent. In the Byzantine period, the age for tonsure was fixed at ten by the 6th *Novella* of Leo the Wise, though there were fluctuations. On the Holy Mountain, on the basis of the Constitutional Charter (article 93), the prospective monk must have reached the eighteenth year of his life; 3) that he have free will and be without defects, mental or other. The monastic confession, like any other legal act must be free of any defective features which would deprive it of due canonical status. Any confession made under conditions of fear, violence or delusion is canonically invalid. Persistence in the monastic life after the repeal of the state created by violence, fear, etc. makes the tonsure valid from the beginning.

As for the rest, there are no other requirements for a man or woman, lay or cleric, to be tonsured as a monk or nun, no matter what bodily afflictions they might have, whatever transgression they may have committed[16] and for whatever crime they may have been sentenced.

The tonsure of a man is carried out by a clergyman of at least the rank of priest, i.e. it may be performed by the abbot, provided he is a hieromonk and has the permission of the bishop.[17] Women are tonsured by the bishop.

---

[16] "It is lawful for a Christian to choose the ascetic life of discipline, and setting aside the turbulent confusion of the affairs of this life to enter a monastery, and to be tonsured according to the monastic schema, whatever transgressions he may have previously committed. For God our Savior said: 'Whoever comes to me, I will not cast out.' As, therefore, the monastic way of life engraves the life of repentance upon us as on a tablet, we receive whoever approaches it sincerely; nor is any one to be allowed to hinder him from fulfilling his intention" (Canon 43 of the Quinisext Synod).

[17] "No monk may be tonsured by a hieromonk without the permission of the bishop" (*The Rudder*, interpretation of Canon 39 of the Apostolic Canons and note 1).

The capacity of monk is conferred in full at the tonsure, and it remains one and undivided. The distinction between monks of the great and small schema, which is encountered from the 9th century on, whereby great schema monks renew their monastic profession more strictly, after many years in the monastic life, has no canonical or legal significance.

"Rasophors," who wear the monastic habit while undergoing their novitiate, do not have the capacity of monks from a canonical or legal point of view.

It is not possible to resign voluntarily from the capacity of monk.

A monk may not undertake secular, military, political or other such concerns. A hieromonk living in a monastery may not bless a marriage. Nor may a monastic act as godparent at a baptism or undertake trusteeship.

CHAPTER FOUR

The Instruments of Church Authority

1 ECUMENICAL SYNODS. As was mentioned above, the Church has its own system of government (πολίτευμα). This term is borrowed from the science of law in which it generally means "the system of the formation and exercise of the constituent will of the state authority in its various functions." The form of the system of government is determined on the basis of its highest or dominant organ.

In the monarchical system of government, where the source of all authority is the monarch, the regime is termed a monarchy. In a democracy, where the source of all authority is the people (δῆμος) the governance is characterized as democratic. These terms, however, are not applied entirely to ecclesiastical organization, since this is arranged by both the human and divine factors.

The highest instrument of authority in the Orthodox Church is a collective one, i.e. the Ecumenical Synod, while in the Church of Rome it is the institution of the Papacy.

The Ecumenical Synod was the highest legislative, administrative and judicial instrument of the ancient, undivided Church and remains so in the Orthodox Church which is the continuation of that Church.

The institution of the Papacy as the highest authority within the Universal Church was unknown in the time of the undivided Church.

According to what was said at the beginning of this chapter, by the system of Church government, we mean the system of the formation and exercise of the constituent will of the ecclesiastical authority in its various functions. The source of the constituent will of the ecclesiastical authority is principally and fundamentally the will of the divine Founder of the Church and, by His authorization, the will of the body of the Hierarchy. Church governance is founded upon a very broad base. This is imposed through its hierarchical organization and the principle of equality and active participation of all the members of the Church in the formation of its life.

The main bases on which the synodal system is based were laid down by the Apostles. The enactment of the institution of the Hierarchy in the Church, by divine right, demanded that the Ecumenical Church be represented by the bishops, in equality and in common, as the bishops possess the fullness of the authorities which derive from the priesthood.

The Ecumenical Synod, therefore, constitutes the highest collective instrument of Church government from the point of view of law.

The Orthodox Church is a spiritual and institutional unity, even if it is divided into individual local autocephalous Churches. All the autocephalous Churches have the same faith, the same sacramental life, the same fundamental principles of Church governance, and they all recognize the Ecumenical Synod as the highest legislative, administrative and judicial collective instrument of the Church. Despite the administrative independence which they enjoy on the basis of the fundamental principles of the arrangements for their internal organization, they automatically acquire their legal unity through the convocation of an Ecumenical Synod.

An Ecumenical Synod is an assembly of the bishops of the Church in one place to confer and arrive at common decisions on matters concerning the whole Church.

For a synod to be recognized as Ecumenical, certain internal and external conditions have to be fulfilled.

The external conditions are that all the local Churches should be represented at the synod, or at least should have been invited and have sent their views on the agenda in written form. The decisions of the synod must be in accordance with the faith and tradition of the Church as witnessed by the "ecclesiastical conscience." The "ecclesiastical conscience" is mainly expressed by the Synod itself, if it is convened legally and is in session freely, without external interference and pressure, either political or of any other kind. The number of members taking part is of no consequence.

The internal conditions are: firstly, the matters under discussion by an Ecumenical Synod must be of a universal nature and of concern to the whole Church. That is to say, They must be matters dealing with the essence of the faith, the fundamental principles of the governance of the Church and Church order in general; secondly, the synod publishing decisions should express in each one of them whatever is contained in divine Revelation, which is preserved in Holy Scripture and Sacred Tradition.

The competence of the Ecumenical Synods extends to:

1. The definition of dogmas of the faith on the basis of the teaching of Holy Scripture and Sacred Tradition. In publishing dogmas, the Ecumenical Synods formulate them as creeds or articles of faith and terms (ὅροι) of faith.

2. The examination and confirmation of pure ecclesiastical tradition, which they distinguish from the false ones.

3. The reviewing and confirmation of the canons of earlier synods.

4. The publication of new canons and positive ordinances for the whole Church on matters of the governance, administration and life of the Church.

5. The definition of ecclesiastical administration in general, especially that of the local Churches, as well as their related competences.

The Ecumenical Synod is the highest judicial authority for ecclesiastical matters, and is over and above all local Churches. It also defines the dignities and the rights of the ecclesiastical hierarchy.

Ecumenical Synods were called by the Roman emperors, who participated in the sessions either personally or through their representatives. Neither the emperor nor his representatives, however, had any right to interfere in the essentials of the matters under discussion. The aim of their presence was to guarantee the legality of the proceedings.

The decisions of certain of the Ecumenical Synods were also signed by dignitaries of the State, together with the bishops. The idea behind the dignitaries signing was not that the emperors reinforced and confirmed the dogmas of the faith and the other decisions through their office, but that they recognized what was affirmed in the synod as undeniable truth, bearing upon the salvation of all Christian peoples, and that, from the point of view of the State, they, therefore, accorded these decisions a status equal to that of civil laws. Today, an Ecumenical Synod is called by the Ecumenical Patriarch.

Both on matters of the faith (terms, ὅροι) and on matters of administration and good order (canons), if the decisions of the Ecumenical Synods were to have universal status and validity, they had to be published officially in whatever was the practice of the time. It follows from this that the protocols of the synodal sessions, the minutes, the speeches, the expositions and so on have no legal force and are of use only in the interpretation of the decisions.

The decisions of the Ecumenical Synods which refer to dogmatic matters (terms, ὅροι), for example the dogma on the Holy Trinity, may not be changed, even by another Ecumenical Synod. However, their decisions concerning administrative and disciplinary matters (canons) may be altered, though only by decisions of another Ecumenical Synod. An Ecumenical Synod may also be called today by the Orthodox Church, given that this Church is the "one, holy, catholic and apostolic Church."

2 LOCAL OR REGIONAL SYNODS. For the whole Church, as has been said, the instrument of highest ecclesiastical authority is the Ecumenical Synod, which, however, only meets as the occasion requires. For the individual local Churches, this instrument is the local synod.

Local synods have their beginning in the ecclesiastical practice of apostolic times. This practice was given canonical and formal shape through the Apostolic Canons. The thirty-seventh Apostolic Canon contains the fundamental ordinance. "Let there be a meeting of the bishops twice a year, and let them examine among themselves the dogmas of faith and resolve ecclesiastical matters which may have occurred." In the 4th century, through canon two of the Second Ecumenical Synod, it was ordained that the synod of bishops of an ecclesiastical region should administer all aspects of the local Church. In the sources, this synod is called either the synod of the eparchy or the metropolitan synod, because the president of the ecclesiastical eparchy was the metropolitan.

Among these synods, there stands out the synod known in the canonical sources as "synod of the diocese," which consisted of all the bishops and metropolitans of a more extensive ecclesiastical region which was earlier called a diocese and later a patriarchate. Because of the latter name, these synods are also known as patriarchal.

A) *The Metropolitan Synod.* A synod of the bishops of a metropolitan region which meets under the presidency of the metropolitan is called a metropolitan or eparchial synod. The competence of these synods extends over all those matters of the ecclesiastical region which exceed the sphere of authority of the bishop.[1]

Canon eight of the Quinisext Ecumenical Synod declares that this synod must definitely convene once a year, while canon six of the Seventh Ecumenical Synod subjects a metropolitan who neglects to call such a synod to canonical reproof.

According to this canon of the Seventh Ecumenical Synod, the competence of these synods falls into two categories: the canonical and the evangelical.

In particular, the interpreters Balsamon and Zonaras consider the following to be canonical matters: judicial jurisdiction, the administration of church property, the election and consecration of bishops, the

---

[1] "It behoves the bishops of every nation to acknowledge him who is the premier (primus) among them and recognize him as their head, and to refrain from doing anything superfluous without his advice and approval; but instead, each of them should do only whatever is necessitated by his own parish and by the territories under him. But neither let the primus do anything without the (advice and) consent of all; for so there will be concord, and God will be glorified through the Lord in the Holy Spirit: the Father, and the Son and the Holy Spirit" (34th Apostolic Canon). Cf. Canon 9 of the Synod in Antioch.

foundation of new episcopal sees, transfer of regional bishops,[2] and vigilance over the bishops, to ensure they take care of the affairs of their sees in accordance with the canons and laws, etc.

They consider evangelical matters to be all those which are concerned with: the administering of the divine mysteries and worship, and especially any questions of faith which might arise; the approval of liturgical books and other writings concerning the faith and the Church; the instruction of the clergy; the religious and moral state of the people; the supervision of the observance of ecclesiastical ordinances and commandments, etc.

For a metropolitan synod to be convened, it must consist of at least three members, i.e. the metropolitan himself and two bishops.[3]

B) *The Patriarchal Synod.* According to the interpretation by Balsamon of the second canon of the Second Ecumenical Synod: "Formerly all the Metropolitans of eparchies were autocephalous, and were consecrated by their own synods," while the bishops were consecrated by the metropolitans and bishops of the metropolitan region. As was mentioned above, the metropolitan convened the metropolitan synods in order to regulate the ecclesiastical affairs of their regions.

In the fourth and fifth centuries, however, the metropolitans of the large cities within the empire acquired even greater power, and the important affairs of the Church were discussed and decided in these cities. Indeed, the metropolitans of the five most important cities in the

---

[2] Interpretation by Balsamon and Zonaras of the 15th Canon of the First Ecumenical Synod.

[3] "... For it behoves that anyone who is going to be promoted to a bishopric be appointed (elected) by bishops, as was decreed by the Holy Fathers assembled in Nicea in the canon saying: 'It is most fitting that a bishop should be installed by all those in the eparchy. But if this is difficult, either because of the urgency of the circumstances or because of the distance to be traveled, at least three should meet together and by their votes combined with those of those absent but taking part in the election by letter, they should carry out the consecration thereafter. But confirmation of what is thus done shall be entrusted to the metropolitan in each eparchy" (Canon 3 of the Seventh Ecumenical Synod). Cf. canons 4 of the First Ecumenical Synod, 13 and 49 of the Synod in Cartagena.

Christian world were called Patriarchs, while with the passage of time, the metropolitans of the smaller cities lost their autonomy, though they retained their former title and their metropolises. The important matters of their ecclesiastical region were now decided by the patriarchal synod, by which the metropolitans were elected, and then consecrated by the Patriarch and the Synod.

The patriarchal synods, under the presidency of the Patriarch, were initially made up of the metropolitans, later of the bishops as well of the patriarchal region, especially those who were, by chance, present at the place where the synod convened.

The patriarchal synod usually met once a year, in June or September, in the city which was the seat of the Patriarch. When this became a permanent, standing synod, it met twice a week, except in the summer months.

It was the responsibility of the patriarchal synods to proceed with: 1) the election of the patriarch; 2) the election and installation of bishops; 3) the promotion of a see to a higher rank in the Syntagmation; 4) the transfer of bishops; 5) the endorsement of the consolidation of two episcopal sees; 6) the foundation of new sees; 7) the ratification of the transfer of the seat of a see to another city; 8) the revision and remedying of decisions taken by the Patriarch which were not in accord with the Holy Canons; and 9) the exercise of ecclesiastical judicial authority in cases brought before it (appeals), as the highest judicial authority.

c) *The Endemousa Synod.* The most ancient of such synods is the Endemousa Synod. When Constantinople became the capital of the Roman Empire, the hierarchs who went there for a variety of reasons remained in the capital for a certain length of time. The Patriarch would invite them to convene and decide on a range of ecclesiastical affairs.

The first such synod for which there is evidence and whose decisions are known to us is the one summoned in 394 by Patriarch Nektarios to discuss the case of Bishops Agapios and Bagadios. With the passage of time, the Endemousa Synod became of exceptional importance for the administration of the Church and for Canon Law. On occasion, this synod also decided on matters of doctrine. The institution of the Endemousa Synod functioned throughout the Byzantine period and for a long time afterwards.[4]

D) *The Greater Synod (Μείζων καὶ Ὑπερτελής)*. According to ancient Canon Law, when the decisions of eparchial or patriarchal synods were questioned, it was possible to have recourse (appeal) to a "greater synod," in which not only the bishops of the eparchy or diocese, but those of the neighboring eparchies or dioceses took part.[5] A greater synod was convened a few years ago in Cyprus, in which Patriarchs Nicholas of Alexandria and Elias of Antioch took part, as did metropolitans from the Patriarchates of Alexandria, Antioch and Jerusalem. It dealt with the case of the defrocking of Archbishop Makarios of Cyprus by three metropolitans of Cyprus and, having decided that the defrocking was uncanonical and non-existent, went on to defrock the three metropolitans. Likewise, a few years ago (1992), a greater and supreme synod was called by the Ecumenical Patriarch Bartholomew in which the Patriarch of Alexandria and the Archbishop of Athens took part. It dealt with canonical matters related to the activities of the Patriarchate of Jerusalem beyond its ground and jurisdiction.

E) *The Permanent Synod.* The Permanent Synod is an institution unknown to classical Canon Law. Nevertheless, it may prove useful when the leaders of the individual local Churches do not have total authority and when rapid decisions need to be taken on matters which require the convocation of a synod.

The president of the Permanent Synod must be the head of the local Church.[6] The members of this may be permanent (as in Constantinople where most of the metropolitans are residents of the city, since they are unable to travel freely to their eparchies and are, therefore, able to participate in the synod on a permanent basis) or non-permanent. In the

---

[4] For more on this, see above, pages 58 ff.
[5] "And if the eparchial Synod bishops should be unable or incompetent to decide settle the charges brought against the bishop and make due correction, then they are to go to a greater synod of the bishops of the diocese (Patriarchate) summoned to try the case ..." (Canon 6 of the Second Ecumenical Synod). Cf. 12 and 14 of the Synod in Antioch.
[6] Cf. Canons 34 of the Apostolic Canons and 9 of the Synod in Antioch.

latter case, bishops who have a see participate in the synod periodically, in predefined numbers (Church of Greece). There is also a mixed system which combines those above, i.e. the synod consists of permanent members and others who take part periodically. It is this mixed system which is in force in the Patriarchate of Moscow.

The institution of the Permanent Synod exhibits certain advantages, but also has its drawbacks, the most important of which is that the synodal bishops are taken away from their eparchies for long periods of time.

The Synod of Excellence ("ἀριστίνδην"), a form of Permanent Synod whose members (the most excellent!) are chosen by the political leadership or by the "first" bishop of the local Church following legislative arrangements on the part of the State, is an innovation unknown to the Canon Law of the Orthodox Church. It is, therefore, uncanonical and unacceptable. It abolishes both the equality of bishops in the priesthood and their joint responsibility (συνυπεύθυνον) in the administration of the Church.

3 The Eparchial Episcopal System of Governance. a) *The Bishop.* In the first years when the Church was being established, each city had its own bishop. Even small towns or places were bishoprics, each of which exercised a certain episcopal jurisdiction, though dependent on the bishop of the city. Due to the persecutions, the presence of a bishop in each location was necessary to hold the people together. Due to this anomalous situation for the Church, it was also difficult to define the limits of the episcopal region, in which each bishop had to exercise his jurisdiction. Confusion and turmoil often resulted within the Church administration, over the ordination of clergy, over priests being subordinate to two bishops, since there were frequently two bishops in one and the same place. When the persecutions of the Christian Church in the Roman State came to an end, the legislative authority of the Church was able to define precisely the bounds within which a bishop could exercise his episcopal jurisdiction. In this way, the canonical, eparchial, episcopal jurisdiction was formed, known as the eparchy.

Initially, the first ecclesiastical communities were founded in the great cities of the Roman empire with their own bishops. However, Christianity also quickly began to flourish in smaller towns and places, to which the bishop of the city on which these small towns were civilly dependent sent clergy to perform the work of the Church until such time as clergy settled there permanently and their own Christian communities were formed, similar to parishes today. In the sources, these communities are called ἐγχώριοι (village) or ἀγροικίαι (farmhouse) or μονοικίαι (one church). Many such parishes were headed by a bishop, dependent upon the regular bishop of the city and called *chorepiscopoi* (suffragans). All these parishes together formed a small ecclesiastical region dependent on the bishop of the city, and this is known today as the episcopal eparchy.

It may be inferred from the decisions of the Fourth Ecumenical Synod that in the fifth century, the episcopal eparchy under the jurisdiction of each bishop consisted of the parish of the city in which the bishop has his seat and of those parishes which were in places civilly subordinate to the city in question.

The bishop in his see is the source of authority and the most important personal instrument of ecclesiastical organization. It is he who exercises the supreme pastoral authority in his see, and he who heads the administration in general, in accordance with the Sacred Canons and the laws of the Church.

B) *The Metropolitans.* In order to preserve ecclesiastical unity between the bishops of an eparchy, synods were convened, which met twice, or at least once, a year, usually in the capital of the eparchy (the metropolis). These synods were presided over by the bishop of the metropolis and made decisions related to the needs of the local Church. The bishop of the capital of the eparchy and president of this eparchial synod was not only charged with the execution of the decisions of the eparchial synods, but also little by little acquired the right to supervise the other bishops of the eparchy. This bishop also mediated in the spiritual communication between the bishops of the eparchy and those of other Churches. It was, therefore, natural that the bishop of the capital, the metropolis (= the mother city) would acquire a certain pre-eminence over the bishops of the eparchy.

The First Ecumenical Synod (325) defined more precisely the eparchial or metropolitan organization, by matching the ecclesiastical organization with the civil, in geographical terms. The term "metropolitan" is first encountered in the fourth canon of the First Ecumenical Synod.[7] The metropolitan was called πρῶτος (first, primate, primus) or πρωτεύων (first ranking) or ὁ τῆς πρώτης καθέδρας (of the first seat).[8]

The metropolitan organization evolved mainly in Asia Minor, and was gradually introduced into the region of Antioch and Egypt, as well as in the West: Italy (after 350), Gaul and Spain (end of the fourth century).

c) *The Exarchs-Patriarchs.* The increase in the number of bishops in the third century, their concentration around the bishop of the capital, the metropolitan and their unity in the synodal system created the basis of the office of metropolitan. At the same period, another higher office began to be created, that of exarch, which developed in full in the fourth century. This office was the precondition for the appearance of a new insignia of rank, that of patriarch.

The term "exarch" goes back as far as classical antiquity. The head or chief among the "chorus" of priests was called the "exarch" *proegemon* (προηγεμών). At the time of the Roman Empire, the title of exarch was given to the highest-ranked officer in the army, the governor of one of those large administrative dioceses into which the empire was divided by Constantine the Great. The term, thus, came into use in ecclesiastical administration, too. In ecclesiastical terms, the title and office had three stages of development.

1. In antiquity, the work of any exarch was understood to be independent of the others.

---

[7] "…but let the confirmation of what is done be given in every eparchy to the metropolitan."
[8] See 34th Apostolic Canon, canons 23, 56 and 98 of the Synod in Cartagena, 16, 18, 19, 20 of that in Antioch, 39 of that in Cartegena et al.

2. Later, the exarch was simply an instrument of patriarchal authority.

3. Later still, to a certain extent the exarch was restored to the initial, independent form of his position. It is the first two stages which will be under examination here.

From the beginning of Christianity, as we see even in the epistles of the Holy Apostles, administrative divisions of the Church conformed to those of the State. The most extensive regions bore the name of entire countries, e.g. the Church of Asia (I Cor. 16:19), those which were slightly smaller, the name of regions, e.g. the Macedonian Church (II Cor. 8:1), and those which were smaller again were called by the name of the metropolises of the main cities of the eparchies, such as the Churches of Thessaloniki (I Thes. 1:1), Ephesus (Rev. 2:1) and so on. All these Churches had their own independent administrations, while the authority to deal with matters of a general and common character was concentrated in the metropolises of the ecclesiastical regions.[9]

Constantine the Great, in his reform of the structure of the State administration, divided the empire into four large sections (*prefecturæ*): those of the East, Illyricum, Italy and Gaul. The Prefectures were divided into Dioceses, the Dioceses into Eparchies, and the Eparchies into Parishes (Παροικίαι). At the head of a Prefecture was the Hyparch, of the Diocese the Exarch, of the Eparchy the Eparch and of the Parish the Parochus (Πάροχος). The various forms of Church administration evolved in the same spirit as that of the civil power.[10]

The Synod of Sardica (347) introduced into ecclesiastical usage the new term of the "exarch of the eparchy," as synonymous with the word "metropolitan." Initially, then, "exarch" meant the same as "primus" or metropolitan of the eparchy. Very soon, however, the meaning of "exarch" was elevated and acquired a position between metropolitan and patriarch. The canonical term "exarch" is mentioned for the first time

---

[9] Acts 20:17 – 35; II Cor. 1:1.

[10] "And if any city has been, or shall hereafter be newly renovated by imperial authority, let the order of the ecclesiastical parishes follow the civil and public order" (Canon 17 of the Fourth Ecumenical Synod). Cf. 38 of the Quinisext.

in the proceedings of the Synod in Antioch (445) where Domnos, the Bishop of Antioch, is thus designated. In his interpretation of canon seventeen of the Fourth Ecumenical Synod, Zonaras says: "Others were also called exarchs, such as the bishops of Cæsarea, Cappadocia, Ephesus, Thessaloniki and Corinth, to whom, it is said, the privilege was given of wearing *polystavria*[11] in their churches."

It is quite clear from this that the bishops of the capital cities of the Dioceses were called "exarchs," that they enjoyed a higher status than that of the metropolitan of the eparchies and that they had a certain independence of action in regards to the metropolitans of the eparchies, which was lost for the latter by the middle of the sixth century. Indeed, mainly because of the political importance of these capital cities, or, as in the case of Jerusalem, because of its great historical sanctity, the heads of the main Dioceses and exarch bishops finally took the title of patriarch.

The second period in the history of the title of exarch began from the time of the Fourth Ecumenical Synod, i.e. from the moment when the patriarchal institution was established in the East. During this period, the heads of the capitals of the main Dioceses developed and reinforced their former authority and took the title, first of archbishop, then later of patriarch. The heads of the other less important Dioceses, the exarchs, in the strict meaning of the word, were placed under canonical dependence on the patriarch and became instruments of patriarchal authority.

The first of the exarchs in the East to gain this superior position was the Exarch of Alexandria, who was called Archbishop in the third century. Second in importance came the Bishop of Antioch. To these two exarchs in the East must be added the following, though of lesser importance: Cæsarea in Pontos, Ephesus, the exarch of Asia, and Heracleia, the exarch of Thrace. It was on these three exarchs that the Church of Constantinople rested in the fifth century and the bishop of the Church of the capital was recognized as the first bishop in the East and Ecumenical Patriarch.[12]

---

[11] *Phelonia* — vestments embroidered with many crosses.

[12] Maximos, Metropolitan of Sardeis, *The Ecumenical Patriarchate in the Orthodox Church*, Thessaloniki 1972, pp. 50–55 (in Greek).

At a later time, the patriarchal representatives who were sent to exercise patriarchal rights were called patriarchal exarchs. Such were the patriarchal exarchs of the monasteries and of the lands and the country of the patriarchal eparchy, as also the commissioners and *loca tenentes* of the patriarch. It was possible for a metropolitan, bishop, abbot, archimandrite, priest, simple monk or even a layman to be a patriarchal exarch.

D) *The Archbishops.* The head of an autocephalous Church is called an Archbishop. In the fourth century, Athanasios the Great addressed Alexander of Alexandria as Archbishop. In certain official cases, the bishops of the most important cities in the Roman Empire, such as Rome, Constantinople, Alexandria, Antioch and Jerusalem, were called Archbishop. In the proceedings of the Fourth Ecumenical Synod, they were called Archbishop, while from the first half of the fifth century the title of Archbishop was awarded to the bishops of the metropolises of the empire in the imperial *novellae* and in important official documents. The Sixth Ecumenical Synod decided that the bishops of Rome, Constantinople, Alexandria, Antioch and Jerusalem were to bear the title of Archbishop as were later the bishops of Cyprus, New Justianopolis, Iberia, Ephesus and Thessaloniki. Of these, the first five also bore the title of Patriarch since the time of the Synod in Chalcedon.

Thus, in the evolution of the title, we see that it was awarded to the presidents of autocephalous Churches and to the bishops of outstandingly important sees. Later, the title was lower than that of Metropolitan. The Metropolitan is the first bishop of a metropolitan eparchy and president of the synod of the eparchy, whereas an Archbishop does not take part in the synod of the eparchy under the Metropolitan, is independent of the Metropolitan and answers only to the Patriarch.

Today, the title of Archbishop is awarded, on the one hand, to the heads of autocephalous Churches (Cyprus, Greece, Poland, Albania) and on the other, in regards to the Patriarchate of Constantinople, to the metropolitans of outstandingly important metropolises (America, Australia, Thyateira, i.e. Great Britain, and Crete), presidents or not of synods of the eparchies. In the Patriarchate of Jerusalem, the Church of Russia and in the other Churches, Slavic and otherwise, the title of Archbishop is lower than that of Metropolitan and higher than that of bishop. In this way, they maintain the ancient canonical tradition of the Church.

E) *Suffragan (Chorepiscopoi) and Auxiliary Bishops.* From about the third century, the institution of suffragan (*chorepiscopoi*) bishops appeared, i.e. bishops of villages, of the countryside, who were dependent on the bishop of the city, who administered the country areas through them. The institution of the suffragan was not entirely canonical, since they were dependent upon the bishop of the city, so that there were two bishops in one and the same eparchy. His consecration was not without a specific place of which he was bishop, so long as he was consecrated to a specific region, even if he was still dependent. Suffragans are not auxiliary bishops in the modern usage, since they did have an area over which they had authority, even though they were dependent on the bishop of the city.

Auxiliary bishops, however, have no jurisdiction over any place and always act on the instructions of the sovereign bishops and within the jurisdictions of the latter. With the passage of time, the institution of suffragans disappeared and was replaced by that of the auxiliary bishops. These latter are awarded the title of a once flourishing eparchy. The institution of auxiliary bishop is, however, uncanonical in the strict sense of ecclesiastical law, since it is not possible for one see to have more than one bishop.

i. *Canonical qualifications for a prospective bishop.* A candidate for the episcopate is required to have not merely the qualifications necessary for all prospective clerics but to have demonstrated these over a long period of time through conscientious and consistently faithful behavior toward himself.

As can be deduced from the canons of the Church, the particular qualities and qualifications of a candidate should be:

a. Appropriate and mature age. In the first years of the Church, only those who had completed their fiftieth year were elevated to the rank of bishop. Later, however, through a *Novella* of Justinian, it was permitted for those who had completed their thirtieth year to be made bishops. Indeed, in a related commentary, Balsamon mentions that according to this *Novella*, a prospective bishop should be "above the age of thirty" and that this *Novella* eliminates the importance and validity of earlier *Novellae*, according to which a man had to have completed his thirty-fifth year in order to be made bishop. According to modern ecclesiastical legislation, the age for candidate bishops varies from thirty-five to forty and is the same in almost all local Churches.

b. The prospective bishop must be known to have remained faithful to the Orthodox faith over a long period of time and to have led a blameless life.

c. According to canon two of the Seventh Ecumenical Synod, a candidate for the episcopate must have a thorough knowledge of Christian teaching and the ecclesiastical canons.

d. If the prospective bishop is not a monk, he must don the monastic habit before his consecration.[13]

Other qualifications for prospective bishops are defined today by the legislation in force in the individual Churches and, therefore, vary.[14]

ii. *Election and consecration of bishops.* The Lord chose the Apostles and the Apostles themselves installed bishops in the Churches they founded, independently of the other Apostles and without prior consultation with the community.[15] During the post-Apostolic period, the neighboring bishops took part in the election and consecration of the bishop, with the consent of the clergy and laity of the see to which the new bishop was elected by the Synod.[16] Concerning the election and consecration of bishops, Cyprian, Bishop of Carthage (third century), says: "We should retain unchanged the divine tradition and Apostolic custom which has survived and is preserved by us and by almost all the

---

[13] "Anyone about to be consecrated bishop must be a monk," *The Rudder*, note on an interpretation of the first Apostolic Canon.

[14] For the conditions prevailing in the Church of Greece, see its Charter in force. For the Holy Archdiocese of America, see Appendix.

[15] I Tim. 4:14; Tit. 1:5; Eusebius, *Eccles. Hist.* III, IV.

[16] Clement of Rome, *Epistle to the Corinthians* 44.

eparchies, and which provide that for the legitimate consecration of a bishop of a certain people, there should gather in one place the neighboring bishops of the same eparchy, so that they may elect the bishop, in the presence of the people, who would have thorough knowledge of the life of each and could testify to all his actions."[17]

The First Ecumenical Synod, through its fourth canon, declares that "... It is most fitting that that a bishop should be installed by all the bishops in the province. However, if this is difficult to arrange on account of urgent circumstances or because of the distance to be traveled, at least three should meet together and by their votes combined with those of those absent but taking part in the election by letter, they should carry out the consecration thereafter. The confirmation of what is thus done shall be entrusted to the metropolitan in each eparchy."

As is clear from this canon of the First Ecumenical Synod, the election of a bishop is now the task of all the bishops of the eparchy and is confirmed by the metropolitan, who, together with at least two other bishops, performs the consecration. The election by the bishops of the synod of the eparchy, without the participation of the people, at least in regards to the voting, appears to have been necessary for the good repute of the Church. In this way, they avoided the clashes and multitude of improprieties which had occurred in former times, when the people were present at the election. "In the past... the voting by the hierarchs took place in the presence of the crowd of citizens, but the divine Fathers did not approve of this, being unwilling to have the life of the clergy disparaged before the laity. And they declared that the bishop should be elected by the bishops of the eparchy in each eparchy... His ordination, i.e. consecration, was entrusted to the first, that is the metropolitan, and not only the consecration but also the ratification of the vote..."[18] If there is not a unanimous decision regarding the bishop to be elected, then according to the sixth canon of the same Synod, the vote of the

---

[17] Cyprian, *Epistola* 68.
[18] Balsamon, interpretation of the fourth canon of the First Ecumenical Synod.

majority prevails.[19] The participation of the people was its testimony on behalf of the candidate, while it was the bishops who voted. It was for these reasons that the Synod in Laodicea declared that it was absolutely forbidden "for the multitude to undertake the elections of those about to be inducted into the ranks of the priesthood."[20]

Despite these decisions by the Church regarding the manner of electing bishops, in certain regions, because of their isolation, the laity continued to be involved in the election of bishops, as, indeed, they were in that of civil leaders. The Seventh Ecumenical Synod, therefore, returned to the subject and repeated the formulation of the fourth canon of the First Ecumenical Synod: that the bishop is elected by the bishops of the eparchy and confirmed by the metropolitan, while it expressly forbids the interference of the civil authorities in this election, repeating the decree of the thirtieth Apostolic Canon.[21]

This manner of election and consecration of bishops by the competent episcopal synod has remained more or less in force throughout the centuries which followed, despite the local, temporal and transient alterations, which were exceptions to the canon.

Today, in the Ecumenical Patriarchate of Constantinople, the bishops are elected and consecrated by the Holy Synod of the Ecumenical Patriarchate, while in the Church of Greece by the Holy Synod of the Hierarchy.

iii. *The consequences of the consecration of a bishop.* A bishop is consecrated to a specific ecclesiastical region and not *ad libertum*. The Church to which someone is consecrated bishop is considered his bride, and he

---

[19] "... If, however, two or three bishops from their own contrariness, oppose the common vote of all, then, provided this vote is reasonable and in accordance with the ecclesiastical canon, let the choice of the majority prevail."

[20] Canon 13.

[21] "Any election of a bishop, priest or deacon by temporal rulers shall be invalid, in accordance with the canon which states: 'If any bishop comes into possession of a church by the aid of the secular rulers, let him be defrocked and excommunicated, and all those who communicate with him, too' ... For he who is to be promoted to a bishopric must be voted for by bishops, as was decreed by the holy Fathers of Nicea ..." (Canon 3 of the Seventh Ecumenical Synod).

is joined to it for life, while the Church, when its bishop dies, is said to be widowed.

A bishop once consecrated, according to canonical ordinances, may not thereafter abandon the administration of the Church entrusted to him. If it should happen that the clergy and people of an eparchy do not recognize a bishop installed by a canonical episcopal synod, he remains in his office, enjoying the rights of the episcopal eparchy assigned to him, while the insubordinate clergy is subject to canonical penance.[22] The bishop retains the office of his authority and the rights attached to it, even when for political reasons, he is not able to occupy the episcopal seat assigned to him.[23] In regards to this, the canons declare that this bishop occupies the seat assigned to him in the synod along with the other bishops.[24]

Once a bishop has been installed in his episcopal seat, he may no longer attempt to be transferred elsewhere. Only the episcopal synod may transfer a bishop and then only for good reason and when it will bring greater benefit to the Church.[25]

---

[22] "If any person, having been ordained bishop, does not undertake the ministry, and the care of the people committed to him, let him be excommunicated until he does undertake it. In like manner a presbyter or deacon. But if he has gone and has not been received, not of his own will but from the perverseness of the people, let him continue to be bishop; and let the clergy of the city be excommunicated, because they have not corrected the disobedient people" (36th Apostolic Canon).

[23] "If any bishop ordained to a parish shall not proceed to the parish to which he has been ordained, not through any fault of his own, but either because of the rejection of the people, or for any other reason not arising from himself, let him enjoy his rank and ministry; only he shall not disturb the affairs of the Church where he should be accorded a congregation; and he shall abide by whatever the full synod of the province shall determine, after judging the case" (Canon 18 of the Synod in Antioch). Cf. canon 37 of the Quinisext.

[24] Canons 37 and 39 of the Quinisext Ecumenical Synod.

[25] "A bishop is not to be allowed to leave his own parish, and pass over into another, although he may be implored by many to do so, unless there be some justifiable cause pressing him, such as if he can confer some greater benefit to them in regard to his appointment because of his devoutness. And this must be done not of his own accord, but by the judgment of many bishops, and at their earnest exhortation" (14th Apostolic Canon).

Through his consecration, a bishop assumes the authority which the Apostles had, since bishops are Apostles' successors, and the Holy Spirit "has made them bishops to be shepherds to the Church of God" (Acts 20:28).

In his eparchy, the bishop is entirely independent, administering his see on his own authority, and no one has the right to place obstacles in his way in the exercise of his duties, provided he exercises his authority within the limits prescribed by the sacred canons. Even more so, no one has the right to interfere in the internal affairs of the administration of the diocese.[26]

It is only the bishop who possesses and exercises episcopal authority in his see, and this is why it is not possible for two bishops to have their sees and seats in the same geographical area.[27] The canons also expressly forbid a bishop to interfere in the affairs of an ecclesiastical region other than his own.[28] This prohibition also applies to an autocephalous archbishop or metropolitan who has no right to interfere in the affairs of the bishops of his own ecclesiastical region, except if a bishop refuses to appoint higher and lower clergy in his see for the performance of spiritual duties, as provided for by the canons, or if he neglects his flock.[29]

A canonically consecrated bishop may not be dethroned and reduced to the rank of presbyter. Canon 29 of the Fourth Ecumenical Synod describes this as sacrilege. According to the provisions of this canon, if a bishop, for good reason, has to cease performing his duties, he is not

---

[26] "Let not a bishop dare to ordain beyond his own limits, in cities and places not subject to him. But if he be confirmed in doing so, without the consent of those persons who have authority over such cities and places, let him be defrocked, and those also whom he has ordained" (35th Apostolic Canon).

[27] Canon 8 of the First Ecumenical Synod.

[28] 16th and 32nd Apostolic Canons; canons 15 and 16 of the First Ecumenical Synod and others.

[29] "If any bishop or presbyter neglects the clergy or the people, and does not instruct them in the way of godliness, let him be denied communion, and if he persists in his negligence and idleness, let him be defrocked" (58th Apostolic Canon); cf. also canon 25 of the Fourth Ecumenical Synod, 19 of the Quinisext, 16 of the First/Second and others.

reduced to the rank of presbyter (since if he is unworthy to celebrate the mysteries as bishop, the same would apply to him as presbyter).

In his eparchy, the bishop has all the rights and duties which derive from this triple office of teacher, hierarch and shepherd-administrator.

iv. *Vacancy of a see.* A see becomes vacant ("widowed") when the bishop departs this life.

A bishop foregoes his see and the administrative authority associated with it, though retaining his priesthood: a) if he is sentenced to be dethroned; b) if he is sentenced to life-long suspension; c) if he is tonsured as a monk; d) if he resigns, which is permissible only in the event that sickness or age make it impossible for him to exercise his administrative duties properly. In these cases, too, the see becomes vacant.

F) **Presbyters.** The rank of presbyter is directly below that of bishop in the hierarchy of the Church and is a rank which was ordained by the Apostles. The presbyter receives his appointment and the confirmation of his election, if he has also been elected by the laity, from the bishop by whom he is ordained and installed in his parish, which he administers and governs in the name of the bishop. He is the direct representative and surrogate of the bishop in the parish area. Within the parish, the priest acts on his own responsibility, but acts on behalf of the bishop from whom he also received the hieratic authority, which he exercises in his own jurisdiction. This hieratic authority is demonstrated through preaching, celebrating and administration. His parish constitutes a small region within that of the whole bishopric and is organically linked to it. Once he has been appointed and installed, he exercises his rights and duties without let or hindrance, by the hieratic authority invested in him at his ordination. The bishop may not suspend a priest simply on his own initiative, nor revoke the authority given to him, except after a judicial verdict, or for serious and sufficient reasons of scandalizing the faithful. Even in this latter case, however, the suspension is only temporary, pending final judgment of the case, since only a judicial verdict can terminate a priest's hieratic authority, which does, indeed, come from the bishop, but in fact originates with the Apostles and is conferred through election and ordination.

G) *Deacons*. Among the fundamental ranks of Church hierarchy, the lowest is that of deacon. The principle task and aim of the deacon is to perform a liturgical ministry.

Deacons have no authority in the Church, but are dependent in everything on the bishops and presbyters. "A deacon does not bless, does not give the blessing, but receives it from the bishop and presbyter; he does not baptize, he does not offer; but when a bishop or presbyter has offered, he distributes to the people, not as a priest, but as one that ministers to the priests" (*Apostolic Constitutions* VIII, 28).

He does, however, have a certain authority in regards to the lower ranks[30] and may take part, with express authorization from his own bishop, in matters of Church administration.[31]

---

[30] "The deacons are also to be honored above the servers and all the lower clergy" (Canon 20 of the Synod in Laodicea).

[31] "A deacon, even if in an office of dignity, that is to say, in whatever ecclesiastical office he may be, is not to sit before a presbyter, unless he is acting as representative of his own patriarch or metropolitan in another city, for then, on the grounds that he is filling the place of the latter, he shall be honored" (Canon 7 of the Quinisext Ecumenical Synod).

PART THREE

AUTHORITY OR ADMINISTRATION IN THE CHURCH

CHAPTER FIVE

Teaching Authority (Prophetic)

Ecclesiastical authority consists of three branches, that is the teaching, priestly and administrative/pastoral. These authorities, which are ministries to the faithful, correspond to the triple office of the Lord as teacher, high priest and king.

The unity of the Church is based on the unity of the faith, and for this reason, a supreme mission of the Church leadership is the development and consolidation of the truth revealed by Christ, so that it remains utterly intact. The instrument through which the unity of the Church is preserved and safeguarded is the bishops, who, above all are obliged to retain the revealed teaching and to bear witness, unfailingly and unerringly, to the truth. Bishops are, therefore, absolutely required to practice this duty, as are such priests and deacons, and even laymen, with the bishop's consent and upon his assignment. "If any bishop or presbyter neglects the clergy or the people, and does not instruct them in the way of godliness, let him be denied communion, and if he persists in his negligence and idleness, let him be defrocked."[1]

It is, therefore, a most important duty of bishops and priests, assisted by the laity, that they should transmit the truth of the word of God through preaching, through publications and through any available means such as radio, television and so on. Another duty of those who

---

[1] 58th Apostolic Canon

hold instructional authority in the Church is the education of young people through catechism, the spread of Christian teaching through mission, the protection of the faithful from false teachers and so on. This task of instruction must be carried out in accordance with the canonical order of the Church.

CHAPTER SIX

Priestly (Teleturgic/Sanctifying) Authority

Teleturgic authority consists of the performance of the mysteries, through which the sanctifying and saving Divine Grace is imparted to the faithful, as well as the other services and prayers performed by bishops and priests according to a specified liturgical order. These services are conducted on behalf of people and things, to be consecrated to God and the Church, or on behalf of particular persons, for the acquisition of divine blessing upon their various relations.

For the mysteries to be valid, it is required that they be conducted by a competent cleric, canonically ordained, and in accordance with the canons and order of services (*typikon*) of the Church. Neither the moral status of the clergyman nor any delusion has any effect whatsoever on the validity of the mysteries and other services, while mysteries conducted by unworthy clerics are entirely valid. Mysteries performed by defrocked priests, or those ordained by a defrocked bishop, are not valid, however. Likewise, those mysteries performed by heretics are invalid, and anyone accepting them, especially ordination, must repeat them on their entry into the Orthodox Church, unless economy is applied.

The full right to perform every mystery and every service in the Church lies with the bishop, while priests receive the right from him to celebrate at all.[1] The right to officiate at certain mysteries and holy cer-

---

[1] "If any one conducts a church of his own, apart from the Church and, scorning the Church, wishes to perform the functions of the Church without a presbyter helping

emonies is reserved for the bishop, in accordance with his archpriestly authority, while the others may be celebrated also by presbyters, who in this regard, however, are subject to the supervision and judicial authority of their own bishop.[2] Deacons cannot perform any rite on their own.

---

with the approval and consent of the bishop, let him be anathema" (Canon 6 of the Synod in Gangra). Cf. 31ˢᵗ Apostolic Canon, Canon 2 of the Synod in Antioch et al.
[2] "Let not priests or deacons do anything without the sanction of the bishop; for he it is who is entrusted with the people of the Lord, and of whom will be required the account of their souls" (39ᵗʰ Apostolic Canon).

CHAPTER SEVEN

Administrative Authority (Royal)

1 **Concerning Church Legislation.** Jesus Christ transferred legislative authority to His Apostles, and from these, it passed to their successors, the bishops, who have exercised it down the centuries, in synod, as they do to this day.

The legislative authority of the Church, based on divine authorization and in accordance with the mission assigned to it, developed over time in a definite and precisely delineated direction. In publishing laws, the instruments of legislative authority in the Church do not act in their own name, nor do they exercise personal rights belonging to them, but they act rather in the name of the Holy Spirit who lives in the Church.

In order for the will and power of the Holy Spirit to be truly expressed in the legislative authority of the Church, the following two main terms must be adhered to: a) that the legislative authority act in the name of the whole Church, as a body guided and given life by the Holy Spirit; and b) that the instruments of this authority be canonically consecrated bishops.

For this reason, it is impossible for a single person, irrespective of whether he holds a prominent episcopal see, to exercise supreme legislative authority over the whole Church. The right to legislate in the Church lies only with the synodal authority. On the basis and in the spirit of the legislation of synodal authority, each bishop may promulgate special laws for his diocese, but these must derive their cause and principle from synodal legislation and in no way deviate from or contravene this.

We have general ecclesiastical legislation in the Church and also particular legislation. What is meant by general ecclesiastical legislation is the laws published by the supreme Church authority. These have absolute validity and status over all members of the Church, though a distinction must be made concerning this general legislation between the ancient general legislation and more recent, i.e. between that developed by the Ecumenical Synods and what followed.

The sacred canons also permit each local Church to regulate its administration within its geographical area in accordance with the existing local relationships. The legislation of the local synods, however, is governed by the general canonical principle that those who promulgate their own particular laws must, above all, have in mind the canons which have status and validity throughout the whole Church and that only in dependence on the general canonical institutions is it possible to publish, within the circle of their jurisdiction, special ordinances, which again may be altered by any canonical regulations which might arise as the situations of the times require. Arbitrary contravention or deviation by a bishop or local Church from the fundamental canonical provisions which have been accepted by the Church as a whole makes the Church in question a schismatic community and any bishop shown to be guilty of such an act is defrocked (Milas).

2 CONCERNING THE ADMINISTRATIVE AUTHORITY OVER PERSONS. General supervision and control over all clergy and monastics, as well as over all the ecclesiastical authorities and organizations subject to the Ecumenical Patriarchate of Constantinople are exercised by the Holy and Sacred Synod and locally by the Eparchial Synods, which are under the Patriarchal Synod. In the autocephalous Church of Greece, they are exercised by the Permanent Holy Synod at the behest of the Holy Synod of the Hierarchy.

In each particular metropolis, the metropolitans exercise similar supervision over the clergy and monastics and organizations under them, acting within the framework set out in the Holy Canons of the Church and in accordance with the instructions of the Holy Synod.

The clergy and monks owe obedience and submission to their bishop, though in the case of uncanonical and illegal behavior on his part, they may communicate their complaints against him by referring the matter to the Permanent Holy Synod.[1]

The Permanent Holy Synod gives leave of absence to metropolitans both at home and abroad.

Permission to travel at home and abroad is given to presbyters and monastics by their own metropolitan.

In general, clergy of all ranks and monastics of the Church of Greece or any other Orthodox Church may not be engaged ecclesiastically, nor even stay longer than two months outside the eparchy to which they belong without written permission from the head of their ecclesiastical authority — for presbyters, deacons and monastics from their own hierarchs and for the latter from the Permanent Holy Synod — and from the metropolitan or bishop of the place of their employment or stay.[2] Permission from the bishop of the region from which the clergy and monastics originated are "the letters of recommendation" which the Church adopted in olden times. These were particularly necessary in the years of the persecutions and great heresies in order to protect the Church from infiltration by suspicious elements.[3]

Should a hierarch lack a proper permit, or have one which has expired, the metropolitan may request the Permanent Holy Synod to remove the disobedient hierarch. In the case of other clergy or monastics, he himself may order them to return to the region to which they belong.

Every monk or nun must be registered at a monastery and must remain there, indeed be forced to do so, if necessary, by the metropolitan. The latter's permission is required for any long-term employment of a hieromonk outside the monastery. For a short stay outside the monas-

---

[1] For the particular regulations in the Holy Archdiocese of America, see its Charter in force in the Appendix, pp. 255ff.
[2] Canons 3, 7 and 8 of the Synod in Antioch. Cod. Just I 3.22. Article 56 of the Charter of the Church of Greece.
[3] Cf. 33rd Apostolic Canon. Canon 13 of the Fourth Ecumenical Synod.

tery, however, a monk needs the permission of his abbot, while a nun is forbidden to spend a night outside her monastery.[4] Likewise, women may not, in principle, spend a night in a men's monastery, nor men in a women's one.[5]

3 **ECCLESIASTICAL JUDICIAL AUTHORITY.** The foundation of ecclesiastical judicial authority was laid by the Founder of the Church, who said to His disciples: "If your brother sins against you, go and tell him his fault, between you and him alone. If he listens to you, you have gained your brother. If he does not listen, however, take one or two others along with you, that every word may be confirmed by the evidence of two or three witnesses. *If he refuses to listen to them, tell it to the church; and if he refuses to listen even to the church, let him be to you as a Gentile and a tax collector.*"[6]

The word "sin" here does not mean the criterion of the conscience nor people's sins from simple internal thoughts, which belong to the sphere of the spiritual guide during confession. Here, we are dealing with external social relations between members of the Church and within its sphere. The Church exercises judicial authority in cases of controversy and discord, which may arise between its members concerning matters of external Church relations. The Church also exercises this authority, not on the basis of any right granted to it by the State or any other such source, but independently and autonomously, on the basis of the direct authority transferred to it by its Founder, Jesus Christ. Consequently, ecclesiastical judicial authority is based on divine right, from which the canonical teaching regarding ecclesiastical judicial jurisdiction was later developed and systematized. With the passage of time, ecclesiastical legislation made provision for and defined all the details considered necessary for the canonical exercise of this jurisdiction.

---

[4] Canon 46 of the Quinisext Ecumenical Synod.
[5] Canon 47 of the Quinisext, 18 of the Seventh Ecumenical Synod et al., *Novella* 133 chap. 3.
[6] Matt. 18:15 – 17.

The right to exercise the judicial office in the Church is held by the bishops.

Through the transfer to the Apostles of the right to "judge your brother" by Jesus Christ, it is clear that the right to do so in the Church belongs to those persons who are successors to the Apostles, i.e. to the bishops. For this reason, the Sacred Canons speak only of the bishops as canonical judges in all differences among the faithful,[7] whose right they recognize absolutely, while threatening with penances those who disdain the bishops and have recourse to another court.[8] Likewise, it is forbidden for lower clergy to set up a court without the bishop.

Everything concerning the Church life of the clergy and laity falls within the competency of ecclesiastical judicial jurisdiction. Due to their position within the Church and their office, the clergy are subject to the ecclesiastical judicial authority, as are the laity, in spiritual matters. Since all matters concerning the faith and the moral life of the Church's members deriving from it are under the supervision of the Church, all contraventions against the faith and Christian religious life fall within its judicial jurisdiction.

A) *Ecclesiastical Courts and Their Competency.* During the first centuries, when the Church was isolated within pagan society and State, it

---

[7] Canon 5 of the First Ecumenical Synod.

[8] "… If, however, certain persons are neither heretics nor excluded from communion, nor condemned, nor previously charged with any offences, should declare that they have an accusation of an ecclesiastical nature against a bishop, the Holy Synod bids these persons to lodge their accusations before all the Bishops involved in the case. But if it so happen that the provincial Bishops are unable or incompetent to decide the case against the Bishop and to make the correction due, then they are to go to a greater Synod of the Bishops of this diocese summoned to try this case. And they are not to lodge the accusation until they themselves have in writing agreed to incur the same penalty if, in the course of the trial, it be proved that they have been slandering the accused Bishop. But if anyone, scorning what has been decreed in the foregoing statements should dare either to annoy the emperor's ears or trouble courts of secular authorities or an Ecumenical Synod, to the affront of all the Bishops of his Eparchy, let no such person be allowed to present any information whatever, because of his having thus insulted the Canons and ecclesiastical discipline" (Canon 6 of the Second Ecumenical Synod).

was forced not to have any communication whatsoever with the pagan civil power. All controversies and differences between Christians arising from their ecclesiastical relationships and also from their mutual social relations were heard before the ecclesiastical court and decided by it. Indeed, during the period of the persecutions this was a need of the Church. Saint Paul wrote to the Corinthians: "When one of you has a grievance against a brother, does he dare go to law before the unrighteous instead of the saints? Or do you not know that the saints will judge the world? And if the world is to be judged by you, are you incompetent to try trivial cases? Do you not know that we shall judge angels? So why not matters of this life? If you have such cases, why do you lay them before those who are least esteemed by the Church. I say this to your shame. Can it be that there is no one among you wise enough to judge between brothers?"[9]

On the basis of this apostolic admonition, we see in the first legislative provisions of the Church that the clergy and Christian laity had recourse to ecclesiastical judicial jurisdiction, i.e. the bishop, not only for their ecclesiastical affairs, but also for civil and social matters.

Thus, in the seat of each bishop, there was not only an ecclesiastical court for the differences and transgressions of members of the clergy, but also a special court which the laity addressed for the resolution of their differences. And they accepted the verdict of the bishop at this trial, as it were, as a settlement of their differences.[10] Of course, the civil power completely disregarded such courts and their verdicts, which had only moral status within the sphere of the Christian community. When, in the fourth century, the Christian Church was granted freedom within the Roman Empire, the decisions of the ecclesiastical courts were taken into account to the same extent as those of the state courts.

As was mentioned above, the competence of the ecclesiastical courts derives from divine law in all matters of the Church. Therefore, it acquires autonomous and independent judicial authority over these matters, with no necessity for this to be recognized by anyone. This jurisdiction was

---

[9] I Cor. 6:1 – 5; I Tim. chaps. 3 and 5.
[10] *Apost. Const.*, book II 44 – 51.

recognized from as early as the time of the first Christian emperors, who forbade civil courts to hear cases which concerned ecclesiastical life.[11] Besides this, however, and with the passage of time, the emperors granted the ecclesiastical courts the right to hear certain secular cases, mainly regarding civil law.

Justinian defined in detail the relations between civil and ecclesiastical courts and published a number of laws on the subject. According to this legislation: 1) all ecclesiastical differences, as well as those concerning the administration of Church property, belong to the jurisdiction of the episcopal court. A clergyman who does not agree with the verdict of the bishop may refer the case to the metropolitan, and thereafter to the patriarch, as the highest judicial authority; 2) a lay person who has a difference with a cleric may have recourse to the judicial aid of the bishop. If the accused does not transfer the case within ten days to the civil court, it is heard by the bishop's court, and then the civil one merely executes the verdict of the bishop; 3) in penal cases involving clergy, both courts, ecclesiastical and civil, may intervene, with the right of appeal if the case is tried by a civil court and the bishop disagrees with the opinion of the highest political official, at which point the patriarch and other higher officials of the Church intervene; 4) all trials involving bishops, whether of an ecclesiastical or civil nature, are heard by their own metropolitan synod. Appeal to the patriarch against the verdict is permitted; 5) no bishop may be called before a civil court as a witness or for any other purpose.

Post-Justinian emperors published protective laws concerning ecclesiastical courts and against any infringement of their rights by civil courts.[12]

During the Byzantine period, ecclesiastical courts also heard judicial cases involving lay people, as well as those between laity and clergy. Indeed, since the ecclesiastical courts of that time handed down verdicts more reliable than those of the civil courts, they were inundated by a host of suits of a private nature. It became necessary, therefore, to define by law

---

[11] Cf. *Codex Theodosianus* XVI *Const.* 1 and *Codex Justinianus* I, 4.

[12] *Novella* of Herakleios (629 AD), *Epanagoge* XI, 11 and 14; *Novella* of John Komnenos (1124 or 1139 AD), *Novella* of Manuel Komnenos (1151 or 1166) et al.

the precise range of the competence of the two courts. The final settlement was reached under Emperor Alexios Komnenos, who, through a *Novella* published in 1086, declared that the ecclesiastical courts would hear all cases concerning the faith, mysteries and Christian morals, as well as cases concerning marriage, while the civil courts would hear all suits of a civil nature. Apart from this, the Church was, from very early times, awarded the right to oversee and protect all the charitable institutions: those of the poor, of the widows and all those supplicating assistance and protection. However, the close bond between the Church and State in the Roman Empire meant that it was not at all easy to distinguish the limits of the competency of the ecclesiastical and civil courts. After the Fall of Constantinople, Mehmet the Conqueror recognized the privileges of the hierarchy in judicial matters which they had enjoyed under the last Roman emperors.

In all the Patriarchates today, and in all the autocephalous Churches of the Orthodox Church, judicial cases both of the laity and clergy are subject to the civil courts. The ecclesiastical courts judge the clergy on violations related to the faith, to the priestly duties and their lives in general. They also hear cases involving the laity in regards to the initial or final procedure for the dissolution of a marriage and transgressions against the faith. Those guilty of crimes against the faith may be punished by exclusion from the sacramental life for a short or long period of time, by excommunication from the communion of the faithful and by denial of Christian funeral and burial rites.

In the Church of Greece, transgressions committed by the clergy and monks in matters related to their duties and the promises made in their confession, and the canonical sanctions involved, are all decided by ecclesiastical courts. A special law regulates the establishment, composition, competence and function of these courts, and until its publication Law 5383/1932, "concerning ecclesiastical courts and the procedure before them" continues to be in force (art. 44 §§ 1 of the Charter of the Church of Greece).

The following ecclesiastical courts operate in accordance with Law 5383:

1. Bishop's Courts.
2. Synodal Courts, of the first instance and appeal.
3. The Courts for the Hierarchy, of the first instance and appeal.
4. The Court for the Members of the Synod.

In accordance with Holy Canons 9 and 17 of the Fourth Ecumenical Synod, the metropolitans of the Church of Greece also have the right of appeal to the Ecumenical Patriarch.

1. *Bishop's Courts.* In the Archdiocese of Athens, and "in each Metropolis, there is a Bishop's Court, with the competence to hear cases involving the clergy, deacons and monastics."

The Bishop's Court, "meeting in session at the Metropolitan's Office at the seat of the Metropolis, consists of the Metropolitan of that see as chairman, or, should he be unable to attend, his lawful deputy as acting chairman, and of two office-holding presbyters from those in the Metropolis area as members" (Article 2).

"In the Bishop's Court, the metropolitan alone has the right to vote, thus giving a judgment. The presbyters who sit with him have a vote which is merely advisory, though they do have the right to record their dissenting opinion, if any, in the minutes. If there is no Metropolitan or if, due to his absence or any other impediment, the court meets in session without him, and thus consists of presbyters, all members have a right to vote in the verdict" (Article 5).

"The Bishop's Court hears any case involving Church offenses wherever these may have been committed by those clergy and monastics under the metropolitan's jurisdciton, as well as those committed within the diocesan region by any clergy or monastics belonging to the jurisdiction of any Metropolitan whatsoever" (Article 7).

Should the transgression committed be too serious for the competence of the Bishop's Court, the latter declares itself not competent and refers the case to the Synodal Court of the first instance.

2. *Synodal Courts of First Instance and Appeal.* The Synodal Court of the First Instance consists of the senior hierarch of the Synod (the vice-chairman of the Synod) as chairman and five other members of the

Synod, chosen by lot at the Permanent Holy Synod's first session of the year after October 1.

The Synodal Court of Appeal consists of the Chairman of the Holy Synod, as chairman and the other six members, after the vice-chairman and the five who sat in the Court of First Instance have been exempted.

The Synodal Court of First Instance hears violations committed by clerics and monastics which have been referred to it by the Bishop's Court, as well as appeals from that court. It also hears cases of simony, in regards to the culpability of the person ordained.

The Court of Appeal hears appeals against the verdicts of the Court of First Instance.

3. *The Court for Hierarchs of the First Instance and Appeal.* The Court of First Instance for Hierarchs consists of the Vice-Chairman of the Holy Synod as chairman and the other eleven members of the Synod, without the Chairman.

The Court of First Instance for Hierarchs hears violations by Hierarchs and is empowered to impose the following penalties: a) censure; b) suspension from all priestly functions for up to six months; c) deposition from the throne; d) defrocking.

The Court of Appeal for Hierarchs consists of the Chairman of the Synod and fourteen members selected by seniority of ordination from among the hierarchs of the state who hold metropolitan sees and are not members of the Permanent Holy Synod. This court hears appeals against the verdicts of the Court of First Instance for Hierarchs.

4. *The Court for Hierarchs who are Members of the Synod.* Should the chairman or members of the Permanent Holy Synod, in the course of their Synodal duties, commit some transgression against an established norm of the Church, a Court is convened, consisting of one third of the metropolitans of the state who have sees, chosen by lot, minus those who were serving in the Synod at the time when the transgressions were committed which gave rise to the trial.

The right of recourse (appeal) to the Ecumenical Patriarch against final judgments which impose suspension, dethronement or defrocking, which is granted to the Metropolitans of Neae Chorae by the Patriarchal and Synodal Act of 1928, is also extended to the Metropolitans of the Autocephalous Church of Greece, thus implementing the ancient practice of the Church and in accordance with canons 9 and 17 of the Fourth Ecumenical Synod.

B) ***Ecclesiasticl Penal Law.*** This part of Canon Law deals with ecclesiastical offenses and the ecclesiastical punishments imposed by the Sacred Canons.

i. *Ecclesiastical infringements.* According to Canon Law, an offense is any transgression by an external action or omission against the ecclesiastical law in force.

The punishment imposed for offenses committed by the clergy are different from those which apply to the laity, because of the difference in the duties of both parties as members of the Church.

ii. *General ecclesiastical infringements.* The most serious ecclesiastical offenses are:

1. Apostasy, i.e. the denial of the Christian faith and the acceptance of another non-Christian confession. Apostasy may arise through the exercise of personal will or through coersion.

In the first case, it is punished through the great excommunication or anathema. This is imposed by a decision of the Synod of the Hierarchy of the Church of Greece, at the recommendation of the Permanent Holy Synod. In the Holy Archdiocese of America by the Holy and Sacred Synod of the Ecumenical Patriarchate, at the recommendation of the Holy Eparchial Synod. In the case of apostasy through coersion, the punishment is lesser.

2. Heresy, i.e. the deliberate and stubborn rejection of or deviation from the dogma of the Orthodox Church and the acceptance of a dogmatically misleading teaching. The punishment imposed is the great excommunication or anathema.

3. Schism, that is the organized rejection of obedience to and compliance with the canonical Church authority. The punishment imposed is defrocking for the clergy and excommunication for the laity.[13]

---

[13] "If any presbyter, despising his own bishop, shall draw people aside, and set up another altar, without finding anything wrong with the bishop in point of piety and

4. Simony, that is that attempt to use Divine Grace for commerce or trade. The name derives from Simon the Magician who tried to bribe the Apostles in order to buy divine authority (Acts 8:9ff).

It is not only the person who ordains or promotes someone to the hierarchy on payment of money who is guilty of simony, but also the person so ordained and anyone who acted on his behalf.[14] Equally, simony is not confined to cases where money changes hands, but also applies to those where any gifts are offered in return for the acquisition or provision of a spiritual office or even when the ordination or promotion is the reward for personal services rendered or because of kinship or friendship, or when someone uses powerful personages for the uncanonical and illegal acquisition of Church offices,[15] or when he uses illegitimate means to attract votes for election to an ecclesiastical office.[16]

Another aspect of the offense of simony is the misuse of judicial jurisdiction and penal authority for base ends, by handing down unjust verdicts or imposing lesser sentences, either through profiteering or

---

righteousness, let him be defrocked, on the ground that he is an office-seeker. For he is a tyrant. Let the rest of the clergy, be treated likewise, and all those who abet him. But let the laymen be excommunicated. Let this, however, be done after a first, second, and third admonition from the bishop" (31st Apostolic Canon). Cf. Canons 6 of the Synod in Gangra, 5 of Antioch, 10 and 11 of Cartagena, 13, 14 and 15 of the First Second, et al.

[14] "If any Bishop should ordain for money, and put to sale a grace which cannot be sold, and consecrate a bishop, or chorepiscopos, or presbyters, or deacons, or any one of the roll of the Clergy with a view to gain; or, for money, nominate a steward, or Ekdikos (advocate), or paramonarios, or any one whatever who is on the roll of the Church with the object of making a shameful profit for himself: let him who is found guilty of this stand in peril of his office; and let him who has been thus ordained have no benefit from such traffic in ordinations or nominations, but, on the contrary let him have no claim upon the dignity or charge he has obtained for money. And if any one should be found negotiating such shameful and unlawful transactions, let him also, if he be a clergyman, forfeit his office, and if he be a layman or monk, let him be anathematized" (Canon 2 of the Fourth Ecumenical Synod). Cf. 29th Apostolic et al.

[15] "If any bishop obtain possession of a church by the aid of the temporal powers, let him be defrocked and excommunicated, and all who communicate with him."

[16] Canon 2 of the Synod in Sardica

personal antipathy.[17] The punishment imposed on the perpetrators of simony is defrocking for the clergy and anathema for the laity.[18]

5. Sacrilege, that is the removal of an object dedicated to divine worship. Sacrilege is not merely an ecclesiastical crime, but is also contained in the common penal code as a particular instance of theft and is punished more severely.

iii. *Misdemeanors by the clergy.* Misdemeanors by the clergy are concerned either with the particular duties of their calling or to general Christian duties which are common to all members of the Church. Those concerned with their particular ecclesiastical duties are:

1. Reordination of a clergyman to the same hieratic rank.[19]

2. Arbitrary celebration of the mysteries and other priestly services by a defrocked clergyman.[20]

3. Ordination or celebration "beyond the parish" (παρ' ἐνορίαν), i.e. exercise by the clergy of their priestly functions outside the limits of their geographical jurisdiction.[21]

4. Abandonment by a clergyman of the post to which he was ordained and acceptance of another without the consent and approval of the competent bishop.

5. Infringement of the secrecy of confession.

6. Non-observance of and disregard for the official liturgical rite and of pastoral duties in general.

7. Squandering Church property, etc.

8. Plotting against the canonical authorities or the establishment of factions.[22]

---

[17] Canon 4 of the Seventh Ecumenical Synod
[18] Canon 2 of the Fourth Ecumenical Synod et al.
[19] 68th Apostolic Canon, canon 48 of the Synod in Cartagena
[20] 28th Apostolic Canon, canon 6 of the Second Ecumenical Synod, canon 4 of the Synod in Antioch.
[21] 35th Apostolic Canon, canons 15 of the First Ecumenical Synod, 2 of the Second Ecumenical Synod, 8 of the Third Ecumenical Synod, 5 of the Fourth Ecumenical Synod et al.
[22] Canons 18 of the Fourth Ecumenical Synod, 34 of the Quinisext et al.

9. Sycophancy, hubris and abusiveness.[23]

10. Adultery.

11. Loose living.

12. Theft.

ii. *Ecclesiastical punishments.* Ecclesiastical punishments are divided into the following categories:

1. Punishments imposed on all members of the Church, clergy and laity alike.

2. Punishments imposed only on the clergy.

3. Punishments imposed on clergy and monastics.

4. Punishments imposed only on monastics.

Ecclesiastical punishments imposed on all members of the Church. After the Lord's crucifixion and resurrection, His authority to forgive sins passed to the Apostles, through them to their successors, the bishops, and at the behest of the latter to presbyters acting in their name. "Whatever you bind on the earth shall be bound in heaven, and whatever you loose on earth shall be loosed in heaven" (Matt. 18:18). Judicial authority in the Church is exercised by the bishops. This authority is exercised also through the mystery of repentance and confession, when they impose on those making their confession the "penances" provided for by the holy canons. These strictures are designed to be corrective, not punitive. The "penances" are: stricter than usual fasting, alms-giving, temporary exclusion from Holy Communion and others. All sins may be pardoned, provided there is genuine repentance.

In the third and fourth centuries, those who were excluded from the Divine Eucharist passed through certain stages before their final rehabilitation. These stages were those of the "lamenting," the "attentive listeners," the "fallen" and the "penitents."

Judicial authority is exercised by the bishops in person through the mystery of repentance, though they may authorize presbyters under them to perform this mystery, by written command or "license."

---

[23] 55th and 56th Apostolic Canons; canons 6 of the First Ecumenical Synod, 21 of the Fourth et al.

Even without the mystery of confession, the bishop may impose the penance of the lesser excommunication, i.e. exclusion from the Holy Liturgy, on persons who have committed sins involving that punishment.

The greater excommunication or anathema is the severest of punishments and consists of the expulsion of the guilty party from the Church for life and the withdrawal of their membership in it. This punishment is imposed as a last resort and only if other measures have proved ineffective.

In the sources, the term excommunication is sometimes used in the sense of the lesser and at others in the sense of the greater, or anathema. The punishment of anathema may be imposed after death, also, though it may likewise be revoked as well.

Another punishment imposed on all members of the Church is denial of Church burial. Those who are thus deprived are: 1) people who have been excommunicated and have not recanted; 2) those who die in a duel or as a result of wounds incurred in one; 3) those who died by their own hand, unless they are not of sound mind or if they repent shortly before they die.

Punishments imposed only on the clergy. Apart from the punishments which may be imposed on any member of the Church, without distinction, there are also others which can be imposed only on the clergy or monastics.

Thus, the clergy are punished:

1. By defrocking, which is the most severe of the punishments imposed upon them. Through this, the clergyman is entirely deprived of his hieratic status and returns to the class to which he belonged before his initial ordination, i.e. to the class of the laity or of monks. Any mystery or priestly function performed by a defrocked priest is invalid, while the defrocked priest who performs such rites becomes subject to further Church punishment,[24] is deprived of the right of appeal[25] and is charged with impersonation.

2. By suspension. It is forbidden for a clergyman under suspension to perform his priestly functions or exercise the duties stemming from

---

[24] 28th Apostolic Canon
[25] Canon 4 of the Synod in Antioch.

his administrative authority for as long as he is subject to this punishment. Since the clergyman who is under suspension still retains the hieratic rank and office, any mysteries and other rites celebrated by him are valid, but his disobedience in performing them makes him liable to further, more severe ecclesiastical punishments.

3. By demoting him to the lowest seniority among those of equal rank of the priesthood (*officium*) with him.

4. By removal from his throne, which applies only to bishops. In this case, his administrative authority is taken away, but his priesthood remains and he is entitled to celebrate rites appropriate to his rank provided he has permission from the bishop in whose see he resides.

5. By a monetary fine.

Punishments imposed on clergy and monastics. These are:

1. Transfer.

2. Removal from office, which is sanctioned by ordinances in the canons for both clergy and monastics.

3. Confinement of unmarried clergy or monastics in the reformatory center of his own or another monastery.

4. Reprimand (censure in the case of bishops) for clergy of all ranks and monastics.

5. Recommendation (supplication) by which those involved are reminded of the duties of the clergy and monastics in the Church according to their position within it. A recommendation is repeated two or three times, following which a more severe punishment is imposed.[26]

Punishments imposed only on monastics. Of these, the most important are the removal of the monastic habit, expulsion from the monastery, excommunication, withdrawal of rations and various penances.

4 CHURCH PROPERTY LAW. A) *The Right of the Church to Hold Property.* In order to achieve its aims in the world, the Church needs the material goods required for this. There is testimony to this

---

[26] 31ˢᵗ Apostolic Canon.

from the apostolic age. Voluntary offerings, regular or exceptional contributions and alms, etc. are the sources of the Church's property.

After the necessary expenses for worship and the maintenance of the clergy had been met, this property was used to further charitable and social aims. For this reason, from the time of Constantine the Great, Roman legislation often approved and protected the increase of Church property and granted it tax exemption.[27]

B) *Ownership of Church Property.* The question arises as to who is the owner of Church property. In the modern era, there has been uncertainty among Western teachers of Church Law regarding the answer to this question and various theories have been propounded on the subject. Some have claimed that the owners of the property of the Church are the ecclesiastical communities present everywhere, others the State and others the whole Church.

According to the Canon Law of the Orthodox Church, all these theories are mistaken. They arose from the various relations of the Church in the West, as well as from those which prevailed at different times between the Church and each State. In regards to this matter, the Canon Law of the Orthodox Church follows the theory of the sources of the Canon Law of the undivided Church. These sources characterize the parish church in any particular place as the owner of the property of that part of the general Church property which it acquired through donations, inheritance, legacies, etc. Each individual parish church, wherever it may be, has all the rights of a legal owner and in itself and in regards to third parties is a sovereign and independent legal entity.[28] This canonical theory of the Church held such sway entirely in Church practice, to the extent that it was strictly forbidden for bishops to use the property of one parish church for the purposes of another, even if both were subject to the same bishop and were, therefore, parts of the same episcopal area.[29] Apart from individual parish churches, the canonical sources also recognize mon-

---

[27] *Codex Theodosianus* XIII, 1, 5.XVI 2. 6. 10 – 14; *Codex Justinianus* 1. 2, 12; 3, 13 …
[28] Canons 24 and 25 of the Synod in Antioch.
[29] Canons 26 and 33 of the Synod in Cartagena.

asteries as having rights of ownership, as well as charitable institutions and all other Church foundations. This theory and principle was accepted in Roman Law, which recognized the legal entity of all the foundations recognized as such by the Church itself. Indeed, one law of Justinian includes the provision that if anyone leaves a legacy in the name of God, that legacy passes into the full possession and ownership of the parish church of the place where the testator lived. "Should anyone leave an inheritance or legacy in the name of our great God and Savior Jesus Christ, we order that the church of the place in which he had his residence shall take the bequest" (*Novella* 131, chap. 9; Basilica L, 3, 10).

c) *Concerning the Acquisition of Church Property.* In the first years of the establishment of the Church, it was maintained through the voluntary contributions of Christians, consisting of objects of various kinds, such as the fruits of the earth (first-fruits), money, etc. Mention is also made of tithes, which were paid by the faithful for the Church and the clergy. These contributions were not compulsory but voluntary and were given from a sense of piety. With the passage of time, the Church also acquired land and farms.[30] At the time of the persecutions, the Church was unable to consider its possessions as its permanent and enduring property. From Constantine the Great, however, it was awarded full legal recognition of Church property, in accordance with the civil laws governing property, so that it enjoyed the rights of ownership over its possessions through the protection afforded it by the State itself, as was the case with any private property. Roman Law distinguishes between the acquisition of possessions because of death (*mortis causa*) and through legal agreements between the living (*actus vivos*). These provisions also govern Church property.

1. Of the various ways in which the Church acquires property through cause of death, the first place is held by inheritance through a will (*ex testamento*). The Church also has the legal right to undisposed inheritance (*ab intestato*), especially that of property belonging to clergy

---

[30] Canon 25 of the Synod in Antioch.

who died intestate. During the Byzantine era, the Church was able to become heir to the property of certain classes of lay people who died without making a will (prisoners, heretics and Jews). The right of the Church to inherit the property of clergy who die intestate is recognized to this day and is regulated by specific laws (in Greece).

Most of the Church's property was acquired by "legacies for reasons of piety" (*legata ab pias causas*). In this case, the Church is not the owner of the property in the legacy, but it, or the competent bishop, merely has the right of ultimate supervision over the legacy. It directs the administration of it and takes any legal measures necessary if the administration is irregular and not in accordance with the stated purpose of the bequest. In this sense, any institutions founded through legacies are known as ecclesiastical institutions (*instituta*). These institutions enjoyed special privileges, especially that of exemption from the Falcidian law. According to this and to later Roman Law, any legacy was valid only provided that the legal heirs received at least one quarter of the whole estate. Otherwise, the heir was authorized to diminish the bequests *pro rata*, until the sum equivalent to that to which he was entitled was made up (*Quarta Falcidia*).

2. The Church also acquires property through legal transactions between the living, especially donations, through purchase and other legitimate dealings by which private individuals acquire the various objects in their possession. Another way in which the Church acquires property is through positive prescription or lapse, i.e. the acquisition and ownership of something through continuous use over a certain period of time.

D) *Administration of Church Property.* During the first years of the Church, the first people to administer its property were the Apostles and thereafter their successors, the bishops, acting as they thought fit and answerable only to God.[31] Later, when the property of the Church had increased considerably, it became impossible for the bishops alone to administer and manage it. For this reason, extra clergy, known as stewards (οἰκονόμοι), were drafted in to assist in the task of administering

---

[31] 38th Apostolic Canon. Cf. 40th and 41st Apostolic Canons and canons 24 and 25 of the Synod in Antioch.

Church property, while in the parishes, where the administration of Church property took on a local character, it was undertaken by the parish priest, who was personally responsible for it to his own bishop. In regards to monasteries, the administration was in the hands of the abbot, with the general supervision over all the Church property in the diocese as a whole resting with the bishop.

Today, administration of Church property is regulated by the relative provisions of each autocephalous Church and through the laws of the State.[32]

E) *Distinctions between Items of Church Property.* Items of Church property are distinguished into:

1. The sacred, i.e. those which are used exclusively for worship. These are further divided into those sanctioned for special rites and consecrated with holy myrrh (the church, the Holy Table, the antimens, sacred vessels, etc.) and those merely sanctified with a blessing or through being located in a particular holy, sanctified place (liturgical books, vestments, icons, etc.).

2. The holy, i.e. all the rest (furniture, non-movable items, etc.).

Sacred items may not form any part of transactions, though holy ones may.

---

[32] For the Church of Greece, see its Charter, art. 17.

PART FOUR

THE LIFE OF THE CHURCH

CHAPTER EIGHT

Marriage

The Church follows Christians from the day when they become canonical members of it to the day of their death. The teaching of Canon Law in this part follows Christians in all phases of their lives as members of the Church and regulates the manner in which they become participants in the rights which the Church provides for its members. It also regulates any relationship with worship or with Canon Law which they may enter upon, either singly or with others as well as the termination or cessation of these rights. Due to restrictions of space, however, we shall be dealing only with marriage in this part.

Marriage is the most ancient institution in the divine law. According to Holy Scripture, God ordained the conjugal bond between man and woman at the creation of the First-Created, Adam and Eve: "And the Lord God said, 'It is not good that the man should be alone. Let us make him a helper fit for him' ... and the rib which the Lord God had taken from Adam, he made into a woman and brought her to Adam. And Adam said: 'This now is bone from my bones and flesh from my flesh ... because of this, a man will leave his father and mother and cleave to his wife and they shall be one flesh ...'"[1] "And God blessed them, saying: 'Increase and multiply and fill the earth.'"[2]

---

[1] Genesis 2:18 – 24.
[2] Genesis 1:28.

According to Holy Scripture, then, marriage is a sacred action of divine authority, linked with the creation of mankind and the world and with God's providence for them. The conjoining of man and woman is aimed at their physical bond, but also the moral bond between two people of opposite sexes, who complement one another, assist one another and are drawn together toward moral perfection. They are joined as "one flesh" and fulfill the purpose of the Creator concerning the human race through procreation, from which arises the duty of the parents to bring up their children "in the discipline and instruction of the Lord."[3] For this reason, God implanted in both genders a very strong feeling of natural, mutual love, so that both were closely interlinked, thus becoming one soul and one body.

Marriage, then, in its pure form, is an arrangement of nature in accordance with the will of God. It is the basis of the family, of that society in which the noblest human feelings are forged and developed. So, by its very nature, marriage is a sacred foundation and the Church has stamped its sanctity by recognizing it as a divine institution and arrangement and by defining the lawful and canonical communal relationship between men and women as a divine mystery. Due to the importance of marriage for the human race, for people's spiritual equilibrium and their relationship to creation and, therefore, to the Creator, Canon Law has systematically set out what is aimed at in marriage.

1 CONCEPT OF MARRIAGE AND JURISDICTION OVER MATTERS RELATED TO IT. Marriage has always had a religious character among a variety of peoples, since the notion of its religious origin has remained alive in their consciousness. Even among the Ancient Romans, where marriage consisted principally of a contract between a man and a woman, moral and religious significance were not absent. According to the Roman jurist Modestinus, marriage is the conjoining of man and woman, the conjointness of life forever, a communion by divine and human law." Three features can be discerned in this definition of marriage:

---

[3] Ephes. 6:4. Archbishop Chrysostomos Papadopoulos, "On Marriage" in Ἐκκλησία 1979, p. 291 (in Greek).

The natural element, i.e. the conjugal union of a man and a woman.

The moral element, i.e. the complete and unbroken cohabitation of the man and woman for the whole of life.

The religious element, which contains the full communion of everything that concerns religion and the law.

This definition has also been included in the canonical collections of the Orthodox Church, being recognized therein as the best interpretation of the essence of marriage.[4]

The Christian Church proclaimed the institution of marriage to be a mystery. Apart from its natural importance, marriage thus acquired supreme moral and spiritual significance, having as its foundation that love between spouses which amounts to self-denial, similar to the love of Christ for the Church.[5] Indeed, it appears that from the first years of the Christian Church, marriage was consecrated through a blessing: "Perform the union after the bishop has agreed, so that the marriage may be according to the will of the Lord rather than by desire," writes Ignatios the God-bearer to Polycarp of Smyrna at the beginning of the second century.[6]

Since marriage as a mystery is viewed as being within the sphere of divine grace, it is included in the liturgical setting of the Divine Eucharist, within which it is also performed. Tertullian (2nd century) is, perhaps, the most ancient witness to the association between marriage and the Divine Eucharist.[7]

From a legal point of view, in the first years of the Church and in later years, marriage was of civil importance, was subject to civil jurisdiction and had no direct connection to the Church. In any case, centuries were to pass before the Roman Empire became fully Christian. Christians,

---

[4] *Nomocanon* XII, XIII. *Syntagma* of Vlastares III, II…

[5] Ephes. 5:25 ff.

[6] Cf. Tertullian, "Letter to his own wife" in which he calls marriage a "mystery." Also Methodios of Olympos, "*The Symposium of the Ten Virgins*"; Basil the Great, Homily 7 *On the Hexaemeron*; Gregory the Theologian, "*Discourse* 40." In many discourses, Saint John Chrysostom calls the marriage honorable "mysteries," et al.

[7] "Unde sufficiamus ad enarrandam felicitatem ejus matrimonii, quod ecclesia conciliat et confirmat *oblatio* et consignat benedicti."

therefore, contracted civil marriages which were also recognized by the Church. Apart from this civil marriage, however, there was also a form of ecclesiastical marriage, as was mentioned above, contracted before the bishop or a presbyter in Church. This Christian marriage, however, was considered in the Roman State to be devoid of any legal status and validity. As far as the civil courts were concerned it simply did not exist, even though it was very widespread.

During the reign of Emperor Justinian, in the first half of the sixth century, the first step was taken to link the civil marriage contract with the ecclesiastical form, in marriages relating to persons of the middle class. Justinian granted the right to members of the middle classes to declare their decision to contract a marriage in church, before the judge in whose area the church lay, who would then engage three or four of the priests serving there and draw up an act of marriage to be signed by him, the couple and the priests. As a consequence of this law of Justinian, Church marriage began to gain ground in the Roman state. Finally, Emperor Leo VI, the Wise, through his *Novella* 89 (of the year 893 AD), declared that only marriages blessed by the Church were legal. From then on, marriage blessed by the Church had both civil and ecclesiastical character and fell, as was to be expected, entirely under the competence of the Church. This state of affairs continued for Christians after the capture of Constantinople by the Ottomans (1453), i.e. during the period of the Ottoman Empire.

Since the Greek revolution in 1821, marriage within the Greek realm has retained its significance as a mystery, in accordance with the spiritual and moral tradition of the Greek nation. It also retains its institutional status, despite the negative attitude expressed in recent years principally by certain of those in legal and other circles toward this status. These circles cleave to the notion of marriage as no more than a contract, a concept which derives from Western Europe and, in particular, from 19th century France.

Article 21 § 1 of the Constitution in force today in Greece (1975) declares that: "The family, as well as marriage, motherhood and childhood years come under the protection of the State." Such recent constitutional reinforcement of the family as the most vital nucleus within society emphasizes the institutional nature of marriage, which is why provision is made to afford it the protection of the State.

Until 1982, when the option of civil or religious marriage was introduced into Greece through law 1250/82, the position had been under existing legislation that marriage could only be legitimate if performed at a service according to the dogma or religion of the prospective couple. Compulsory religious marriage for Christians, Jews and Muslims is still required in the Islamic countries of the Near and Middle East, as well as in Israel. In recent years, religious marriage was compulsory in civil law only in Greece and Spain in Europe, but this condition was abolished in 1982 and 1978 respectively. Compulsory religious marriage was a remnant of an era when it was entirely expected that citizens would belong to some religion and would follow its law on marriage. Nowadays, in Europe and the Americas, the position of the State in regards to religious or civil marriage, while differing widely in detail, comes in two main forms: one is where civil marriage is compulsory and the other where there is an option between civil and religious.

Compulsory civil marriage is required in the states of Central Europe, mainly in all Communist States, as well as in most countries of South America and some in Asia and Africa.

Historically, compulsory civil marriage was instituted during the French revolution and has since developed into a battleground against the Churches in the cultural field. The religious wedding ceremony, in accordance with the principle of total separation between Church and State in these countries, is totally ignored by the State. The system of compulsory civil marriage requires that the civil wedding take place before the religious ceremony, in the presence of a Registrar or Mayor. This arrangement comes from the view that only the State is the source of law, and that the Church has no legislative authority over the marriage of its members. The demand on the part of the State, however, for exclusivity in the matter of marriage, among other things, is an insult to freedom of belief and conscience, as well as to freedom of worship, which are guaranteed by the 1945 Charter of the United Nations (article 18 of the Declaration of the UN), by the 1966 UN Convention on Human Rights (article 18) and by the final act of Helsinki (1975).

The option between religious and civil marriage has been established in two-thirds of the countries of the world, among which are the most developed. According to this arrangement, those about to wed have the right to choose to celebrate their marriage either only before a clergyman, provided he be competent according to the canons of their religion, or only before the Registrar of Municipal Authority. This type of marriage is encountered in two forms, the Roman and the English.

In the Roman model, the state, on the basis of a concordat with the Vatican, recognizes a marriage celebrated in accordance with the provisions of Canon Law. This marriage held to be valid today in Italy, Portugal, Spain and Santo Domingo.

The English model of optional religious marriage exists in the Anglo-American sphere of law, particularly in Britain, the Scandinavian countries, the Commonwealth, certain states of South America, the United States of America and in other countries, i.e. in most countries in the world. In this form of marriage, the prospective spouses have the right to choose the manner in which their marriage will be contracted, either before a representative of their religion or before the State registrar. Choosing a religious wedding does not in the least affect the legal content of the marriage. In regards to the impediments to marriage, the possibility of contracting marriage and the consequences of marriage, as well as whatever is connected with marriage and divorce, the civil law is valid for all citizens, without any exception whatsoever, and independent of religion. Moreover, the competence of the Church in regards to the requirements for contracting marriage, its consequences and its dissolution is not affected by State law. No clergyman may be forced to conduct a religious wedding ceremony when there is a religious impediment which, according to the teaching and order of the cleric's religion may not be overlooked. The requirement for the marriage to be recognized by the State is that there should be no impediment in civil law.

According to the most recent laws in these countries, acknowledgement of the marriage by the registrar is compulsory. This acknowledgement is merely a formal declaration, rather than a necessary component.

As was mentioned above, the voluntary choice between civil and religious marriage was introduced into Greece in 1982, through Law 1250. Two forms of marriage are established by this law, which ordains that: "Marriage is performed either by the simultaneous declaration by the prospective couple that they agree to this (civil wedding), or by a religious ceremony conducted by a priest of the Orthodox Church or by a functionary of another dogma or religion known in Greece. The declaration takes place at a public celebration, in the presence of two witnesses, before the mayor or president of the community of the place where the marriage is conducted, or before their legal deputy and these are obliged to draw up the relative act immediately. The requirements of the religious ceremony and any related matter are laid down by the order of service (*Typikon*) and rules of the dogma or religion according to which the ceremony is held, provided these comply with public order. The religious functionary is obliged to draw up the relevant act immediately. The performance of a civil wedding does not prevent a religious ceremony taking place for the same marriage, in accordance with the religion and dogma of the spouses (article 1367 of the *Civil Code*).

By Law 1250/82, it is also ordained that "a marriage which occurs without any of the types envisaged in article 1367 being observed at all is null and void."

According to current legislation on the valid contracting of marriage, the following requirements are demanded:

1. There must be consent between the prospective spouses, without conditions or a time limitation. The relevant declarations are to be made in person (article 1350 of the *Civil Code*).

2. The prospective spouses must be of legal age, i.e. must have completed their eighteenth year (article 1350 of the *Civil Code*).[8]

---

[8] Article 12 of the law "on Family Law" replaced, as stated above, the revoked article in the *Civil Code* which had read: "Terms for contraction. For the contraction of a mar-

3. "Should the prospective spouses be minors, the court, having first heard them and the persons exercising care over them, may allow the marriage even before the completion of the legal age, provided the ceremony is deemed necessary for a pressing reason" (article 1350 of the *Civil Code*).[9]

Should an underage couple desire to celebrate their marriage with a religious ceremony, without the permission of the Court, a bishop may, by economy, issue a special license. Whenever the pressing need arises for the bishop to issue a special license to minors without the permission of the Court and because of exceptional and unusual circumstances, he may do so at his pastoral discretion, provided he has first referred the case to the Holy Synod for its permission for such a wedding by economy and if the parents of the underage couple agree (Encyclical 2355/26-4-83 of the Holy Synod of the Church of Greece). According to the Holy Synod, significant reasons for granting a marriage license to an underage couple are: a) if the woman is pregnant; b) military call-up; c) emigration; d) elopement; and e) conflict between the families.

4. The ability to make a legal contract is required: "Whoever is unable to enact a legal contract cannot contract a marriage. Marriage is, however, allowed for people who are incapacitated in regards to the law (Article 1351 of the *Civil Code*).

2 THE FORMAL REQUIREMENTS FOR THE PERFORMANCE OF MAR-RIAGE. Until the new law was passed, article 1368 of the *Civil Code*, concerning the marriage of Orthodox Christians, contained the follow-

---

riage it is required that the man should have completed his eighteenth year and the woman her fourteenth." In Byzantium, it had been the fourteenth year for the man and the twelfth for the woman.

[9] This was enacted through article 12 of the law on Family Law, which replaced the repealed article 1352, which read as follows: "A minor with limited ability to make legally binding agreements may contract a marriage with the consent of the person exercising paternal authority, or the mother who has the minor in care, or whoever has the supervision or guardianship. If they refuse consent, the court may, at a hearing of the closest relations, provided this is feasible, grant a marriage license if this is enjoined by the interests of the minor."

ing provision: "License from a bishop is required for the performance of the marriage ceremony. Celebration without a license does not entail invalidity..." The new law states: "For the wedding ceremony to be performed, either civil or as a service of the Eastern Orthodox Church, a license is required from the Mayor or President of the Community of the last domicile of each of the persons who intend to marry."

The new law also amends article 1370 of the *Civil Code* in stating: "It is obligatory for a marriage license to be issued (by the Mayor or the President of the Community) provided it has been ascertained that the conditions for the forthcoming marriage have been investigated and the banns posted. If there is serious reason, the banns may be omitted." It does not follow from the law that if a religious marriage ceremony is performed without a license from the Mayor or President of the Community it is invalid, nor are any strictures to be applied to the detriment of the Mayor, President of the Community or Priest of the Orthodox Church.[10] License from a bishop for a religious marriage is required, however, by article 49 of the law 590/77 "concerning the Charter of the Church of Greece," and this has not been repealed. However, a few months after the new law was passed, and because of the displeasure engendered and the pointless aggravation caused by the necessity of obtaining a license from the Mayor or President of the Community in order to be granted a license from the bishop for those interested in a religious marriage, this requirement — for the civil license — was revoked. Granting a bishop's license retains the process as it was before Law 1250/1982 (encyclical 2329/20-10-82 of the Holy Synod of the Church of Greece) and, following the amendment of article 1368 of the *Civil Code*, the priests of the Orthodox Church in Greece continue to celebrate weddings only by license of the bishop, the responsibility for complying resting with them.

Before a religious marriage service is celebrated, it must be announced, which ought to happen either by publication in a daily newspaper or, in areas where there is no daily press, by posting the banns on the churches of

---

[10] Opinion by G. Lilaios, special legal advisor to the Church of Greece.

the parishes through which the issuing of the license is activated (Encyclical Note of the Holy Synod of the Church of Greece, serial no. 1392/21-4-83, cf. art. 1369 of the *Civil Code*). If the marriage is not formalized within six months from its publication, the latter must be repeated.

During the time of Great Lent and the other fasts, the canons do not, in the first place, allow a wedding to be celebrated, though permission may be given in urgent cases.

A marriage between heterodox Christians or members of a non-Christian religion is celebrated according to the Dogma or religion of the parties of each of the parties approaching marriage, provided this is legally recognized in Greece.

By a decision of the Permanent Holy Synod of the Church of Greece, and in accordance with Law 1329/1983, in order for a marriage to take place, the priest has to inquire of the prospective couple as to the surname which all children resulting from the marriage will bear in common, i.e. whether they will be given the surname of their father, their mother or a combination of the two. Should the parents fail to declare a surname for their children, then by default the children will bear the surname of their father (encyclical 2374/28-12-1983).

The Church has no involvement in any engagement performed before marriage. If, in contravention of this, an engagement is celebrated separate from marriage, the local bishop shall declare it invalid and the priest shall be punished.

3 **IMPEDIMENTS TO MARRIAGE.** Impediments to marriage are such circumstances as prevent the contracting of a marriage.

The impediments can be divided into: revocatory and dilatory.

Revocatory impediments prevent marriage on pain of annulment, while dilatory ones do, indeed, prevent a marriage being contracted, though if it is performed, despite their existence, it is not annulled. The revocatory impediments are divided into absolute and relative, depending on whether marriage is absolutely forbidden to any person at all or to any person in particular.

A) *Absolute Revocatory Impediments.* i. *Prematurity.* The invalidity of the marriage is lifted if, after the fact, a court grants a license or if the husband recognizes the marriage once he has reached the age of consent (18 years) (article 1373 of the *Civil Code*).

ii. *Lack of consent between the prospective spouses.* The invalidity of the marriage is lifted in this case if there follows full and free agreement between the spouses (article 1373 of the *Civil Code*).

iii. *Inability to enact legally binding contracts.* The annulment of the marriage is lifted if the husband recognizes it when he is of an age to enact legally binding contracts (article 1373 of the *Civil Code*).

iv. *Absence of consent of the guardian to a person under judicial protection.* The annulment of the marriage is lifted if the guardian, the court or the person himself, when he is of age, ratifies the marriage (article 1373 of the *Civil Code*).

v. *Marriage of a Christian to a member of another religion.* There is an impediment against a religious marriage but not against a civil one (Encyclical 2320/19-5-82 of the Holy Synod).

vi. *A legally valid marriage.* "A second marriage may not be contracted before the irrevocable dissolution or the annulment of an existing one. Spouses may repeat their wedding ceremony even before the marriage is annulled" (Article 1354 of the *Civil Code*).

vii. *A previous third marriage.* There is an impediment against a religious marriage but not against a civil one (Encyclical 2320/19-5-82 of the Holy Synod).

viii. *The priesthood and the monastic tonsure.* A religious, though not a civil, marriage is not permitted for clergy of all ranks and monastics of the Orthodox Catholic Church (Encyclical 2320/19-5-82 of the Holy Synod).

B) *Relative Revocatory Impediments.* The relative impediments prevent marriage between certain persons. Some of these arise from kinship relationships and others from other causes.

By "kinship" is meant the relationship which exists between two persons through the descent of one from the other, the descent of both from a third, through the bonds between two or three families or through a relationship similar to kinship.

According to this, kinship is: 1) kinship by blood, i.e. consanguinity; 2) kinship by marriage between members of two or three families, i.e. affinity; 3) spiritual kinship; 4) adoption.

i. Consanguinity is the mutual relationship between two persons by reason of the descent of one from the other, or the descent of both from a third. Persons in this relationship are called relatives, being of the same blood.

The degree of relationship is the proximity or distance by birth between two persons and the unbroken and continuous series of degrees is called the line (τάξις, *linea*, *ordo*). It is divided as follows:

a) A direct (*recta*) line and in particular (I) the line of ascent (*ascendentalis*) starting from a particular person and linking other persons in a direct line without interruption of the degrees of birth, i.e. father, grandfather, great-grandfather, etc., and (II) the line of descent (*descendentalis*), starting from a particular person and linking other persons in a direct line, i.e. son, grandson, great-grandson, etc.

b) Collateral lines (*obliquæ*, *transversales*, *collaterales*), which include persons belonging to varying lines of kinship, all of which lead back, through common descent, as to an origin or root, to one and the same person, the founder of the family. This collateral kinship exists between a person and brothers, uncles, etc. The distance of the consanguinity is determined by degrees which are themselves defined by the number of consecutive births. That is to say that each birth constitutes a degree.[11]

The fewer births there are interspersed between blood relatives, the closer is the relationship deemed to be, while the more there are, the more distant the relationship. According to the legislation now in force, blood relationship in direct line is an impediment to marriage without limit, while collateral is an impediment up to and including the fourth degree (i.e. first cousins) (Article 1356 of the *Civil Code*).

---

[11] "Each birth constitutes a degree." Demetrios Chomatinos: "*On the Degrees of Kinship.*" E. 421.

ii. Affinity is the kinship between two families which arises from marriage. In determining the degrees, account is taken of the number of births, while the spouses are considered one person and, therefore, one birth. "Marriage between relations by affinity is not permitted in direct line without limit and collaterally until the third degree" (Article 1357 of the *Civil Code*). For the celebration of a religious marriage, there is also an "impediment against marriage between a relative up to and including the second degree of the one spouse with a relative by blood up to and including the second degree of the other spouse ..." (Article 1358 of the *Civil Code*). This article has been revoked by the new law and, therefore, does not apply to civil marriages.

iii. There is an impediment to the marriage of a person born out of wedlock and his descendants with those from a father who has recognized that person as his child and relatives by blood in a direct line without limit and in a collateral line up to and including the fourth degree. (Article 1359). Article 13 of the law concerning Family Law revokes this article in regards to the term "out of wedlock," though the impediment remains for civil marriage as an impediment of consanguinity.

iv. "There is an impediment to marriage between a person adopted and his descendants and the person who adopted. This impediment remains in force even after the dissolution of the adoption" (Article 1360 of the *Civil Code*).

v. A religious marriage, though not a civil one, may not be contracted between a godparent and godchild or its mother (revoked Article 1361 of the *Civil Code*).

vi. "A religious marriage may not be contracted between a guardian and his descendants and his ward until the guardianship has been formally completed" (revoked Article 1362).

vii. A religious marriage may not be contracted between two people convicted of adultery with each other (revoked Article 1363).

viii. A religious marriage may not be contracted by clergy of any degree and monastics of the Orthodox Church (revoked Article 1364 of the *Civil Code*).

In regards to the impediment of adultery in particular (article 1363 of the *Civil Code*), the Church may apply economy depending on the case and in accordance with the judgment and pastoral discretion of the local bishop, or, should he be hesitant, of the Holy Synod.

The principle of economy may also be applied in cases of spiritual relationship (Article 1361 of the *Civil Code*).

It is, however, self-evident that the retention by the Church of the impediment to marriage of a clergyman of any degree, or of a monastic, which has been revoked by the new law, involves the imposition of canonical sanctions and, in particular, the punishment of defrocking for a priest and removal of the habit for a monastic who wishes to perform a (civil) marriage (Encyclical 2320/19-5-1982 of the Holy Synod).

c) *Dilatory Impediments.* The sole dilatory impediment to the performance of a religious marriage is the so-called year of mourning, which has been abolished for civil marriages through the new law on Family Law. According to the revoked Article 1365 of the *Civil Code*, "a woman may not contract marriage before the passage of ten months from the irrevocable dissolution or annulment of her previous marriage. The prohibition does not apply if the woman has given birth before the passage of ten months." This impediment came from the Canon Law of the Church and was adopted as a law in order to avoid confusion over paternity of any children which might be born during that period.

However, even for the performance of a religious wedding ceremony, economy might be applied in this instance, too (Encyclical 2320/19-5-1982 of the Holy Synod).

A civil marriage which has been performed and not dissolved by death or divorce counts as a legal previous marriage (Encyclical 2320/19-5-1982 of the Holy Synod).

CHAPTER NINE

Divorce

B y its very nature, marriage and the goal to which it aspires are indissoluble until the end of the lives of the spouses. However, marriage must also fulfill the terms contained in the definition of it in Roman law, i.e. the natural, moral and religious term.

The indissolubility of marriage is a divine command: "Those whom God has joined, let no one put apart" (Matt. 19:6).

The indissolubility of marriage was further sanctioned and strengthened by the Church, which considered it a great mystery of nature which, through Christianity, also acquired a religious character, symbolizing the union between Christ and the Church.

A legally contracted marriage, therefore, can only be ended by death or some other event which removes the, so to speak, religious idea of the indissolubility of marriage, overturns the moral and religious basis, and is, in human weakness, death in another sense.

The teaching of the Orthodox Church is founded both on this meaning attributed by it to marriage, as a mystery of the New Testament, and on the importance of marriage in the family, society and religion, as well as on the positive teaching of the New Testament (Matt. 2:32 and 19:3 – 9; Rom. 7:2; I Cor. 7:15 and 39).

Although the Orthodox Church has always looked unfavorably on divorce and has stressed the moral obligation of the partners within it, in accordance with the words of the Gospel, not to dissolve the marriage bond which has once been tied, it realized early that it was not possible to overlook human weakness and accepted in principle the possibility of the dissolution of the marriage of the spouses in this life and their remarriage.

According to the law now in force, marriage is dissolved by an irrevocable judicial decision which is final, once it has been shown that at least one of the reasons envisaged by the law exist. These are:

1 IRRECONCILABLE BREAKDOWN OF THE MARRIAGE. Either of the two spouses may seek a divorce when the relationship between them has broken down to such an extent, in regards to the person of the defendant or of both spouses, that continuing in the married state would, with justification, be unbearable for the plaintiff..." (Article 1439 of the Civil Code).

Unless the defendant proves otherwise, evidence of breakdown is in the case of: 1) bigamy; 2) adultery; 3) abandonment; 4) plotting against the life of the plaintiff by the defendant; 5) separation of the spouses for a period of at least four consecutive years. In this last case, divorce may still be sought even if this reason for the breakdown concerns only the person of the plaintiff. The completion of the time of the separation is not affected by short intervals in which attempts at reconciliation have been made by the spouses.

2 DISAPPEARANCE. "Either of the spouses may seek a divorce when the other has been declared to be of no known whereabouts" (Article 1440 of the Civil Code).

3 DIVORCE BY CONSENT. "When the spouses agree on divorce, they may seek it by a common application which is heard in accordance with the procedure of a voluntary legal action..." (Article 1441 of the Civil Code). In order for a divorce by consent to be granted, the marriage must have lasted at least one year before the deposition of the application.

According to Roman law (*Novella* 27 of Alexios I) and during the years of Ottoman rule, divorce hearings came under the jurisdiction of the ecclesiastical courts. According to the law in force in Greece today, these hearings, for the dissolution of religious and not only civil marriages, are held in civil courts and, in particular in the courts of the first instance. Hearings for the dissolution of a religious marriage, however, must be preceded by an attempt at reconciliation between the separated spouses by their own bishop (i.e. of the residence of the man). To this effect, an application must be submitted by the interested parties to the competent bishop, who is entitled to hold this for three months while he acts to reconcile the spouses. Should the attempt at reconciliation fail, the bishop returns the application to the court, noting upon it the failure to bring about an accord.

When the judicial decision announcing the divorce is published, it is thereafter irrevocable; the public prosecutor sends a copy to the bishop of the residence of the man and the latter declares the marriage is also dissolved spiritually. If the marriage has been celebrated by a religious ceremony, the bishop is the person competent to dissolve it, as a consequence of the religious ceremony. The civil court undertakes as a commission the procedure of publication of the divorce as well as the examination of the differences between the spouses who are seeking the divorce. The authority who actually dissolves the marriage, however, is the bishop, who is obliged to accept the findings of the preceding judgment of the court.

A marriage which is dissolved and then recontracted between the same persons is considered to be a new marriage, and therefore, for it to be regarded as valid, the same necessary prerequisites and absence of impediments are required as in the case of any marriage.

The legal consequences of a divorce affect the divorced parties and also the children born of the marriage. Through divorce, all marital bonds of any description are loosed and the spouses revert to their relationship as before marriage. They are free to enter a second or third marriage, if the one dissolved is the first. The inheritance and property affairs created by the divorce are dealt with by Family Law. Even after divorce, the kinship relationships remain. Thus, the children of the first marriage, for example, are siblings with those of the second, etc.

PART FIVE

RELATIONS BETWEEN CHURCH AND STATE

CHAPTER TEN

Ecclesiastical and Political Authority

The Church of Christ is one in the world, destined to exist until the
end of time, to direct people's will in accordance with the will of
God and to introduce all people into the kingdom of God. For this reason, the Church bears the character of absolute necessity.

In order to accomplish this mission, the Church is obliged to enter
into communication with the State and thereafter with all religious confessions which are outside its communion. Hence, certain legal relations
arise between Church and State, as well as with the various heterodox
religious confessions.

In the various systems of Ecclesiastical or Canon Law, these relations
are characterized as external Ecclesiastical Law, in order to distinguish it
from internal Ecclesiastical Law, which is concerned with the canonical
relations of the members with their Church.

The Church and State derive their authority from one and the same
source. The Church was founded by God, and the birth of the State is a
product of the will of Divine Providence for the world. Despite this, relations between them are distinguished in a fundamental manner. Each is
self-sufficient and independent in the sphere of its jurisdiction.

In the first place, the difference resides in their foundation. The
Church was founded directly by God (Matt. 16:18) and equipped by
Him with a particular organization (Matt. 18:20; Acts 15:28), while the
states were founded indirectly by Him, by inculcating in people the

propensity for cohabitation and union, whence sprang each of the states, which were organized through human laws.

Another difference is the following: the Church is not limited in space or time, but was destined for all the peoples of the earth at all times, but each political region extends over a particular area and includes a particular people or peoples within precisely drawn borders.

Moreover, there is only one Church and can be only one, while there are many states. The Church remains the same, unaltered and continuous, existing throughout the centuries; states, however, are formed and disappear, stripped of their particular characteristics.

The most fundamental difference between Church and State, however, is the goals they seek to achieve. The Church has the salvation of people and the world in Christ as its aim and mission and to prepare people to be worthy of the inheritance of Christ even in this life, while the State is called upon to ensure a quiet and regular life on earth within its boundaries. In order to achieve their aims, each has at its disposal its own means, though those of the Church are spiritual and those of the State earthly and material.

The difference between Church and State justifies the self-sufficiency and independence of each within its sphere of jurisdiction.[1] Christ drew the boundaries between Church and State precisely, stressing the independence and self-sufficiency of each: "Render unto God that which is God's and unto Caesar that which is Caesar's" (Matt. 22:21).

One consequence of this principle ought to be the avoidance, on the one hand, of any attempt to merge the two organizations, either by the subjection of the Church to the State (Caesaro-Papism), or through the subjection of the State to the Church (Papo-Caesarism, hierocracy, theocracy) and, on the other, the establishment of harmonious cooperation between the two organizations, i.e. the principle of mutualism or reciprocal benefit (συναλληλία). Emperor Justinian, in the prologue to his sixth *Novella*, recognizes two powers on earth derived from God:

---

[1] Milas et al.

"the priesthood and the kingdom," i.e. the ecclesiastical and the state. The former is concerned with spiritual matters and the latter with material. This position is the basis of the parallel, without subjection, and independent exercise of powers for the good of mankind and also of the system of mutualism (συναλληλία) in relations between Church and State. Unfortunately, this fundamental and golden rule in relations between Church and State has not always proved capable of achievement, especially in the West.

The relations formed over the centuries between the Church and the various states might be distinguished basically into two systems, i.e. those of subordination and those of parallelism. In the first of these are classified firstly the hierocratic and secondly the statist in its three forms, i.e. Caesaro-Papism, territorialism and the absolutism of the Catholic countries. In the second, that is the systems of parallelism are classified the system of *homotaxis* (όμοταξία), i.e. equality of order, the system of total separation of Church and State, the system of mutualism and the system of "State holding in law." The last is statist, even though it is generally included in the systems of parallelism.

1 Systems of Subordination. In the systems of subordination, a fusion occurs between the two organizations, Church and State, either through the subjection of the State to the Church (hierocratic system or Papism, παποκρατία) or through the subjection of the Church to the State (statism, Caesaro-Papism, πολιτειοκρατία).

a) *The Hierocratic System (Caesaro-Papism, παποκρατία).* The hierocratic system, formed under the influence of the ideas of Saint Augustine, consists in total subjection of the State to the Church This was applied in the West.

According to this, the hieratic power, and the Pope in particular, is considered the peak of all earthly authority, spiritual and state. The secular leaders are subject to the hieratic power, which also characterizes the laws of the State as being in accordance with or opposed to Divine Will. Depending on this characterization, the citizens of the State are obliged to conform to it or not. The implementation of the hieratic system has varied at different periods in history.

B) *The Statist System (πολιτειοκρατία)*. Diametrically opposed to the hieratic system is the statist, by which the Church is subjected to the State. In the person of the highest officer of the State are concentrated both political and ecclesiastical authority. This system appears in three different forms, i.e. as:

i. Caesaro-Papism. According to this system, the ruler is also the highest ecclesiastical authority, taking care not only of secular matters and the provision of material goods for the citizens of the state but also of their souls. One state which retains the Caesaro-Papist system to this day is Great Britain, where the monarch is the head of Church and State, as is the case in Sweden.

ii. Territorialism. According to this system, which made its appearance in Protestant countries, the Church is subject to the State and is run by civil servants, while its members are obliged by the State to carry out their ecclesiastical obligations. In this system, the State also exercises the legislative ecclesiastical authority.

iii. Absolutism in Catholic countries. This statist system appeared in the mostly Catholic states of France, Bavaria and Austria. According to this system, through religious compulsion, all ecclesiastical matters were made subject to the State, not excepting the religious life of the citizens.

2 SYSTEMS OF PARALLELISM. The systems of parallelism have the characteristic that the one authority is clearly distinguished from the other and that they follow parallel but separate paths, independently of the relations which link them. These systems are classified into:

A) *The System of Homotaxia*. According to this system, the State does not exercise any authority over the Church, nor the Church over the State, but both organizations are considered equivalent. The boundaries of the jurisdiction of the Church and the State are defined through accords, contracted by their representatives. These accords are known as Concordats.

B) *The System of Total Separation between Church and State.* According to this system, the State regards religion as a purely personal matter and the Church as a legal entity in private law, as an association like any other of the same kind.

In certain cases, the State maintains a well-disposed neutrality toward the religious confessions within its realm (e.g. the United States of America) or indifference toward the Church (France). In other cases, this separation conceals a clearly hostile attitude of the State toward the Church and is no more than a cover for conducting official or unofficial persecution (the Soviet Union and the other Communist states).

C) *The System of Mutualism (συναλληλία).* This system prevailed in the Christian Roman Empire (Byzantium), for as long as it endured. According to the well-known ordinance of Justinian in the prologue to his sixth *Novella*, there are two authorities on earth, derived from God, "the priesthood and the kingship," clearly distinguished, but co-operating for the good of mankind and concerned with spiritual and material affairs respectively. The Church is a prime source of law and legislates independently of the State in synod (sacred canons). The State also legislates on ecclesiastical matters, though in accordance with the Canon Law of the Church and an agreement with it. The sacred canons are compulsory in their application by the Church, while they are recognized by the State as having the force of laws of the state (Justinian). In the event of a conflict between the sacred canons and the laws of the State, the sacred canons have precedence over the side of the State.[2]

D) *The System of "State Holding in Law."* According to this system, the Church is, on the one hand, clearly distinguished from the State, but enjoys special protection by it. The position of the Church within the

---

[2] "Ordinance III of the 2nd title of the *Novella* orders that the canons and dogmas of the seven synods be observed as Holy Scripture. In book 1 of the codex title III ordinance 44 and in the 1st and 4th ordinance of the first title of the *Novella*, it states that the canons are to be observed as laws and also that the laws follow the canons. And in book 1 of title II ordinance 12 it states that "formulations of the State which conflict with the canons are invalid" (Nomocanon of Photios, title 1 chapter 2, in Rallis and Potlis, *Syntagma of the Sacred Canons*, etc. vol. 1, p. 36).

State is a privileged one of a legal entity or organization The relations between Church and State are not, however, arranged by a concordat, but unilaterally, by the State, through the Constitution and the laws of the State, sometimes following an agreement with the Church. This system involves the danger of developing, to a greater or lesser extent, into outright statism, even though it is included among the systems of parallelism, since it binds the Church to the State entirely, in return for State protection.

The system of "State holding in law" is expressed: i) by the proclamation of a certain Church as the predominant religion; ii) by the exercise of supervision over it; and iii) by moral and material support of it.

i) Recognition of one Church as the predominant or official religion (*jus reformandi*) is made through the constitution. Other churches and religions are also free and enjoy the protection of the law, but the State affords special treatment to the predominant religion.

ii) Supervision of the Church on the part of the State (*jus inspeciendi* or *jus suspremae inspectionis*) is supervision of the so-called external affairs (*sacra externa*) of the Church.

In the course of this supervision, the State does not intervene in the so-called internal affairs of the Church (*sacra interna*), i.e. whatever concerns dogmas, worship, ordinations, internal administration and so on.

iii) This moral and material support toward the Church and the imposition of respect toward it (*jus advocatiæ*) is granted by the State, either directly or indirectly (penalties for mockery of the official religion, holidays on Sundays and feasts, penalties for impersonating ecclesiastical office, participation of the State in the execution of the verdicts of the ecclesiastical courts, material support from the public purse for the salaries of the clergy, etc.). Of course, such moral and material support is given to the Church in many countries of the European Union (Belgium, Sweden and others), in recognition of the beneficial affect of the Church on society, and to this end it is not necessary for the State "to hold by law" the Church and legislate for its subservience.

APPENDIX

Institutions of
the Ecumenical Patriarchate

1 THE PRESENT SITUATION. The Ecumenical Patriarchate, which occupies the first place in the canonical structure of the Orthodox Church, an organization of divine law, appears in the Turkish Republic as a legal entity under the form of a free Church within a religiously indifferent state (*état laïque*), the citizens of which are, in the great majority, Muslims.

Secondly, its eparchies or dioceses in Europe, Asia, Australia and America have the same status of free Churches within States of the same form, in which, with few exceptions, almost all the citizens are Christians, or have the character of a free Church within states of which the official religion is Roman Catholicism, Anglicanism or Lutheranism or, finally, have the form of an official religion, as in Greece and Finland.

The Patriarchate functions today in accordance with the sacred canons, the ecclesiastical ordinances, Church customs and with certain traditional features preserved from the General Regulations of the 19th century and the first part of the 20th. The latter are adapted in an ecclesiastical spirit to conditions as they present themselves.

2 THE PATRIARCH. The Patriarch, primus (πρῶτος) in the Orthodox Church, bears the official title of "... (Name), by the grace of God Archbishop of Constantinople, New Rome and Ecumenical Patriarch."

The election of the Patriarch is conducted by the Endemousa Holy Synod, in which the active metropolitans staying in Constantinople take part. To this synod is sent the *sympsephon*[1] of the Hierarchy of the Throne Abroad. The requirement for laity to be present (19th century National Regulations) at the meeting for the election of the Patriarch has already lapsed.

According to the view of the Turkish state, any prospective Patriarch must be a citizen of the Turkish Democracy.

After the election, there follows the ecclesiastical establishment or enthronement. A civil establishment has already ceased to be performed.

The seat of the Patriarch is the Patriarchate in the Fanar, while his summer residence is in the special patriarchal apartments in the Holy Theological School in Halki.

As Archbishop of Constantinople, the Patriarch has direct pastoral jurisdiction over the Archdiocese of Constantinople, which includes the communities of Constantinople, Galata and Katastenou.

He is assisted in his task by hierarchical vicars, i.e. assistant bishops, or sometimes by metropolitans, who may or may not be members of the synod, and who are in charge of, or act as supervisors for, churches or areas.

By exception, he continues to wear the external cassock of a clergy-man, being the only one, as head of a religion, to have permission to appear as such outside holy premises within the Turkish Democracy, following a law on priestly garb dating from 1935.

3 THE HOLY SYNAXIS OF THE HIERARCHY. Every two years since 1992, on September 1st, the Holy Synaxis of the active hierarchs of the Throne from around the world has been called in the Patriarchate. The aim of this is "mutual information and support and exchange of views on their sacred duties, the promotion and effective execution of these, the furtherance of the task of the Church in general, for the good

---

[1] This is the vote from the metropolitans not present, outside Turkey, and is counted together with the vote of the majority.

of the Christ-loving people entrusted in wisdom to each hierarch, for the renown of the Mother Church and the glory of the holy Name of God."[2]

4 THE HOLY SYNOD. Around the Patriarch and under his chairmanship, there is the permanent and regular Holy Synod, consisting of twelve members. In the Holy Synod, Metropolitans take part who have eparchies within the confines of the Turkish Democracy.[3]

The length of service of the Metropolitans at the Holy Synod is one year, with six metropolitans being replaced every six months. Except for the eight "of the Elders" (γεροντικαί) and certain other Metropolises, the order contained in the *Syntagmation* (the list of eparchies) is no longer followed in this, and instead, after the aforementioned, the date of the consecration of the hierarchs is taken into account.

In the absence, since 1923, of the Mixed Council, laymen do not participate directly in the ecclesiastical administration in the Ecumenical Patriarchate.

5 SYNODAL COMMITTEES. Under the auspices of the Holy Synod, reporting and in reference to it, there are the Synodal Committees, which today number twenty-six.

These are the following: 1) Financial Committee; 2) Auditing Committee; 3) the Committee for the Holy Monastery of the Holy Trinity of Halki; 4) Canonical Committee; 5) Committee for Inter-Orthodox Affairs; 6) Committee for the Eparchies of the Throne Outside of Turkey and Orthodox Mission; 7) Committee for the Institutions of the Throne Outside of Turkey; 8) Committee for Inter-Christian Relations; 9) Committee for Dialogue with non-Chalcedonian Churches; 10) Committee for Dialogue with the Roman Catholic

---

[2] Patriarchal Letter of Invitation from His All-Holiness the Ecumenical Patriarch Bartholomew (490/18-4-1996). It has been announced unofficially that this Synaxis will develop into the Synod of the Hierarchy.

[3] Since March 2004, the Ecumenical Patriarch has invited six Metropolitans who have eparchies in Turkey and six from abroad as members of the Permanent Holy Synod.

Church; 11) Committee for Theological Studies; 12) Committee for the Holy Mountain; 13) Committee for the Publication of the Periodical "Orthodoxia"; 14) Committee for the Publication of the Hemerologion (Year Book) of the Ecumenical Patriarchate; 15) Committee for Spiritual Diakonia; 16) Committee for Monasteries; 17) Committee for the Restoration, Maintenance and Preservation of the Patriarchal Church and Buildings; 18) Committee for the Patriarchal Archives and Library; 19) Committee for the Sacristy and the Holy Chrism; 20) Committee for the Holy Water; 21) Committee for Divine Worship; 22) Committee for the Liturgical Kanonion; 23) Committee for Dialogue with Islam; 24) Committee for Legal Counsellors; 25) Committee for Pensions and Medical Insurance; and 26) Committee on the Holdings of the Ecumenical Patriarchate.

6 **THE SYNODAL OFFICE AND PATRIARCHAL OFFICE (*PROTOSYNKELLIA*) OF THE GRAND CHANCELLERY.** Serving in the Synodal Office are the chief secretary (archimandrite), the under-secretary and the codicographer (both usually deacons).

Private Patriarchal Office. The director here is usually a Metropolitan of the Throne.

The First Patriarchal Office constitutes the central Service through which the personal and official correspondence of the Patriarch to the outside world generally is conducted as well as any tasks related to the proceedings and decisions of the Holy Synod, be this registration, composition, typing and dispatch. The director usually bears the *officium* of Grand Protonotarios.

In parallel with the Synodal Department, there is also the Department of the Grand Chancellery, run by the Grand Chancellor (Μέγας Πρωτοσύγκελλος). Linked to this are the Grand Archdeacon (Μέγας ἀρχιδιάκονος), second (δευτερεύων), third (τριτεύων), deacon-in-line (διάκονος τῆς σειρᾶς) and patriarchal deacons, the Patriarchal Central Ecclesiastical Committee, the Department of Religious Certificates, the Turkish Office, the Archives, the Patriarchal Library, the Accounts

Department and Treasury, the Office of the Holy Theological School and Spiritual Diakonia and the Patriarchal church.

7 METROPOLISES-ARCHDIOCESES. There are four active metropolises in Turkey today: Chalcedon, Derka, the Prince's Islands (Πριγκηπονννήσων) and Imbros and Tenedos. The other Metropolitans in Turkey bearing titles of Metropolises from the *Syntagmation* are also considered active, though now without a flock.

Other Eparchies of the Throne are: In Greece, those of the Neae Chorae, the administration of which, through the Patriarchal and Synodal Act of 1928, was delegated to the Church of Greece, in the capacity of steward; the semi-autonomous Church of Crete, consisting of the Archdiocese of Crete and seven metropolises (bishoprics until 1962); the four Metropolises of the Dodecanese Islands;[4] the Archdiocese of America, with more than ten Bishops, now Metropolitans, of eparchial dioceses and Auxiliary Bishops; the Metropolis of Toronto (Canada); the Metropolis of Buenos Aires (South America); the Metropolis of Panama and Central America; and the Metropolis of Hong Kong and the Far East.[5]

Through the Archdiocese of America, the following eparchies in North America are subject to the jurisdiction of the ecclesiastical competence of the Ecumenical Patriarchate:

1. The Ukrainian Orthodox Church in Canada (Metropolis).
2. The Ukrainian Orthodox Church in America (Archdiocese).
3. The American Carpatho-Russian Orthodox Greek Catholic Diocese of the United States of America.
4. The Albanian Orthodox Diocese of America.
5. The Belorussian Council of Orthodox Churches of North America (bishopric).

Also subject to the Ecumenical Patriarchate is the Archdiocese of Australia, with four auxiliary bishops, founded in 1924 as a Metropolis, but named Archdiocese in 1959, and the Metropolis of New Zealand.

---

[4] Since 2004, five.
[5] Since 2004, the Metropolis of Korea, also.

In Europe, the Archdiocese of Thyateira and Great Britain, with seven auxiliary bishops and seven Metropolises, i.e. those of: a) France, b) Germany; c) Austria; d) Sweden; e) Belgium, founded in 1969 by special Tomes; f) Switzerland, founded in 1982; g) Italy, founded in 1991; and h) Spain and Iberia, founded in 2003, as well as the Russian Exarchate in Western Europe, subject through the Holy Metropolis of France to the Ecumenical Patriarchate; the autonomous Archdiocese of Finland and the autonomous Metropolis of Estonia. Also subject to the Ecumenical Patriarchate is the Holy Metropolis of New Zealand (founded in 1970). Since 1995, the Ecumenical Patriarchate has accepted under its canonical jurisdiction groups of Orthodox Ukrainians of the Diaspora and has chosen two metropolitans as head of them, with an archbishop and three bishops.

The monasteries of the Holy Mountain are directly linked to the Patriarchate, as are the Monastery of St. John the Theologian, Patmos, and the Patriarchal Exarchate of Patmos, the Holy Monastery of Saint Anastasia in Halkidiki and the Holy Monastery of the Vlatades (Μονή Βλατάδων) in Thessaloniki.

The Ecumenical Patriarchate is permanently represented at the World Council of Churches in Geneva (1915).

8 HIERARCHY-CLERGY. Subject to the Ecumenical Patriarchate are the Archbishops and Metropolitans of the Eparchies of the Throne, of the first title (Archbishop) given to the heads of autonomous Churches or to Metropolitans with wider ecclesiastical jurisdiction, such as those of America, Australia, Thyateira or Crete.

Apart from the autonomous Church of Finland and the Archdiocese of America, where there is the institution of the eparchial bishop, all bishops within the jurisdiction of the Patriarchate are titular, auxiliaries of the Patriarch, the Metropolitans or the Archbishops.

The election of all those elevated to the rank of hierarch is conducted by the Holy Synod of the Patriarchate, on the basis of the preconditions embodied in the sacred canons, with the exception of the Church of

Crete, which embarks on these acts through its own Holy Synod, in accordance with the relevant provisions of its Charter. The Archbishop of Crete is elected by the Patriarchal Synod. The same canonical qualifications are required for the election of bishops as those for other hierarchs.

Since 1923, the Patriarch, the Metropolitans and the Bishops within the Turkish Republic have been restricted to the performance of their religious and spiritual duties only. All the clergy of the Patriarchate within the Turkish Republic have worn black civil clothing outside church since 1935. The same is true of almost all the eparchies of the Throne, except Greece.

9 ECCLESIASTICAL OFFICES. Patriarchal offices are awarded to clergy and laity who belong to the Metropolises of the Throne and other Orthodox Churches.

Ecclesiastical offices awarded to the laity, having lost their real function, are more of an honorary nature.

With few exceptions, it is now only the ordained clergy within the Patriarchate and some lay personnel who have offices which correspond to their ecclesiastical function.

10 HOLY MONASTERIES. For the study and settlement of matters referring to monasticism, the Ecumenical Patriarchate has the Committee for Monasticism and the Committee for the Holy Mountain, which report to the Patriarch and the Holy Synod.

Apart from the eight monasteries in Turkey, the twenty monasteries on the Holy Mountain are directly subject to the Ecumenical Patriarch, as are the Monastery of Patmos, the Monastery of Saint Anastasia the Farmakolytria in Halkidiki and the Monastery of the Vlatades in Thessaloniki; there are two Patriarchal Stavropegic Monasteries in America: a) the Monastery of the Entry of the Mother of God, in Malbis Plantation, Daphne, Alabama; b) the Monastery of the Divine Transfiguration of the Saviour in Union Town, Pennsylvania; and c) the Monastery of Chrysovalantou, in Astoria, NY, and its Dependencies; in the Archdiocese of Thyateira and Great Britain, the Monastery of St. John the Forerunner; in the Metropolis of France, the Orthodox Patriarchal Center at Taisé (1965) and the Holy Monasteries of Saint Nicholas, the Dormition of the Mother of God, Saint Anthony, the Divine Protection (Ἁγία Σκέπη) and the Transfiguration of the Savior. Similarly, there are eparchial Monasteries, some for men others for women, subject to the various Archdioceses or Metropolises of the Patriarchal Throne, as well as Dependencies (*Metochia*) of other Churches or Monasteries, within the jurisdiction of the Ecumenical Patriarchate.

11 DIVINE WORSHIP. No permit has been given to the Ecumenical Patriarchate since 1923 to found a new church within the Turkish Republic: all that is allowed is the repair of those which are already in existence. Outside that country, churches are being built, either in the Byzantine style or in that of contemporary models. In regards to the interior decoration of the churches, an attempt is being made to maintain the Byzantine tradition.

The holy Mysteries and the other sacred Offices are performed according to the *Typikon* of the Great Church of Christ. Sermons are preached on a more or less regular basis.

12 SOCIAL ACTIVITY. The task of organized charity is carried out within the Turkish Republic by charitable institutions which are not directly linked to the Church administration, but to the Orthodox community. Almost every community has its Charitable Association, soup kitchen, cultural clubs for the young and various other associations. Similar work is also being carried out abroad in the eparchies of the Throne.

13 ECCLESIASTICAL/THEOLOGICAL LETTERS. Certain rights have been recognized for the Greeks in the Turkish Republic within the educational sphere, not in regards to the Ecclesiastical Authority, but the Community.

Ecclesiastical education is served within the jurisdiction of the Ecumenical Patriarchate by Ecclesiastical Schools or Seminaries, such as the Athonias School (the Holy Mountain), the Patmian Ecclesiastical School, the Ecclesiastical School in Crete and certain others. The Theological School in Halki is linked to the Patriarchate. Other Theological Schools are: the Russian Orthodox Institute of Saint Sergius in Paris (1925), the Holy Cross Theological School in Brookline, Mass., North America (1937) and the Apostle Andrew Theological School of the Archdiocese of Australia. Mention must also be made here of the Patriarchal Institute for Patristic Studies, at the Holy Stavropegic Monastery of the Vlatades in Thessaloniki.

Important auxiliary tools and resources for theological studies are the libraries of the Patriarchate, of the Theological School of Halki, of the Theological Schools and Seminaries mentioned above, of the Monasteries of the Holy Mountain and Patmos, of the Patriarchal Institute for Patristic Studies in the Monastery of the Vlatades in Thessaloniki, etc., as well as the periodicals published by the Patriarchate or its Archdioceses or Metropolises.

The Ecumenical Patriarchate had at its disposal its own patriarchal press, which ceased to function in 1923, was reestablished in 1951 and then abolished again in 1964.[6]

---

[6] The data above concerning the institutions of the Ecumenical Patriarchate were taken from the book *The Ecumenical Patriarchate* (in Greek), Athens 1967, by Professor Vasileios Stavridis, and from the *Hemerologion* of the Ecumenical Patriarchate for the year 2004.

The Charters of
the Holy Archdiocese of America

1 CHARTER OF THE GREEK ARCHDIOCSE OF NORTH AND SOUTH
AMERICA (NEW YORK, 1923). † The Ecumenical Patriarch Meletios
promulgates

THE CHARTER
OF THE GREEK ARCHDIOCESE OF NORTH AND SOUTH AMERICA

ARTICLE I. A Religious Association is founded under the title of
THE GREEK ARCHDIOCESE OF NORTH AND SOUTH AMERICA, for the
sake of the Christians living there who belong to the Holy Orthodox
Eastern Church, and having Greek, exclusively or primarily, as its liturgical language, the tongue in which the Holy Gospels and the other
books of the New Testament were written.

ARTICLE II. Aim. The aim of this Church is to build the religious
and moral life of the Greeks and of Orthodox American citizens, of
Greek descent, on the basis of the Holy Scriptures, the Terms/Oroi
(ὅροι) and Canons of the Holy Apostles and of the Seven Ecumenical
Synods of the Ancient, Undivided Church, as these are interpreted in
the practice of the Great Church of Christ in Constantinople.

ARTICLE III. Administrative dependence. By canonical and historical right THE GREEK ARCHDIOCESE OF NORTH AND SOUTH AMERICA
is subject to the Supreme Spiritual and Ecclesiastical Supervision of the
Ecumenical Patriarchate of Constantinople.

ARTICLE IV. Administrative division. The Archdiocese as a whole is divided into four episcopal areas.

1. That of New York. This includes the States of:

NEW YORK, with the Communities in the city of New York and Brooklyn and the Communities of: Schenectady, Syracuse, Rochester, Buffalo, and Endicott.

CONNECTICUT — Stamford, New Haven, Ansonia, Waterbury, New Britain, Danielson, Norwich and Thompsonville.

NEW JERSEY — Newark, Orange, New Brunswick, Trenton, Paterson and Passaic.

PENNSYLVANIA — Philadelphia, Reading, Bethlehem, Altoona, Wilkesbarre, Pittsburgh, Vandergrift, Erie, New Castle, Monessen, Woodlawn and Ambridge.

WEST VIRGINIA — Wheeling, Weirton and Clarksburg.

VIRGINIA — Norfolk, Richmond.

MARYLAND — Baltimore.

DISTRICT OF COLUMBIA — Washington.

KENTUCKY

NORTH CAROLINA

SOUTH CAROLINA — Charleston.

GEORGIA — Savannah, Atlanta and Augusta.

MISSISSIPPI

FLORIDA — Jacksonville, Tarpon Springs, Pensacola.

THE REALM OF MEXICO AND THE COUNTRIES OF CENTRAL AND SOUTHERN AMERICA.

2. That of Boston. This includes the States of:

MAINE, with the Communities of Biddeford and Lewiston.

NEW HAMPSHIRE — Manchester, Nashua, Dover and Somersworth.

VERMONT

MASSACHUSETTS — Boston, Lynn, Peabody, Worcester, Fitchburg, Holyoke, Springfield, Webster, Clinton, Somerville, Cambridge, New Bedford, Lawrence, Brockton, Ipswich, Chicopee Falls, Marlboro and Southbridge.

RHODE ISLAND — Providence, Newport and Pawtucket.
and the Communities of Montreal, Toronto and Fort William in Canada.

3. That of Chicago. This includes the States of:

MINNESOTA, with the communities of Minneapolis and Duluth.

WISCONSIN — Milwaukee, Racine, Fond du Lac and Sheboygan.

MICHIGAN — Detroit and Flint.

IOWA — Sioux City, Mason City and Waterloo.

ILLINOIS — Chicago, Chicago Heights, Moline, Joliet and Rockford.

INDIANA — Gary and Indianapolis.

MISSOURI — Saint Louis and Kansas City.

NORTH DAKOTA

SOUTH DAKOTA

KANSAS

NEBRASKA — Omaha.

OKLAHOMA — Oklahoma City.

ARKANSAS — Little Rock.

LOUISIANA — New Orleans and Shreveport.

TEXAS — Dallas, Fort Worth and Houston.

OHIO — Cleveland, Toledo, Akron, Youngstown, Canton, Columbus, Cincinnati, Dayton, Warren, Martin's Ferry and Lorraine.

TENNESSEE — Memphis and Nashville.

ALABAMA — Birmingham and Mobile.

and the Community of Winnipeg in Canada.

4. That of San Francisco. This includes the States of:

WASHINGTON — Seattle.

OREGON — Portland.

MONTANA — Great Falls.

NEVADA — McGill.

UTAH — Salt Lake City and Price.

COLORADO — Denver and Pueblo.

CALIFORNIA — San Francisco, Oakland, Los Angeles and

Sacramento.

ARIZONA

WYOMING

NEW MEXICO

ALASKA

and Western Canada (BRITISH COLUMBIA)

The New York episcopal area holds the position of Archdiocese and has as its head the Archbishop of America. The other three are Bishoprics, each of them under its own bishop, who has the name of the seat of his Bishopric as his pastoral title.

ARTICLE V. The Untransferability of the Archbishop and Bishops. In accordance with the divine and Sacred Canons, the Archbishop and Bishops are untransferable. In the event of the Archiepiscopal Throne becoming vacant, one of the three Bishops may be elected Archbishop, in observance with the relative ordinances concerning the election of Bishops in the present Charter.

ARTICLE VI. Leave of Absence for Bishops. Each bishop is entitled to one month's leave of absence from his duties annually. For any longer period of time, which may not exceed four months, permission is required from the Holy Synod of the Archdiocese.

ARTICLE VII. The Synod of the Archdiocese. The Archbishop, together with the three Bishops, constitute the Synod of the Greek Archdiocese of North and South America, which, in accordance with the relative provisions of the Sacred Canons of the Orthodox Eastern Church, meets twice a year: once before Pascha and once in the fall, where the Archbishop decides.

This Synod has all the authority and responsibilities which are assigned by the Sacred Canons to the "Synod of the Eparchy", and is also accountable to the Synod of the Metropolitans of the Ecumenical Throne around the Patriarch for the unswerving observation of the divine Dogmas and Sacred Canons of the Orthodox Eastern Church.

In the event of a tied vote in the Synod, the opinion supported by the Archbishop, who is also the President, prevails.

Should the Archbishop be absent or unable to attend, his place in the presidency is taken by the Bishop with seniority of consecration.

ARTICLE VIII. Jurisdiction and Competence of the Bishops. Each of the Bishops, has, in his own diocese, the authority and responsibilities allotted to the Episcopal Office by the divine and Sacred Canons and the centuries-long practice of the Church and also the right to be installed upon the Holy *Synthronon*.

Among these rights and duties are: the sanctification and consecration to worship of the churches and of the houses of prayer; the appointment to them of priests, deacons and other clergy to celebrate and chant; the organization of a properly-conducted and well-ordered administration for the good of all; the issuance of licenses for the performance of the mystery of Marriage and the Letters of Divorce for those marriages which have been competently declared dissolved; the distribution to the priests of the Myrrh of the Holy Chrism, which the Archbishop receives from the Ecumenical Patriarch.

ARTICLE IX. Order of Commemoration. In the mysteries and the services, priests and deacons shall commemorate their Canonical Bishop, the Bishops shall commemorate the Archbishop and the Archbishop the Ecumenical Patriarch.

ARTICLE X. Spiritual Court. In each Bishopric, there functions a Spiritual Court, consisting of at least two office-holding priests and the Bishop as President, or his representative and surrogate according to the order of the Church. This court hears all the canonical offences of the Clergy in the first instance, except those which lead to defrocking.

ARTICLE XI. The Spiritual Courts of the Dioceses do not try cases in which a preliminary hearing has formed the opinion that the accused may be subject to the punishment of defrocking. They forward such cases to the Holy Synod of the Archdiocese.

An appeal may be made to the Holy Synod of the Archdiocese, within 31 days of their being served, against decisions of the Spiritual Courts of the Bishoprics calling for a suspension of more than two months. An appeal may be made to the Holy Synod of the Ecumenical Patriarchate, within 91 days, against decisions of the Holy Synod of the Archdiocese which involve defrocking or suspension for more than one year.

ARTICLE XII. Local Ecclesiastical Assemblies. Each of the Four Dioceses has its own Ecclesiastical Assembly, consisting of all the canonical clergy of the Bishopric and of one elected lay representative from each incorporated Holy Church, to be elected by the parish Council.

Each of these Ecclesiastical Assemblies meets by invitation of the competent Bishop, who is also its President, or by his representative and surrogate should he be absent. It convenes regularly once a year, in the month of May, and extraordinarily as often as the Bishop deems proper. A quorum is formed when in the presence of the Presiding Bishop, or his Substitute, twelve members are present in person, of whom at least six must be clergymen.

ARTICLE XIII. General Ecclesiastical Assembly. The General Assembly of the whole of the Greek Archdiocese of North and South America consists of the Archbishop, the Bishops and 24 elected members, 12 from the clergy and 12 from the laity. The former and the latter are elected in groups of six by each of the four Ecclesiastical Assemblies.

The General Assembly meets regularly once every two years, in the month of September, at the invitation of the Archbishop, and in extraordinary session following a relevant decision by the Synod of the Archdiocese.

The President of the General Assembly is the Archbishop, or, in his absence, whichever of the Bishops present has seniority of consecration. A quorum is formed when in the presence of the Presiding Archbishop, or the Presiding Bishop, and at least one other Bishop twelve members are present in person, of whom at least six must be clergymen.

ARTICLE XIV. Proxy Representation by Reason of Distance. In both the Local Assemblies of each Bishopric and in the General Assembly of the whole Archdiocese, those Clergy and Churches who have the right to participate may be represented by duly authorized persons, the Clergy by a Clergyman and the Laity by a Layman.

In a vote the proxy for the absent members also casts their vote, except in the case of the nomination of a Bishop, when each of those present has only one vote.

Once authority to be a proxy has been given and recognized by the Assembly, it may not be recalled and remains in force throughout the proceedings of the Assembly.

In the event that the competent Assembly should fail to establish, in all detail, rules of composition or procedure for the Body of the Assembly, this shall be done by the local bishop or his surrogate.

ARTICLE XV. The Tasks of the Assemblies. It is the right and duty of each Committee of the Ecclesiastical Assemblies to audit the whole of the Ecclesiastical financial management and to pass ordinances, in agreement with the local Bishop, respecting the management of ecclesiastical institutions, in accordance with the Sacred Apostolic and Synodal Canons and conforming to the relevant Laws of the United States. Ratification of these ordinances by the Archiepiscopal Synod is a prerequisite for their implementation.

Provisions of individual parish Charters which contravene the divine and Sacred Canons and the Laws of the United States are, *per se,* invalid.

The General Assembly takes decisions and ratifies measures of common action throughout the whole Archdiocese, always with the aim of achieving greater progress in the realization of the religious, moral and social task set out in article II.

ARTICLE XVI. Election of the Archbishop and Bishops. Given that today there is only an Archbishop, canonically elected by the Holy Synod in Constantinople, the three Sees of Chicago, Boston and San Francisco, founded by a Patriarchal and Synodal resolution in addition to the Archdiocese of New York shall be filled for the first time as follows:

Following the legal ratification of this Charter, which also defines the boundaries of each Bishopric, the special Ecclesiastical Assembly of Chicago shall meet first at the invitation and under the chairmanship of the Archbishop, in order to propose three candidates for this Bishopric, taken from a list of the Clergy of the whole Archdiocese who hold a recognized degree from an Orthodox Theological School, being of blameless life and with ecclesiastical experience, and already approved by the Ecumenical Patriarch and his Holy and Sacred Synod. From these three, the Synod shall elect the Bishop by canonical vote.

ARTICLE XVII. Once the thrones of the three sees have been filled in this way, elections in future, in the event that one of them, or the Archdiocese falls vacant, shall occur as follows: within three months at the most, the local Ecclesiastical Assembly, called by the Locum Tenens and under his chairmanship, and at the behest of the Synod, shall propose three candidates from the list already approved by the Holy and Sacred Synod of the Ecumenical Patriarchate in Constantinople. From these, the Synod around the Archbishop will elect the Bishop, or in the case of the Archdiocese, the Archbishop. This election will be announced to the Synod of the Ecumenical Patriarchate for ratification.

ARTICLE XVIII. Should the person thus elected and ratified be the Archbishop, he is consecrated by the Ecumenical Patriarch. Should he be a Bishop, the Patriarch merely gives his permission for the consecration.

ARTICLE XIX. Should a second see become vacant before another Episcopal throne is filled, the two remaining bishops cannot now constitute a Synod by themselves. In this case, after the proposal of candidates by the special local Assembly, the election shall take place for the first of the sees to fall vacant. This election shall take place in the Synod around the Ecumenical Patriarch, with the votes of the Bishops in America being counted for the majority (*sympsephon*). Thereafter the election of the second Bishop shall proceed, functioning in accordance with Article XVII, again by the Synod around the Archbishop.

ARTICLE XX. Executive Council. An Executive Council functions within the Archdiocese of New York and in each of the three Bishoprics. In the Archdiocese of New York, this Council consists of the Archbishop, as President, and four ranking Clergymen of the Archdiocese appointed by the Archbishop and four distinguished Lay members, proposed by the Archbishop and approved by the Local Ecclesiastical Assembly.

The same provision is in force for each Executive Assembly of each

Bishopric, the only difference being that the members, Clergy and Laity, may number only three each, should there be a lack of a greater number of Priests in the seat of the Bishopric and its surrounding area.

ARTICLE XXI. The appointment of Clerical and Lay members of the Executive Council is for a term of two years. The Vice-President of the Council is the highest ranking clergyman among these members, who also retains his voting rights as a member. The Executive Council elects the Treasurer and the Secretary from its members.

The jurisdiction of the Executive Council extends over all matters of the Association, except those which, according to the Canons of the Church, are considered to lie within the exclusive competence of the Bishop, acting either alone or in concert with the Spiritual Court. The Bishop also has the right to enact regulations within his sphere of jurisdiction, provided they do not contravene the present Charter.

ARTICLE XXII. Loca Tenentes. If the Archdiocese falls vacant, the Bishop with seniority of consecration shall act as locum tenens. Should the Bishoprics of Boston and Chicago fall vacant, the Archbishop acts as locum tenens, because of proximity. For the same reason, in the case of San Francisco, the locum tenens shall be the Bishop of Chicago.

ARTICLE XXIII. Seminary. The Greek Archdiocese of North and South America has its own Seminary for the education of the Clergy. This Seminary is headed by a Board of Trustees, of which the Archbishop is President. This Board consists of four Clerical members and three Lay, appointed by the Archbishop or the Synod, once formed, from the best educated Clergy and Laity in the Archdiocese of New York.

The Administrative Organization of the Seminary and the curriculum is drawn up by the Board of Trustees and approved by the Archbishop, or the Synod of the Archdiocese, when this has been formed.

The Seminary has a special Fund, the resources of which are to be used exclusively for educational purposes, for the instruction of the Clergy and Teachers.

ARTICLE XXIV. Concluding Articles. Ordained Clergy of the Greek Archdiocese of North and South America are appointed to their ministries without any involvement whatsoever on the part of civil Authorities. The guiding Law for the whole of the administration are the Sacred Apostolic and Synodal Canons, as well as the competently applied regulations which are in accordance with the Sacred Canons and the Laws of each State where the administration of the Church extends.

ARTICLE XXV. Any regulation of any Ecclesiastical Organization whatsoever which contravenes either the Laws of the United States or the Sacred Canons of the Orthodox Church is of itself invalid.

ARTICLE XXVI. Until the election of the Bishops and the formation of the Holy Synod, the General Assembly, the Spiritual Court, the Executive Council and the Seminary shall be regulated by the ordinances of the previous, temporary Charter.

ARTICLE XXVII. The present Charter has been passed in the General Assembly, convened in accordance with Article IV of the Temporary Charter of the Greek Archdiocese of North and South America, and is subject to review, should this be deemed reasonable, no sooner than two years after the implementation of its legal ratification.

In the month of December 1922, indiction vi.
† Meletios, Patriarch of Constantinople declares,

signed:
† Nikolaos of Caeasarea,
† Kallinikos (?) of Kyzikos

2 CHARTER OF THE GREEK ORTHODOX ARCHDIOCSE OF NORTH AND SOUTH AMERICA (1927). † VASILEIOS, by the grace of God Archbishop of Constantinople, New Rome, and Ecumenical Patriarch, having approved the following with the Holy and Sacred Synod around us endorses:

THE CHARTER
OF THE GREEK ARCHDIOCESE OF NORTH AND SOUTH AMERICA

ARTICLE I. A Religious Association is founded under the title of THE GREEK ARCHDIOCESE OF NORTH AND SOUTH AMERICA, for the sake of the Christians living in America who belong to the Holy Catholic and Apostolic Eastern Orthodox Church of Christ, and having Greek, exclusively or primarily, as their liturgical language, the tongue in which the Holy Gospels and the other books of the New Testament were written.

ARTICLE II. Aim. The aim of this Church is:

a) to maintain and spread the Orthodox Christian Faith, on the basis of Holy Scripture, Sacred Tradition, the Terms/Oroi (ὄροι) and Canons of the Holy Apostles and of the Seven Ecumenical Synods of the Ancient, Undivided Church, as interpreted in practice by the Great Church of Christ in Constantinople.

b) to build the religious and moral life of the Greek Orthodox American citizens and those Orthodox of Greek descent, in accordance with the faith and traditions of this Church.

c) to teach the original language of the Gospel.

ARTICLE III. Canonical dependence. By canonical and historical right, the Greek Archdiocese of North and South America is subject to the supreme spiritual and ecclesiastical supervision of the Ecumenical Patriarchate of Constantinople.

ARTICLE IV. Administrative Division. The Archdiocese as a whole is divided into four episcopal areas.

I. That of New York. This includes the following States with the Communities now existing in them and those that will be established in the future:

1) The District of the State of New York lying south of the Albany to Buffalo New York Central railway line.[1]

2) The District of the State of Connecticut lying south of and includ-

---

[1] Where parishes within the same state belong to different dioceses, diocesan boundaries are delineated with precision. Otherwise states within each diocese are named without cities, obviously in anticipation of parishes to be established in the future.

ing the city of Bridgeport.

    3) The State of New Jersey

    4) The State of Pennsylvania

    5) The District of the State of Ohio lying to the south of the New York Central railway line.

    6) The State of West Virginia

    7) The State of Virginia

    8) The State of Maryland

    9) The State of Delaware

    10) The District of Columbia

    11) The State of North Carolina

    12) The State of South Carolina

    13) The State of Georgia

    14) The State of Florida

    15) All the countries of Central and South America, together with the islands.

    II. That of Chicago. This includes the following States with the Communities now existing in them and those that will be established in the future:

    1) The State of Illinois

    2) The State of Minnesota

    3) The State of Wisconsin

    4) The State of Michigan

    5) The State of Iowa

    6) The State of Indiana

    7) The State of Missouri

    8) The State of North Dakota

    9) The State of South Dakota

    10) The State of Kansas

    11) The State of Nebraska

    12) The State of Oklahoma

    13) The State of Arkansas

    14) The State of Texas

15) The State of Louisiana

16) The State of Mississippi

17) The State of Alabama

18) The State of Tennessee

19) The State of Kentucky

20) The District of the State of Ohio lying north of the New York Central railway line, including the Communities upon this line.

21) The States of Manitoba and Saskatchewan in Canada.

III. That of Boston. This includes the following States with the Communities now existing in them and those that will be established in the future:

1) The State of Massachusetts

2) The State of Rhode Island

3) The State of Vermont

4) The State of New Hampshire

5) The State of Maine

6) The District of the State of Connecticut lying north of and excluding the town of Bridgeport

7) The District of the State of New York lying north of the Albany to Buffalo New York Central railway line upon this line.

8) The States of Quebec and Ontario in Canada.

IV. That of San Francisco. This includes the following States with the Communities now existing in them and those that will be established in the future:

1) The State of California

2) The State of Oregon

3) The State of Washington

4) The State of Montana

5) The State of Idaho

6) The State of Wyoming

7) The State of Nevada

8) The State of Utah

9) The State of Colorado

10) The State of Arizona

11) The State of New Mexico

12) Alaska

13) The States of Alberta, British Columbia and the Northern Territory in Canada

14) Mexico

The New York episcopal area holds the position of Archdiocese and has as its head the Archbishop of America. The other three are Bishoprics, each of them under its own bishop, who has the name of the seat of his Bishopric as his pastoral title.

ARTICLE V. The Untransferability of the Archbishop and Bishops. In accordance with the Divine and Sacred Canons, the Archbishop and the Bishops are untransferable. In the event of the Archiepiscopal Throne becoming vacant, one of the three Bishops may be elected Archbishop, in observance with the relative ordinances concerning the election of Bishops in the present Charter.

ARTICLE VI. Leave of Absence for Bishops. Each bishop is entitled to one month's leave of absence from his duties annually. For any longer period of time, which may not exceed three months, permission is required from the Holy Synod of the Archdiocese. In the case of absence of Bishops outside America, the canonical permission of the Ecumenical Patriarch and of his Holy and Sacred Synod must be sought, directly for the Archbishop and through the Archbishop for Bishops.

ARTICLE VII. The Holy Synod of the Archdiocese. The Archbishop, together with the three Bishops, constitute the Holy Synod of the Archdiocese of North and South America.

In accordance with the relative provisions of the Sacred Canons of the Orthodox Eastern Church, it meets regularly twice a year: once before Pascha and once in the fall, and also in extraordinary session when need arises at a time and place appointed by the Archbishop. Similarly, the Holy Synod may be called into extraordinary session when a majority of its members shall judge this necessary.

This Synod has all the authority and responsibilities which are assigned by the Sacred Canons to "The Synod of the Eparchy," and is also accountable to the Synod of the Metropolitans of the Ecumenical Throne around the Patriarch for the unswerving observation of the divine Dogmas and Sacred Canons of the Orthodox Eastern Church.

In the event of a tied vote in the Synod, the opinion supported by the Archbishop, who is also the President, is adopted.

Should the Archbishop be absent or unable to attend, his place as President is taken by the Bishop with seniority of consecration.

ARTICLE VIII. Jurisdiction and Competence of the Bishops. Each of the Bishops, has, in his own diocese, the authority and responsibilities allotted to the Episcopal Office by the Divine and Sacred Canons and the centuries-long practice of the Church and also the right to be installed upon the Holy *Synthronon*.

Among these rights and duties are: the sanctification and consecration of the churches and houses of prayer for worship; the establishment and appointment to them of priests, deacons and other clergy to celebrate and chant; the organization of a properly-conducted and well-ordered administration for the good of all; the issuance of licenses for the performance of the mystery of Marriage and the Letters of Divorce for those marriages which have been competently declared dissolved; the distribution to the priests of the Myrrh of the Holy Chrism, which the Archbishop receives from the Ecumenical Patriarch.

ARTICLE IX. Order of Commemoration. In the mysteries and the services, priests and deacons must commemorate their Canonical Bishop, the Bishops shall commemorate the Archbishop and the Archbishop the Ecumenical Patriarch.

ARTICLE X. Spiritual Court. In each Bishopric, there functions a Spiritual Court, consisting of the Bishop as President and at least two office-holding priests appointed and dismissed by the Bishop. In the event of the President being absent or unable to attend, his substitute presides. In this court, only the Bishop has a decisive vote, while the other members have an advisory vote. When a priest presides over the Spiritual Court as substitute for the Bishop all the members of the Spiritual Court have a decisive vote. The Spiritual Court in each Bishopric court hears all the canonical offences of the Clergy in the first instance, except those which lead to defrocking.

ARTICLE XI. The Spiritual Courts of the Bishoprics do not try cases in which a preliminary hearing has formed the opinion that the accused may be subject to the punishment of defrocking. They forward such cases to the Holy Synod of the Archdiocese.

An appeal may be made to the Holy Synod of the Archdiocese within 31 days of their publication, against decisions of the Spiritual Courts of the Bishoprics calling for a suspension of more than two months. An appeal may be made to the Holy Synod of the Ecumenical Patriarchate, within 91 days, against decisions of the Holy Synod of the Archdiocese which involve defrocking or suspension for more than one year.

ARTICLE XII. Marriage, in both its ecclesiastical and spiritual aspects is subject to the Church Authorities.

ARTICLE XIII. **Local Ecclesiastical Assemblies.** Each of the Four Bishoprics has its own Ecclesiastical Assembly, consisting of all the canonical Parish Priests who are clergy of the Bishopric and of one elected lay representative from each incorporated Holy Church, to be elected by the parish Council from its members, or the Members of the Community or from Orthodox Christians from another city or the city in which the Local Assembly takes place, but of necessity being in proper standing as regards the Orthodox Greek Church.

Each of these Ecclesiastical Assemblies meets by invitation of its own Bishop, who is also its President, or by his representative and surrogate should he be absent. It convenes regularly once every two years, in the month of September, and extraordinarily as often as the Bishop deems proper. A quorum is formed when in the presence of the Presiding Bishop, or his Presiding Surrogate, twelve members are present in person, of whom at least six must be clergymen.

ARTICLE XIV. **General Ecclesiastical Assembly.** The General Assembly of the whole of the Greek Archdiocese of North and South America consists of the Archbishop, the Bishops and 24 elected members, 12 from the clergy and 12 from the laity. The former and the latter are elected in groups of six by each of the four Ecclesiastical Assemblies, either from their Members or from elsewhere, but of necessity being in proper standing as regards the Orthodox Greek Church.

The General Assembly meets regularly once every three years, in the month of September, at the invitation of the Archbishop, and in extraordinary session following a relevant decision by the Holy Synod of the Archdiocese.

The President of the General Assembly is the Archbishop, or, in his absence, whichever of the Bishops present has seniority of consecration. A quorum is formed when in the presence of the Presiding Archbishop, or the Presiding Bishop, and at least one other Bishop twelve members are present in person, of whom at least six must be clergymen.

ARTICLE XV. Proxy Representation by Reason of Distance. In both the Local Ecclesiastical Assemblies of each Bishopric and in the General Ecclesiastical Assembly of the whole Archdiocese, those Clergymen and Laymen who have the right to participate may be represented, the Clergy by a Clergyman and the Laity by a Layman, officially authorized and in proper standing ecclesiastically.

In a vote, the proxy for the absent members also casts their vote, though never more than three, including his own, except in the case of the nomination of Bishops, when each of those present has only one vote.

Once authority to be a proxy has been given and recognized by the Assembly, it may not be recalled and remains in force throughout the proceedings of the Assembly.

In the event that the competent Assembly should fail to establish, in all detail, rules of composition of the Body of the Assembly or its procedure, this shall be done by the local bishop or his substitute.

ARTICLE XVI. The Task of the Assemblies. 1) THE LOCAL ASSEMBLIES. The right and duty of each Episcopal, Local Ecclesiastical Assembly are: a) to audit the whole of the Ecclesiastical financial management; b) to pass ordinances, in agreement with the local Bishop, respecting the management of the ecclesiastical, educational and charitable institutions of the Bishopric, in accordance with the Sacred Apostolic and Synodal Canons, the relevant laws of the United States and the decisions of the General Ecclesiastical Assemblies of the whole Archdiocese; c) to elect, as foreseen in Article XIV, representatives with a double number of supernumeraries for the General Ecclesiastical Assembly of the whole Archdiocese; and d) to elect the lay Members of the Joint Council of the Bishopric, as foreseen in Article XXI, together with a certain number of supernumeraries.

Provisions of individual parish Charters which contravene the Divine and Sacred Canons and the Laws of the United States are, *per se*, invalid. Ratification of the Charter of any Community by its own Bishop is a prerequisite for their implementation.

2) GENERAL ASSEMBLIES take decisions and ratify measures of common action throughout the whole Archdiocese, always with the aim of achieving greater progress in the realization of the religious, moral and social task of the Church set out in Article II.

ARTICLE XVII. The decisions of the General Ecclesiastical Assembly take precedence over those of the Local Ecclesiastical Assemblies. Decisions of the Local Ecclesiastical Assemblies take precedence over the General Community Assemblies. Any differences between the General Ecclesiastical Assembly and the Holy Synod of the Archdiocese over matters of jurisdiction are referred to the Ecumenical Patriarchate.

ARTICLE XVIII. **Election of the Archbishop and Bishops.** In the event that a bishopric, or the Archdiocese, falls vacant, the election of the Archbishop or Bishop shall be held as follows: Within of no more than three months, without fail, the local Ecclesiastical Assembly, meeting under the presidency of the Locum Tenens and at his invitation, following an order from the Holy Synod of the Church of America, shall nominate three candidates from among the clergy of the Archdiocese of North and South America, holders of degrees from a recognized Orthodox Theological School, of blameless life and successful service to the Church in the America, of five years in the case of a prospective Bishop or seven in the case of the Archbishop and, as appearing in the catalogue of the

Holy Synod of the Church of America, already approved by the Holy and Sacred Synod of the Patriarchate of Constantinople. In the case of filling the vacancy of the Archdiocese, candidates may also be drawn from the other active Metropolitans of the Ecumenical Throne. From the three candidates, the Holy Synod of the Archdiocese of North and South America will elect the bishop, or, in the case of the Archdiocese, the Archbishop. Such an election shall be announced by the Holy Synod of the Archdiocese to the Ecumenical Patriarchate for ratification.

ARTICLE XIX. Should the person thus elected and ratified be the Archbishop, he is consecrated by the Patriarch. Should he be a Bishop, the Patriarch merely gives his permission for the consecration.

ARTICLE XX. Should a second see become vacant before another episcopal throne is filled, so that the two remaining bishops cannot now constitute a Synod by themselves, the election of candidates nominated by their own local Ecclesiastical Assembly for the first of the two vacant sees shall be held by the Synod around the Ecumenical Patriarch, with the votes of the Bishops in America being counted for the majority (sympsephon). Thereafter the election of the second Bishop shall proceed in accordance with Article XVIII, again being held by the Holy Synod around the Archbishop.

ARTICLE XXI. Joint Council. A Joint Council functions within the Archdiocese of New York and in each of the three Bishoprics. In the Archdiocese of New York, this Council consists of the Archbishop, as President, and four ranking Clergymen of the Archdiocese appointed by the Archbishop and four distinguished Lay members, proposed by the Archbishop and approved by the Local Ecclesiastical Assembly.

The same provision is in force for each Joint Council of each Bishopric, the only difference being that the members, Clergy and Laity, may number only three each, should there be a lack of a greater number of Priests in the seat of the Bishopric and its surrounding area.

ARTICLE XXII. The appointment of Clerical and Lay members of the Joint Council is for a term of two years. The Vice-President of the Council is the highest ranking clergyman among these members, who also retains his voting rights as a member. The Joint Council elects the Treasurer and the Secretary from its members.

ARTICLE XXIII. **Loca Tenentes.** If the Archdiocese falls vacant, the Bishop with seniority of consecration shall act as locum tenens. Should the sees of Boston and Chicago fall vacant, the Archbishop acts as locum tenens, because of proximity. For the same reason, in the case of San Francisco, the locum tenens shall be the Bishop of Chicago.

ARTICLE XXIV. The Greek Archdiocese of North and South America, in order to fulfill its purpose as described in article II has at its disposal: holy churches, schools and charitable institutions, missions, publications and all other legitimate means, while it takes particular care for the functioning of a Seminary to meet its needs.

ARTICLE XXV. Ordained Clergy of the Greek Archdiocese of North and South America are appointed to their ministries without any involvement whatsoever on the part of civil Authorities. The guiding Law for the whole of the administration shall be the Sacred Apostolic and Synodal Canons, as well as the competently applied regulations which are in accordance with the Sacred Canons and the Laws of each State where the administration of this Church extends.

ARTICLE XXVI. Any regulation of any Ecclesiastical Organization whatsoever which contravenes either the Laws of the United States or the Sacred Canons of the Eastern Orthodox Church is of itself invalid.

ARTICLE XXVII. No clergyman or layman can be a ranking or even an ordinary member of the Greek Orthodox Church of America unless he is a member of the Greek Orthodox Church of Christ, and no-one may remain in office or be an ordinary member of the Church of America if he ceases to be in order with it.

ARTICLE XXVIII. The present Charter, consisting of XXVIII articles, has been read and passed by article and in total in the Third General Assembly of the Archdiocese of North and South America, convened in accordance with Article XIII of its Charter of 11 August 1922 in the Cathedral Church of Saint Basil, Chicago, on the 12th, 13th, and 14th of October, 1927. Approved and ratified by the Patriarch and

Synod, with certain amendments also, it comes into effect and will be replaced by the Constitution of the Holy Canons of the Greek Orthodox Church in America, which, following a decision of the same General Assembly, will be drawn up by a Special Committee, elected by the Holy Synod of the Church of America and will come into effect, without being ratified by another General Assembly of the Archdiocese, once it has been approved and ratified by the Ecumenical Patriarchate.

In the month of July, 1927, Indiction xi:
signed
† Vasileios, Patriarch of Constantinople declares.

† Veniamin of Nicea
† Agathangelos of Chalcedon
† Photios of Derkon
† Nikodemos of Prousa
† Amvrosios of Neocæsarea
† Thomas of Princeponesa
† Germanos of Sardeis and Pisidia
† Evgenios of Silivria
† Kyrillos of Rodopolis
† Gennadios of Ilioupolis
† Iakovos of Imvros and Tenedos

† Maximos of Philadelpheia,
Chief Secretary to the Holy and Sacred Synod,
declares this to be a true copy from the official Codex.

3 CHARTER OF THE GREEK ORTHODOX ARCHDIOCSE OF NORTH AND SOUTH AMERICA **(1931).** † Photios, by the Grace of God Archbishop of Constantinople, New Rome, and Ecumencal Patriarch, with our Holy and Sacred synod around us having approved the following we ratify:

Protocol No. 28

THE CONSTITUTION
OF THE GREEK ARCHDIOCESE OF NORTH AND SOUTH AMERICA

ARTICLE I. The Greek Orthodox Archdiocese of North and South America, which constitutes a Religious Association under the name of GREEK ARCHDIOCESE OF NORTH AND SOUTH AMERICA, is an Eparchy of the Most Holy Apostolic and Patriarchal Throne, which is a member and the first-throne See of the body of the One, Holy, Catholic and Apostolic Orthodox Eastern Church, the Head of which is Christ. This Archdiocese is administered on the basis of the present Constitution and the Regulations foreseen by it.

ARTICLE II. The Greek Archdiocese of America includes all the Orthodox living in the American Continent and the islands lying off it which, as their liturgical language, have exclusively, or principally, Greek, in which the Holy Gospels and the other Sacred Books of the New Testament were written.

Other Orthodox Communities in America, of different races, may belong, on application, to this Archdiocese, with the approval of the Ecumenical Patriarchate, which thus exercises the canonical and historical right of its spiritual jurisdiction over the Orthodox Communities in the Diaspora. In this event, they may retain their own liturgical languages.

ARTICLE III. In accordance with the canons and practice of the Church, the Greek Archdiocese of North and South America is under the spiritual and ecclesiastical dependence of the Ecumenical Patriarchate of Constantinople and its jurisdiction and supervision.

ARTICLE IV. The purpose of this Archdiocese is:

I) To retain and spread the Orthodox Christian Faith, on the basis of the Holy Scriptures, Holy Tradition and the Terms and Canons of the Holy Apostles and the Seven Ecumenical Synods of the ancient, undivided Church, as these are interpreted in fact by the Great Church of

Christ in Constantinople.

II) To build up the religious and moral life of Orthodox Christians, in accordance with the faith and traditions of this Church.

III) To teach the original language of the Gospel.

These duties will be set out in greater detail through a special Regulation.

ARTICLE V. In order to fulfill the aim expressed in article IV, the Archdiocese has at its disposal holy churches, schools and charitable institutions, publications and all other legal means.

Special Regulations will be written for each of these Institutions and means.

ARTICLE VI. The administration is exercised by the Archbishop, who has all the authority and duties, in accordance with the Sacred Canons and the practice of the Great Church. The Archbishop is responsible to the Ecumenical Patriarch and His Holy and Sacred Synod.

One auxiliary bishop may be appointed to the Archbishop.

ARTICLE VII. The Archbishop is elected by the Holy Synod of the Ecumenical Patriarchate, as is the Auxiliary Bishop, on the recommendation of the Archbishop.

No one may be nominated or elected Archbishop or Auxiliary Bishop unless he has been awarded a degree by a recognized Orthodox Theological School, has been tested in the lower orders of the priesthood for not less than five years and who is not less than thirty years of age.

ARTICLE VIII. At the Archdiocese, there is an Office, the function of which will be organized in accordance with a special Regulation.

ARTICLE IX. For the fulfillment of the aims of the Archdiocese of America set out in the present document, Ecclesiastical Conferences are to be held, of which the composition, time and place of meeting, responsibilities and any other relationship and detail of their function will be determined by a special Regulation.

ARTICLE X. Together with the Archbishop, a Mixed Council assists the Archdiocese in the realization of its aims, especially in the administration of Church property, as will be determined in a special Regulation.

The Mixed Council will be responsible for the inauguration of a General Church Fund and for the pensions of the Holy Clergy.

Temporarily, and until the publication of this Charter, this work will continue to be undertaken by the existing Mixed Council of the Archdiocese, in accordance with provisions XXI and XXII of the Charter in force until now.

Should any member of the temporary Council resign or be absent for whatever other reason, the Archbishop appoints his replacement.

ARTICLE XI. In each Community belonging to this Archdiocese there is a Council to work for the aim determined in the above article, the competence, duties and general functions of which Council shall be defined in a special Regulation.

ARTICLE XII. For the fulfillment of the religious needs of Christians who are not organized into religious Associations, the institution of a Mission is to be founded, functioning in accordance with a special Regulation.

ARTICLE XIII. For the promotion and systematic organization of the Schools, there shall be a Higher Council for Education in the Archdiocese, presided over by the Archbishop, which will function in accordance with the provisions of a special Regulation.

ARTICLE XIV. For the systematic religious education of the children of the Church there will function, in the Archdiocese and in a manner specified by a special regulation a Catechetic Schools Service with a governing Council.

ARTICLE XV. In accordance with the Sacred Canons and the Law of the Church Spiritual Courts function in the Archdiocese of America for the purpose of maintaining order and discipline within it. The composition, extent of competence, procedure, punishments, operation and all other details relating to these Courts shall be determined by a special Regulation.

ARTICLE XVI. Marriage, as well as Divorce, as regards their ecclesiastical and spiritual aspect, are subject to the Church Authorities.

A special Regulation, published by the Archdiocese, will regulate matters of Marriage and Divorce in detail.

ARTICLE XVII. General Provisions. The Regulations envisaged in articles IV, V, VIII, IX, X, XI, XII, XIII, XIV, XV and XVI shall be drawn up by Committees appointed by the Archbishop of America and presided over by him, and shall constitute an integral part of this present Charter, once they have been approved by Ecumenical Patriarchate. The regulations shall define the composition of the responsible Councils, their duties and competence, and also the details, in general, of their *modus operandi*.

ARTICLE XVIII. Any necessary addition or detail of the present Constitution shall, in each instance, be determined by a decision of the Mixed Council of the Archdiocese.

Any provision of the special Regulations or decision of the Mixed Council which conflicts with the present Charter is invalid.

ARTICLE XIX. The Clergy of the Archdiocese of America are appointed to their duties through an act of the canonical and legal Ecclesiastical Authority, while the law guiding the whole administration of the Archdiocese of America shall be the Sacred Apostolic and Synodal Canons and the Regulations put into practice in accordance with them and with the practice of the Church as each has been interpreted by the Ecumenical Patriarchate.

ARTICLE XX. No clergyman or layman can become an officer or even ordinary member of the Greek Orthodox Archdiocese of America unless he belongs to the Orthodox Church of Christ, and no-one may remain in his office or even as an ordinary member of the said Archdiocese, if he ceases to be in proper standing in regard to it.

ARTICLE XXI. Any provision of any Church Organization whatsoever which conflicts with the laws of the United States or the Sacred Canons of the Orthodox Eastern Church is of itself invalid.

ARTICLE XXII. The present Charter, consisting of twenty-two Articles and drawn up on the basis of a proposal by the competent special Committee, in accordance with article XXVIII of the Charter of the Archdiocese of North and South America at present in force and approved and ratified Synodally by His All Holiness the Ecumenical Patriarch comes into effect. It may be amended as regards non-fundamental provisions by a special Committee, appointed by the Archbishop, provided any such amendment is validated and applied after it has been approved by the Ecumenical Patriarchate.

In the month of January (10), Indiction XIV (1931)
† Patriarch of Constantinople PHOTIOS declares

signed
† Thomas of Pringhiponnisa
† Germanos of Sardeis and Pisidia
† Evgenios of Silyvria
† Kyrillos of Rodopolis
† Gennadios of Helioupolis
† Leontios of Theodoroupolis
† Meletios of Christoupolis
† Polykarpos of Myra
† Dorotheos of Laodicea

4 CHARTER OF THE GREEK ORTHODOX ARCHDIOCSE OF NORTH AND SOUTH AMERICA (1977). † Demetrios, by the Grace of God Archbishop of Constantinople, New Rome, and Ecumencal Patriarch.

THE CHARTER
OF THE GREEK ARCHDIOCESE OF NORTH AND SOUTH AMERICA

ARTICLE I. Preamble. The Holy Archdiocese of North and South America, being by law a religious corporation under the name "Greek Orthodox Archdiocese of North and South America," is a province within the territorial jurisdiction of the most Holy Apostolic and Ecumenical Patriarchal Throne of Constantinople which is the first-ranking see of the body of the Holy Catholic and Apostolic Eastern

Church whose head is Christ. The Archdiocese is governed by the holy canons, the present charter and the regulations promulgated by it and as to canonical and ecclesiastical matters not provided therein, by the decisions thereon of the Holy Synod of the Ecumenical Patriarchate.

The Archdiocese of North and South America serves all of the Orthodox living in the western hemisphere.

ARTICLE II. Purpose. The purpose of the Archdiocese is to administer the life of the church in the Americans according to the Eastern Orthodox faith and tradition, sanctifying the faithful through the divine liturgy and the holy sacraments and edifying the religious and ethical life of the faithful in accordance with the holy scriptures, the decrees and canons of the holy apostles and the seven ecumenical councils of Ancient Undivided Church, as interpreted by the practice of the Great Church of Christ in Constantinople. As to its ecumenical activities, both inter-Christian and inter-religious, the Archdiocese shall follow the position and guidelines established by the Ecumenical Patriarchate.

ARTICLE III. Jurisdiction. The Archdiocese of North and South America is by canonical and historical right under the supreme spiritual, ecclesiastical and canonical jurisdiction of the Ecumenical Patriarchate.

ARTICLE IV. Organization. The Archdiocese is comprised of dioceses, the number, diocesan sees and boundaries of which are designated by the Archdiocesan Council subject to approval and ratification by the Ecumenical Patriarchate. The Archdiocese shall be located in New York City and at the outset shall be comprised of nine dioceses, seven in the United States, one in Canada and one in South America.

The present dioceses are as follows: Chicago, Boston, San Francisco, Charlotte, Pittsburgh, Detroit, Denver, Toronto and Buenos Aires.

The Archdiocese of North and South America also embraces within its spiritual aegis and administration other Orthodox groups, parishes and dioceses that have voluntarily submitted to its jurisdiction subject to the approval of the Ecumenical Patriarchate which exercises canonically and historically ecclesiastical authority and jurisdiction over the Orthodox in the diaspora.

ARTICLE V. **Administration of the Archdiocese.** The Archbishop presides over and administers the Archdiocese, exercising the said highest ecclesiastical authority with the Synod of Bishops and is responsible therefore to the Ecumenical Patriarchate.

ARTICLE VI. **The Synod of Bishops.** The Archbishop and the bishops constitute the Synod of Bishops of the Archdiocese of North and South America. The Archbishop convenes and presides over the Synod of Bishops according to the holy canons of the Eastern Orthodox Church at least twice annually, before Easter and in the autumn and specially whenever the Archbishop deems it necessary or Ecumenical Patriarchate request. The Archbishop determines the place of such meetings.

The Synod of Bishops has all the authority and responsibility which the holy canons prescribe to the provincial synod, as modified herein by this charter. It is furthermore responsible to the Ecumenical Patriarchate for the firm observation and preservation of the divine doctrines and holy canons of the Eastern Orthodox Church.

ARTICLE VII. **Rights and Responsibilities of the Archbishop.** The Archbishop, in his capacity as Archbishop and Exarch of the Ecumenical Patriarchate, is charged as follows:

1. To be responsible to the Ecumenical Patriarchate for the proper and effective administration and activity of the Archdiocese of North and South America.

2. To oversee and coordinate with the Synod of Bishops and the Archdiocesan Council the preservation and promotion of the unity of the Archdiocese and is responsible therefore to the Ecumenical Patriarchate.

3. To exercise and perform all the rights and duties of an archbishop in accordance with the holy canons.

4. To submit to the Ecumenical Patriarchate an annual report as to the state of the Archdiocese.

5. To oversee the activities of the bishops and assist and cooperate with them in the implementation of their common programs through which the unity of the Archdiocese may be preserved.

6. To consecrate and enthrone bishops in their sees.

7. To bear with the Synod of Bishops the responsibility for the administration, maintenance and growth of the Archdiocesan institutions.

8. To preside over Pan-Orthodox committees and councils and to represent the Archdiocese and Ecumenical Patriarchate when so directed before ecclesiastical and civil authorities.

9. To preside over the Archdiocesan Clergy-Laity Congress and the various boards and commissions of Archdiocese.

10. To cultivate and strengthen the bond of unity between the Archdiocese and the Ecumenical Patriarchate.

ARTICLE VIII. Rights and Responsibilities of the Bishops. After enthronement, each bishop in his has the rights and responsibilities of a bishop in accordance with the holy canons and ancient practice of the church, as modified herein by this charter. Among the rights and responsibilities of a bishop are to consecrate and sanctify for worship churches and houses of prayer, administer his diocese in an orderly and harmonious manner, convene and preside over the Spiritual Court of First Instance in his diocese, issue permits for the performance of the sacrament of marriage and decrees of divorce on marriages that are validly dissolved, distribute to the priests the myrrh of holy chrism which is received by the Archbishop from the Ecumenical Patriarchate, ordain deacons and priests in his diocese, after they are approved by the Synod of Bishops to which each candidacy is submitted and in the interim, between meetings of the Synod of Bishops, with the approval of the Archbishop to whom the responsibility is delegated.

ARTICLE IX. Order of Commemoration. During sacraments and ceremonies, priests and deacons commemorate the Archbishop and their bishop, the bishops commemorate the Archbishop, and the Archbishop commemorates the Ecumenical Patriarch.

ARTICLE X. Spiritual Courts. A Spiritual Court of First Instance functions within each diocese. It is comprised of clerical members selected by the bishop, who presides over it and hears cases involving family problems, divorce, as well as moral and disciplinary offenses of clerics and laity.

The Spiritual Court of Appeals is comprised of the Archbishop, who presides over it, the members of the Synod of Bishops and the Chancellor of the Archdiocese as secretary. It is convened twice annually when the Synod of Bishops meets and hears all appeals from decisions of the Spiritual Courts of First Instance. The operating procedures of the spiritual courts will be formulated by regulations hereinafter promulgated.

Matters involving bishops will be judged and determined by the Synod of Bishops convening in such instances as a spiritual court in accordance with the provisions herein.

ARTICLE XI. Archdiocesan Clergy-Laity Congress. The Archdiocesan Clergy-Laity Congress is convened biennially and presided over by the Archbishop. It is concerned with all matters, other than doctrinal or canonical, which affect the life of the church including its unity, uniform administration, education and financial programs.

The decisions of the Archdiocesan Clergy-Laity Congress are submitted to the Ecumenical Patriarchate for approval and ratification. Following their approval, the decisions must be faithfully adhered to by all parishes regardless of whether or not they were represented at the Archdiocesan Clergy-Laity Congress at which they were adopted.

ARTICLE XII. Diocesan Clergy-Laity Assembly. Each diocese shall have a Diocesan Clergy-Laity Assembly convened annually, presided over by its bishop and comprised of the priests and the presidents, or their representatives, of the parishes of the diocese.

The Diocesan Clergy-Laity Assembly is concerned with matters involving the better organization and productivity of parish activities in accordance with existing church practices.

Regulations hereinafter promulgated shall set forth its manner of operation.

ARTICLE XIII. The election of the Archbishop is the exclusive privilege and right of the Holy Synod of the Ecumenical Patriarchate. The Synod of Bishops and the Archdiocesan Council have an advisory voice concerning the person of the Archbishop to be so elected. The Archbishop must be a Greek Orthodox Christian, be a graduate of a recognized Orthodox school of theology, have a fluent knowledge of English, be a cleric of deep faith, have proven ability in administration, be fully aware of ecclesiastical affairs in the United States and be totally committed to the Ecumenical Patriarchate.

ARTICLE XIV. Election of Bishops. Bishops shall be chosen from the list of celibate candidates for the Episcopal office of the Archdiocese of North and South America. The election thereof is the exclusive privilege and right of the Holy Synod of the Ecumenical Patriarchate.

The Synod of Bishops in consultation with the Archdiocesan Council shall nominate three candidates. The Holy Synod of the Ecumenical Patriarchate will elect one of them.

Candidates must be graduates of an Orthodox school of theology, must have a fluent knowledge of the English language and the spoken language of the lands to which they will be assigned, have had a period of service of more than five years in the Archdiocese of North and South America and shall not be less than 35 nor more than 55 years age.

ARTICLE XV. Archdiocesan Council. The Archdiocesan Council is comprised of the Archbishop as president, the bishops, and the clergy and laity from each diocese selected in accordance with regulations hereinafter promulgated. The Archdiocesan Council is convened by the Archbishop and meets as often as necessary but at least semiannually. It is concerned with matters and problems that affect the life and growth of the church and takes such decisions thereon as are required.

In the event that legislation becomes necessary between Archdiocesan Clergy-Laity Congresses, the Archdiocesan Council shall exercise such interim legislative authority when so convened by the Archbishop and advised as to the necessity therefor.

Regulations hereinafter promulgated shall set forth its manner of operation.

ARTICLE XVI. Diocesan Council. The Diocesan Council is comprised of the bishop as president and clergy and laity selected in accordance with the regulations hereinafter promulgated.

It meets at least annually and in special sessions as often as the bishop deems necessary. The Diocesan Council is a consultative and advisory body to the bishop.

Regulations hereinafter promulgated shall set forth its manner of operation.

ARTICLE XVII. Hierarchical Vacancies. In the event of a vacancy in the office of the Archbishop, the bishop first in order of seniority of consecration becomes temporary *locum tenens* until the Holy Synod of the Ecumenical Patriarchate designates a *locum tenens*.

In the event a diocesan see becomes vacant, the Archbishop designates the *locum tenens* who serves until his successor has been elected.

ARTICLE XVIII. Education. The Archdiocese shall establish and administer such educational institutions as may be necessary, including afternoon and day parish schools, schools such as the present St. Basil's Academy and colleges and seminaries such as the present Hellenic College and Holy Cross School of Theology.

The Archdiocese shall publish educational, religious and spiritual materials to fulfill the needs of Orthodox faithful.

ARTICLE XIX. Institutions. The existing Archdiocesan institutions and any to be established in the future are the concern and responsibility of the Archdiocese. The establishment of new institutions requires the approval of the Synod of Bishops and Archdiocesan Council.

ARTICLE XX. Assignment and Transfer of Priests. The assignment and transfer of priests and deacons within each diocese is the right of the local bishop. As to transfers between dioceses, the Synod of Bishops shall have the responsibility, except that between meetings of the Synod of Bishops, the Archbishop shall have the right after consultation with the two bishops involved.

ARTICLE XXI. Regulations. Regulations as required to implement this charter and govern the Archdiocese shall be proposed by the Archbishop and presented to the Archdiocesan Council which shall consider, adopt, and present them to the next Archdiocesan Clergy-Laity Congress for approval. The said regulations, which must be in conformity with the charter herein, shall then be presented to the

Ecumenical Patriarchate for approval and ratification.

ARTICLE XXII. Language of the Charter. The languages of this charter and any regulations hereunder promulgated shall be Greek and English. In the event of a need for interpretation, the English text shall be deemed the official and legal text.

ARTICLE XXIII. Implementation. This charter was prepared by the Archdiocesan Council under its interim legislative authority between Archdiocesan Clergy-Laity Congresses. It was submitted to the Ecumenical Patriarchate which has studied, modified it, and granted it in its present form to the Archdiocese. It becomes fully operative three months after the granting thereof by the Ecumenical Patriarchate.

ARTICLE XXIV. Revision. The charter herein may be revised upon the request of the Archdiocesan Clergy-Laity Congress as the need therefore arises. Revisions thereto shall be submitted to the Ecumenical Patriarchate for approval and ratification.

In the Patriarchate, 29 November, 1977
† Demetrios Patriarch of Constantinople signed

declares

† Meliton of Chalcedon	† Kyrillos of Chaldia
† Maximos of Laodicea	† Maximos of Sardeis
† Ieronymos of Rodopolis	† Photios of Imvros and Tenedos
† Maximos of Stavroupolis	† Chrysostomos of Myra
† Gabriel of Colonia	† Kallinikos of Lystra
† Constantinos of Derka	† Vartholomaios of Philadelpheia

5 **CHARTER OF THE GREEK ORTHODOX ARCHDIOCSE OF AMERICA** (2003). † Bartholomew, Archbishop of Constantinople, New Rome, and Ecumenical Patriarch.

Protocol No. 1048/2002

CHARTER
OF THE GREEK ARCHDIOCESE OF AMERICA

ARTICLE 1. **Preamble and Canonical Jurisdiction.** a. The Holy Greek Orthodox Archdiocese of America ("Archdiocese"), with its headquarters located in the City of New York, New York, United States of America, is an Eparchy of the most Holy Apostolic and Patriarchal Ecumenical Throne of Constantinople ("Ecumenical Patriarchate"), which is the first-ranking See of the One Holy, Catholic, and Apostolic Church, whose head is Christ.

b. The Archdiocese, being Hierarchical, as an Eparchy of the Ecumenical Throne, is governed by the Holy Scriptures, Sacred Tradition, the Holy Canons, this Charter, the Regulations promulgated pursuant hereto ("Regulations"), and as to canonical and ecclesiastical matters not provided for herein, by the decisions of the Holy and Sacred Synod of the Ecumenical Patriarchate ("Holy Synod").

c. The Archdiocese receives within its ranks and under its spiritual aegis and pastoral care Orthodox Christians, who either as individuals or as organized groups in Dioceses and Parishes have voluntarily come to it and which acknowledge the supreme spiritual, ecclesiastical and canonical jurisdiction of the Ecumenical Patriarchate. In the case of the coming to the Archdiocese of organized groups, either Orthodox or heterodox, the opinion and approval of the Ecumenical Patriarchate is required, as it exercises its ecclesiastical jurisdiction over the Orthodox in the Diaspora.

d. The Archdiocese serves and pastors to the Orthodox Christians who live in the United States of America.

ARTICLE 2. **Mission of the Holy Archdiocese.** a. The mission of the Archdiocese is to proclaim the Gospel of Christ, to teach and spread the Orthodox Christian faith, to energize, cultivate and guide the life of the Church in the United States of America according to the Orthodox Christian faith and Sacred Tradition.

b. The Archdiocese sanctifies the faithful through the Divine Worship, especially the Holy Eucharist and other Sacraments, building the spiritual and ethical life of the faithful in accordance with the Holy Scriptures, Sacred Tradition, the doctrines and canons of the Ecumenical and local Synods, the canons of the Holy Apostles and Fathers of the

Church and of all other Synods recognized by the Orthodox Church, as interpreted by the Great Church of Christ in Constantinople.

c. The Archdiocese serves as a beacon, carrier and witness of the message of Christ to all persons who live in United States of America, through Divine Worship, preaching, teaching and living the Orthodox Christian faith. As to its intra-Orthodox, intra-Christian and inter-religious activities, the Archdiocese follows the positions and guidelines established by the Ecumenical Patriarchate.

ARTICLE 3. Organization of the Holy Archdiocese. a. The Archdiocese, being the Eparchy of the Ecumenical Throne in the United States of America, is one unified entity in its entirety. It is comprised of the New York based Direct Archdiocesan District ("Archdiocesan District"), and Metropoles, the number, seat, and boundaries of which are designated by the Sacred Eparchial Synod of the Archdiocese ("Eparchial Synod"), in consultation with the Archdiocesan Council ("Archdiocesan Council"), and are submitted for evaluation and decision to the Ecumenical Patriarchate.

b. The Archdiocese of America has its seat in New York City and is incorporated in the State of New York. It is presently comprised of the Direct Archdiocesan District and eight (8) Metropoles. These Metropoles, which also are incorporated, are (according to the order of the English alphabet) the following: Atlanta, Boston, Chicago, Denver, Detroit, New Jersey, Pittsburgh and San Francisco.

c. The Direct Archdiocesan District and each Metropolis, being incorporated and recognized by civil law, are administered by their respective hierarch according to the Holy Canons, the Ecclesiastical Regulations, and the provisions of this Charter.

ARTICLE 4. System of Governance of the Holy Archdiocese.

a. Comprised of the Archbishop as President and the Metropolitans as its members, the Eparchial Synod constitutes the ecclesiastical instrument of governance of the Archdiocese.

b. Presided over and represented by its President, the Archbishop, the Eparchial Synod has the ecclesiastical and canonical responsibility for the Archdiocese to the Ecumenical Patriarchate, which is its superior ecclesiastical authority.

ARTICLE 5. The Holy Eparchial Synod of the Holy Archdiocese.

a. The Archbishop as President and the Metropolitans as members constitute the Holy Eparchial Synod of the Holy Archdiocese of America ("Eparchial Synod"). The Archbishop convenes and presides over the meetings of the Eparchial Synod which shall meet in regular session, according to the Holy Canons of Orthodox Church, twice annually, in the spring and in the autumn. The Eparchial Synod may also meet in special session if a special need arises, or if the Ecumenical Patriarchate requests it, in which case the meeting is obligatory. The Eparchial Synod may also be especially called at the request of the Archbishop or of a majority of its members, with the agenda topics specified.

b. The Eparchial Synod has all of the authority and responsibility that the Holy Canons and this Charter ascribe to the "Eparchial Synod." All legal issues, which affect the Archdiocese as a whole and its Metropoles are within the exclusive jurisdiction of the Eparchial Synod. Through its president, the Eparchial Synod shall inform the Ecumenical Patriarchate about the issues discussed and the decisions made at its meetings.

c. Regulations hereafter promulgated by the Eparchial Synod and approved by the Ecumenical Patriarchate shall govern its manner of operation.

ARTICLE 6. Responsibilities and Rights of the Archbishop. The Archbishop of America presides over the Holy Eparchial Synod and is the Exarch of the Ecumenical Patriarchate in the United States of America. In his capacity as Archbishop, as President of the Eparchial Synod and as Exarch of the Ecumenical Patriarchate, among other rights and responsibilities, the Archbishop:

1. Exercises and performs all of the rights and duties designated for his office by the Holy Canons.

2. Is responsible together with the Eparchial Synod over which he presides, to the Ecumenical Patriarchate concerning the canonical and orderly functioning, life, governance and activities of the one and uni-

fied Archdiocese.

3. Reports to the Ecumenical Patriarchate, to which he forwards an annual report on the status of the entire Archdiocese.

4. Is directly responsible for pasturing and governing his own Archdiocesan District.

5. Oversees and coordinates, together with the Eparchial Synod and the Archdiocesan Council, the work which is planned and carried out in each Metropolis, through which the unity of the unified Archdiocese is secured and enhanced.

6. Ordains and installs the Metropolitans in their eparchies.

7. Supports his fellow Hierarchs in a brotherly manner as they implement the unified programs of the Archdiocese.

8. Presides over the Eparchial Synod, the Archdiocesan Clergy-Laity Congresses, the meeting of the Archdiocesan Council and the boards of the trustees of the major institutions and organizations of the Archdiocese.

9. Represents the Archdiocese and the Ecumenical Patriarchate in their dealings with all ecclesiastical and civil authorities in the United States of America.

10. Presides as Exarch of the Ecumenical Patriarchate over Pan-Orthodox councils, meeting and assemblies and promotes and fosters harmony and cooperation among all Orthodox Christians in the United States of America.

11. Is responsible for intra-Christian and inter-religious activities in the United States of America.

12. Cultivates and strengthens even more the existing bond of unity between the Archdiocese and the Ecumenical Patriarchate.

13. Carries out and implements the provisions of this Charter.

ARTICLE 7. Responsibilities and Rights of the Metropolitans.

a. Each Metropolitan within his ecclesiastical district and the Archbishop in his Direct Archdiocesan District have the rights and responsibilities of a Bishop in accordance with the Holy Canons and the long-established life, praxis and order of the Church as well as the provisions of this Charter, including the exclusive right to occupy the throne behind the altar (*Synthronon*).

b. Among the rights and responsibilities of each Metropolitan are the following:

1. To be a member of the Eparchial Synod and participate in its work, forwarding to the Archbishop an annual report regarding the progress of the work of his Metropolis.

2. To ordain deacons and priests for his Metropolis, following his submission of their candidacy to the Eparchial Synod and the Eparchial Synod's approval.

3. To consecrate and sanctify for worship churches and chapels.

4. To administer his Metropolis in a considered, orderly, harmonious and fiscally responsible manner for the common good.

5. To convene and preside over the Spiritual Court of First Instance in his Metropolis.

6. To issue permits for the celebration of the sacrament of marriage and decrees of ecclesiastical divorce in the event of the dissolution of marriage.

7. To distribute to the parish priests the *Myron* (Holy Chrismation Oil) which is received from the Holy and Great Church of Christ through the Archbishop, and

8. To have his *pheme* (Bishop's anthem) canonically chanted during the Divine Liturgy. His *pheme*, however, shall not include *hypertimia* (supreme honor) and *exarchia* (exarchy).

c. During the periods between meetings of Eparchial Synod, the Archbishop having received to this end its authorization of the Eparchial Synod, issues the ordination permit as well as the permit to the Metropolitans of the unified Archdiocese of America for their canonical (annual) or extraordinary absence outside the United States.

ARTICLE 8. Order of Commemoration. During Divine Worship, the Sacraments and the Sacred Services, Priests and Deacons commemorate their canonical Hierarch. The Archbishop and the Metropolitans commemorate the name of the Ecumenical Patriarch at the liturgical exclamation of the "en protois mnestheti ..." ("first of all remember Lord ..."). The Auxiliary Bishops commemorate the name of their respective Hierarch. At the Great Entrance of the Divine Liturgy, after the commemoration of their Archbishop and Patriarch, the Metropolitans also commemorate their Archbishop in America.

ARTICLE 9. Spiritual Courts. a. A Spiritual Court of First Instance functions within the Archdiocesan District and within each Metropolis. Each Spiritual Court is comprised of four senior clergy selected by the Hierarch, who presides over it, and hears cases involving family problems, divorce, and moral and disciplinary offenses of clergy and lay persons. The Court decrees the measures of correction and healing as by the Holy Canons and Tradition of the Orthodox Church.

b. The Spiritual Court of Second Instance (Appeals) is comprised of the Archbishop, who presides over it, the members of the Eparchial Synod and the Chancellor of the Archdiocese as secretary. In the absence of the Archbishop for good cause, the first ranking among the Metropolitans shall preside. It is convened when the Eparchial Synod meets, and hears at the Second Instance all appeals of decisions from the Spiritual Courts of the First Instance. The Hierarch who was the judge of the First Instance Court shall not participate in the decision of the Spiritual Court of the Second Instance (Appeals).

c. Appeals from the rulings of the Spiritual Court of the Second Instance (Appeals) involving Clergy and Laity may be submitted to the Ecumenical Patriarchate for review. The decisions of the Ecumenical Patriarchate regarding these appeals are final and irrevocable.

d. According to ecclesiastical authorization granted to it, the Eparchial Synod convenes as a Spiritual Court of First Instance for cases involving Metropolitans and Bishops.

e. Acting as a Second Instance Court and a Court of Appeals, the Holy Synod of the Ecumenical Patriarchate hears and judges irrevocably those cases.

f. The Eparchial Synod Submits any charges, which require defrocking of clergy to the Ecumenical Patriarchate. The proposed defrocking can only be determined by the Holy and Sacred Synod of the Ecumenical Patriarchate.

g. The operating of the Spiritual Courts will be based upon Regulations hereafter promulgated by the Eparchial synod and approved by the Ecumenical Patriarchate.

ARTICLE 10. Archdiocesan Clergy-Laity Congress. a. Archdiocesan Clergy-Laity Congresses ("Congress") are convened at least triennially and presided over by the Archbishop. Except for dogmatic or canonical matters, they are concerned with all other matters which affect the life, mission, growth and unity of the Archdiocese of America, and especially the uniform administration of the Archdiocesan District, the Metropoles and Parishes, the educational programs, financial programs, and philanthropic concerns of the Archdiocese, and the more active participation of Archdiocese in the life of the United States of America. The Congress makes such decisions as it deems appropriate.

b. The Congress is presided over by the Archbishop and is comprised of the members of the Eparchial Synod, the Auxiliary Bishops, the members of the Archdiocesan Council, and clergy and lay representatives of the Parishes of the Archdiocese.

c. The decisions of the Congress are submitted by the Eparchial Synod through its President, the Archbishop, to the Ecumenical Patriarchate for approval. In the event that no response is received from the Ecumenical Patriarchate within ninety (90) days following the receipt of the decisions by it, the decisions shall be deemed approved. Following their approval, the decisions must be faithfully and firmly adhered to by all Parishes whether or not they were represented at the Congress, and regardless of whether they voted with the minority.

d. Regulations hereafter promulgated shall set forth the composition, functioning, and frequency of convening of the Congress.

ARTICLE 11. Local Clergy-Laity Assemblies. a. The Archdiocesan District and each Metropolis shall have a Clergy-Laity Assembly ("Assembly") convened and presided over by its local Hierarch. The Assembly is comprised of the priests and lay representatives of the

Parishes within its jurisdiction and the members of the Local Council.

b. Except for dogmatic or canonical issues, the local Assemblies are concerned with matters affecting the life and growth of the Archdiocesan District or the Metropoles as may be applicable and the unity thereof. They deal with local matters including the uniform governance of the Parishes, educational programs, financial programs and philanthropic concerns, as well as with the better organization and effectiveness of the Parishes.

c. Each Assembly may propose to the Archdiocese items for inclusion in the agenda of the upcoming Congress.

d. Regulations hereafter promulgated shall set forth the composition, functioning, and frequency of convening of the Assembly.

ARTICLE 12. Loca Tenentes. a. In the event of a vacancy in the office of the Archbishop, the member of the Eparchial Synod first in order of seniority of episcopal ordination, or — if he is impaired — the next in rank, becomes the *locum tenens* by designation of the Ecumenical Patriarch, until the election of the new Archbishop.

b. In the event a Metropolitan See becomes vacant, the Archbishop, in consultation with the Eparchial Synod, designates the Metropolitan of an adjacent See as the *locum tenens* who serves until a successor is elected.

ARTICLE 13. Election of the Archbishop. a. The election of the Archbishop is the exclusive privilege and the canonical right of the Holy Synod. The Eparchial Synod, as well as the Archdiocesan Council, have an advisory opinion regarding the person of the Archbishop to be elected. This opinion will be submitted in writing to the Holy Synod in a timely fashion, or it may be submitted by a special delegation, so that it may be duly evaluated on the basis of meritocratic criteria.

b. A candidate for the office of Archbishop must be a person of deep faith and ethos, a Greek Orthodox Christian, a graduate of an academically accredited Orthodox school of theology of the highest level, and have all the qualifications as provided by the Holy Canons for Hierarchical office. Also, the candidate shall have a fluent knowledge of spoken and written English and Greek, have proven ability in administration and pastoral work, and be totally committed to the preservation of unity within the Archdiocese as well as to its bond of unity with the Ecumenical Patriarchate. In addition, he shall not be less than forty (40) years of age and have had a period of successful service in the Archdiocese of no less than five (5) years, or to have proven, direct, substantive and broad knowledge of the life and status of the Church in America.

c. Those fulfilling the above conditions are candidates regardless of the place of residence or service during the time of the election.

ARTICLE 14. Election of a Metropolitan. a. In every regular meeting and in consultation with the Archdiocesan Council, the Eparchial Synod reviews and modifies, through additions and deletions, the list of those eligible for the office of Metropolitan. The Auxiliary Bishops are automatically included in this list by virtue of their office. The Eparchial Synod submits the list so completed to the Ecumenical Patriarchate for its approval. The list becomes definitive after its ratification by the Ecumenical Patriarchate and is then officially published by the Archdiocese.

b. Immediately following a vacancy in the See of a Metropolis, but no later than forty (40) days thereafter, the Archbishop convenes the Eparchial Synod in a timely fashion, for the purpose of nominating, after soliciting the opinion of the members of the Archdiocesan Council, three persons, out of whom one shall be elected to fill the vacancy of the Metropolis. The nominees are taken from the above mentioned list of those eligible, pursuant to the procedure provided for by the Regulations of the Eparchial Synod.

c. The list of three nominees thus established is submitted to the Ecumenical Patriarchate. According to the existing practice, the Holy and Sacred Synod of the Ecumenical Patriarchate elects one of the three as the new Metropolitan.

d. A nominee for the office of the Metropolitan shall be a person of deep faith and ethos, a Greek Orthodox Christian, a graduate of an academically recognized and accredited Orthodox school of theology of the highest level, have a fluent knowledge of spoken and written English and Greek, and have a proven ability in administration and pastoral work. In addition, the nominee must have all the pertinent qualifications defined by the Holy Canons, shall not be less than thirty-five (35) years of age, and shall have had a period of sufficient service in the Archdiocese.

e. Those fulfilling the above conditions are candidates and included in the list of eligible candidates regardless of the place of residence during the time of the election.

ARTICLE 15. Elections of Auxiliary Bishops. a. For the election of Auxiliary Bishops the same procedure shall be followed as for the election of Metropolitans (see Article 14).

b. Regulations regarding the Auxiliary Bishops shall be promulgated by the Eparchial Synod and put into effect after its approval by Ecumenical Patriarchate.

ARTICLE 16. Assignment and Transfer of Clergy. a. The assignment and transfer of Clergy within the Archdiocesan District and each Metropolis is the exclusive right and privilege of the respective Hierarch.

b. The initial placement of a clergyman is made by the Archbishop in consultation with the Metropolitan in whose Metropolis the clergyman will be placed. The assignment will be made the Archbishop or the Metropolitan in whose Archdiocesan District or Metropolis the Clergyman will serve.

c. The transfer of clergy between Metropoles (or between the Archdiocesan District and Metropolis) is the right of the Hierarchs involved who will effectuate all transfers according to the ecclesiastical regulations in force. All transfers and assignments shall be communicated to the Archdiocese for its information and use.

ARTICLE 17. Archdiocesan Council. a. The membership of the Archdiocesan Council is comprised of the Archbishop as President, the Metropolitans and Auxiliary Bishops and representatives of the clergy and laity from the Parishes of the Archdiocesan District and of each Metropolis.

b. The Archdiocesan Council is convened by the Archbishop and meets in regular session at least twice a year and in special session as often as is considered necessary.

c. Except for dogmatic and canonical matters, which are within the competence of the Ecumenical Patriarchate, the Archdiocesan Council is concerned with matters and issues that affect the life, growth and unity of the Holy Archdiocese of America, and makes such decisions thereon as it deems necessary. The Archdiocese Council functions as the advisory and consultative body to the Archbishop and to the Eparchial Synod.

d. The Archdiocesan Council is concerned with the Archdiocesan ministries, institutions, and financial affairs of the Holy Archdiocese of America. Together with the Eparchial Synod, the Archdiocesan Council is concerned with the interpretation and implementation of the decisions of Congress, as well as the Regulations adopted pursuant to this Charter on matters within its jurisdiction. The Archdiocesan Council has such duties and responsibilities as set forth herein, as well as those provided for under any Regulations pertaining to it in matters within its jurisdiction.

e. In the event that action becomes necessary between Congresses, the Archdiocesan Council shall exercise the authority of the Congress when so convened by the Archbishop and advised as to the purpose and necessity therefore.

f. Specific Regulations shall set forth the composition, functioning, jurisdiction, and convening of Archdiocesan Council.

ARTICLE 18. Local Councils. a. The Local Council of the Direct Archdiocesan District and of each Metropolis ("Local Council") is the consultative and advisory body to its respective Hierarch. Except for dogmatic and canonical matters, it is concerned with matters and problems that affect the unity, life and growth of the corresponding ecclesiastical area and is comprised of the respective Hierarch as chairman and clergy and laity of his area as members.

b. The Local Council shall meet in regular session at least semi-annually and in special session as the local Hierarch deems necessary.

c. The Local Council is concerned with the ministries, institutions, programs, and financial affairs of the corresponding ecclesiastical area. It has the duties, responsibilities and competence designated to it and provided for under the Regulations pertaining to it.

d. Specific Regulations shall set forth the composition, functioning, jurisdiction, and convening of the local council.

ARTICLE 19. Education. a. The Archdiocese establishes and oversees educational institutions, both religious and cultural, which offer Catechetical training and Greek *paideia*, as may be necessary, such as the present Holy Cross School of Theology and Hellenic College.

b. The Archdiocese also establishes educational programs, which may be necessary to serve its cultural, catechetical, educational and other needs.

c. The Archdiocese publishes such religious and educational materials as may be appropriate to the fulfillment of its mission.

d. Regulations hereafter promulgated shall provide for the establishment and functioning of all necessary educational institutions, as well as the formation of related programs.

ARTICLE 20. Ministries and Institutions. All major existing or future institutions of the Archdiocese shall be the property and responsibility of the Archdiocese (see Article 17, d), while those of a local nature shall be the respective property and responsibility of each local ecclesiastical administration (see Article 18, c).

b. The establishment of new institutions, including, but not limited to, educational, recreational, charitable, retirement homes and the like, as well as the dissolution of such institutions, requires prior approval of the Eparchial Synod and the consent of the Archdiocesan Council or the Local Council as may be applicable.

c. The manner of operation of such institutions shall be pursuant to Regulations hereafter promulgated.

ARTICLE 21. Holy Monasteries. a. Monasteries and organized communities of monastics function according to the long established, canonical tradition and practice of the Church. As such, they are ecclesiastical institutions, functioning under the direct canonical jurisdiction and supervision of the Hierarch in whose jurisdiction they are located.

b. Monasteries are founded by the local Hierarch, following approval of the Eparchial Synod. Canonically, their administration and financial affairs are the responsibility of the local Hierarch, whose name is to be commemorated during Divine Worship.

c. The Monasteries that operate in the United States of America continue the long established monastic life and witness. They function according to the prevailing Monastic Law and the letter and spirit of the Regulations that define their operation.

d. Regulations for the establishment, organization and operation of Monasteries shall be promulgated by the Eparchial Synod and approved by the Ecumenical Patriarchate.

ARTICLE 22. Regulations. a. All regulations pertaining to the implementation of this Charter shall be in conformity with the Holy Canons, Sacred Tradition and the long existing life and practice of the Holy Orthodox Church, as developed in the framework of the Ecumenical Patriarchate, and in conformity with the letter and spirit of this Charter.

b. Regulations for the implementation of this Charter shall be proposed, approved, and ratified as follows:

1. Regulations pertaining to the operations of the Eparchial Synod, the Spiritual Courts and the Monasteries shall be promulgated by the Eparchial Synod and approved by the Ecumenical Patriarchate.

2. Regulations pertaining to the composition of the Archdiocesan Council and the Local Councils shall be promulgated by the Congress; Regulations pertaining to the functioning of these bodies shall be promulgated by the Archdiocesan Council.

3. All other Regulations, including those pertaining to the composition, the frequency of meetings and the manner of functioning of the Congress, Assemblies and Parishes of the entire Holy Archdiocese, shall be proposed by the Archdiocesan Council and promulgated by the Congress.

4. All regulations mentioned in the above paragraphs 2 and 3 and in general, all Regulations pursuant to the present Charter shall be submit-

ted by the Eparchial Synod, through its President, to the Ecumenical Patriarchate for final review and approval. In the event that no response is received from the Ecumenical Patriarchate within ninety (90) days following the receipt of the Regulations by it, they shall be deemed approved.

c. Until the adoption and approval of Regulations under this Charter, all existing Regulations shall continue in full force and effect. However, in the event of a conflict between this Charter and any such Regulations, the provisions of this Charter shall prevail.

d. The present Charter and all Regulations adopted and approved pursuant to this Charter shall be published by the Archdiocese.

e. The Archdiocesan Council shall interpret all Regulations except those approved and ratified pursuant to the provisions of Articles 5, 9, and 21 hereof.

Article 23. Language and Authentic Text. The languages of this Charter and any Regulations hereunder promulgated shall be English and Greek. The English text, as approved by the Patriarchate, shall be deemed the legal and governing text. In the event of need, this Charter shall be authoritatively interpreted by the Ecumenical Patriarchate.

Article 24. Implementation. This present Charter is granted to the Archdiocese of America by the Ecumenical Patriarchate and is effective immediately.

Article 25. Amendment. The present Charter regulating the affairs of the Holy Archdiocese of America as an ecclesiastical institution, may be amended in its entirety or in part after a proposal of the Holy Eparchial Synod submitted to the Ecumenical Patriarchate following the appropriate procedure in the Archdiocesan Council and the Archdiocesan Clergy-Laity Congress, and after the approval of the Holy and Sacred Synod of the Ecumenical Patriarchate to which the proposal has been submitted.

In the year of our Lord 2003, on the 18th day of the month of January. The Archbishop of Constantinople, New Rome and Ecumenical Patriarch Bartholomew declares

† Chrystostomos of Ephesus
† Photios of Heracleia
† Constantine of Derkon
† Germanos of Theodoropolis
† Theoklitos of Metre and Athyra
† Cyril of Imvros and Tenedos
† Iakovos of Pringhiponnison
† Demetrios of Sebasteia
† Irinaios of Myriophyton and Peristasis
† Chrysostom of Myra
† Apostolos of Moschonissia
†Theoliptos of Iconium

This is a true copy given at the Patriarchate on the 18th day of January 2003 by the Chief Secretary of the Holy and Sacred Synod,
† Meliton of Philadelpheia.

Index

Confessor 125
Niketas: —, Metropolitan of Herakleia 63;
  —, Metropolitan of Thessaloniki 64
Nikodemos, Hieromonk 27, 87, 243
Nikon 84, 86
Nomocanon 21, 62, 64, 65, 67, 68, 75, 76, 81,
  82, 83, 84, 85, 86, 88, 104, 106, 111, 187, 209
Novella 21, 67, 68, 70, 71, 81, 110, 111, 126,
  131, 132, 149, 150, 166, 169, 170, 180, 188,
  200, 206, 209
novitiate 131, 132, 133
nun 53, 132, 165, 166

O

obedience 35, 131, 165, 173
obligation 10, 199, 208
observance 14, 15, 21, 83, 101, 102, 104, 107,
  108, 112, 140, 175, 226, 236
offense 19, 97, 128, 171, 173, 174, 251, 261
office 7, 25, 36, 58, 64, 73, 88, 91, 102, 106,
  111, 116, 117, 119, 121, 124, 128, 138, 145,
  153, 155, 156, 159, 167, 171, 174, 178, 210,
  216, 217, 219, 220, 227, 237, 242, 245, 247,
  253, 254, 258, 263, 264; divine offices 119
Old Testament 5, 13, 14, 15, 29, 36, 53
ordinance 3, 20, 21, 22, 29, 30, 32, 33, 34, 35,
  36, 37, 38, 39, 51, 55, 56, 57, 58, 60, 63, 65,
  67, 68, 69, 70, 71, 75, 76, 79, 80, 81, 84, 88,
  89, 90, 92, 93, 94, 100, 101, 102, 103, 107,
  108, 112, 121, 125, 137, 138, 140, 153, 164,
  178, 209, 213, 226, 229, 232, 236, 239
ordination 35, 39, 43, 46, 49, 54, 116, 124,
  125, 126, 127, 128, 143, 151, 155, 161, 172,
  174, 175, 177, 210, 260, 263
organ 21, 28, 42, 75, 96, 135
organization 3, 5, 6, 11, 12, 13, 15, 16, 17,
  22, 24, 25, 28, 29, 32, 39, 47, 55, 66, 73, 74,
  76, 93, 96, 115, 116, 117, 126, 129, 130, 131,
  135, 136, 144, 145, 164, 205, 206, 207, 208,
  210, 213, 227, 237, 246, 252, 259, 263, 268
Orthodox Institute of Saint Sergius 221
Orthodox Patriarchal Center 220
Otto, King 111
Ottoman Empire 91, 92, 188
ownership 179, 180, 181

P

Pachomios, St. 55, 130

Paisios, Patriarch of Alexandria 60
Palestine 38
Pamphylia 44
Pandectæ 69, 78, 81, 84
Panteleimon, Metropolitan of Corinth 89
Papacy 13, 135
parallelism 207, 208, 210
parish 123, 124, 125, 139, 144, 146, 153, 155,
  175, 179, 180, 182, 194, 228, 229, 233, 238,
  240, 249, 252, 254, 256, 260, 262, 263, 266,
  268; — councilors 124
participation 121, 123, 130, 136, 151, 152,
  210, 262
Pascha iii, 42, 52, 226, 236
pastors 121, 256
Patmian Ecclesiastical School 221
Patmos 90, 218, 219, 221
patriarch 33, 43, 44, 46, 47, 50, 51, 54, 55,
  56, 57, 58, 59, 60, 63, 64, 65, 70, 72, 73, 74,
  78, 81, 82, 83, 85, 87, 91, 108, 118, 120, 138,
  141, 142, 145, 146, 147, 148, 156, 169, 171,
  172, 213, 214, 215, 216, 218, 219, 223, 226,
  227, 230, 232, 236, 237, 241, 242, 243, 245,
  248, 251, 255, 258, 261, 263, 270; **Ecumenical** — 59, 72, 74, 91, 118, 138, 142,
  147, 171, 172, 213, 215, 219, 223, 227, 230,
  232, 236, 237, 241, 245, 248, 251, 255, 258,
  261, 263, 270; — **of Alexandria** 142; — **of
  Constantinople** 33, 43, 44, 47, 50, 54, 56,
  64, 70, 78, 85, 87, 232, 243, 248, 255
Patriarchal Institute for Patristic Studies 221
patriarchate vi, 28, 34, 43, 47, 57, 58, 59, 60,
  64, 73, 74, 89, 90, 91, 92, 94, 95, 96, 112,
  139, 142, 143, 147, 148, 152, 164, 170, 213,
  214, 215, 216, 217, 218, 219, 220, 221, 173,
  221, 220, 223, 227, 230, 233, 238, 240, 241,
  243, 244, 245, 247, 248, 249, 250, 251, 252,
  253, 254, 255, 256, 257, 258, 259, 261, 262,
  264, 265, 266, 268, 269, 270; **Ecumenical**
  — vi, 28, 34, 60, 74, 90, 91, 92, 94, 95, 96,
  112, 147, 152, 164, 173, 213, 215, 216, 217,
  218, 219, 220, 221, 223, 227, 230, 233, 238,
  240, 241, 243, 244, 245, 247, 248, 249, 250,
  251, 252, 253, 254, 255, 256, 257, 258, 259,
  261, 262, 264, 265, 266, 268, 269; — **of
  Alexandria** 142; — **of Antioch** 142; — **of
  Constantinople** 47, 57, 64, 73, 148, 152,
  164, 223, 233, 241, 244; — **of Jerusalem**

About the Author
PANTELEIMON RODOPOULOS
Metropolitan of Tyroloë and Serention
and University Professor

1 STUDIES AND ACADEMIC CAREER. Panteleimon Rodopoulos, who was christened Evangelos, was the scion, on his father's side, of an ancient, distinguished family from Arcadia, a member of which was also the great Metropolitan of Corinth, Kyrillos II Rodopoulos (1819 – 1836), who played an important role in the affairs of the Greek Renaissance struggle (1821), in the Capodistrian and Ottoman periods which followed and, as Chairman of the Holy Synod, was the first signatory of the Protocol of Greek Independence.[1] Metropolitan Panteleimon's mother's family — also distinguished — came from the island of Tinos. Born in Athens in 1929, he is the son of Alexandros Rodopoulos, a doctor, and Eleni, née Santamouri, who was very well-educated for the time, holding a degree from the Arsakeion School of Athens.

In Athens, he attended primary and secondary school and was an outstanding pupil at all levels. In the Fourth Class of Secondary school, he was the best student in a school (9th Secondary School of Athens) numbering some one thousand eight hundred pupils, many of whom now hold leading positions in society and remember him still, always speaking well of him.

Thereafter, he studied Theology at the University of Athens, from which he graduated in 1952 with a First Class Honours degree. Like his

---

[1] Methodios Fouyas, Ἡ Ἱστορία τῆς Ἀποστολικῆς Ἐκκλησίας τῆς Κορίνθου, 2nd ed., Athens 1997, pp. 266 – 70.

fellow-pupils, his fellow-students at the University remember him as dignified, polite and unassuming, outstanding at his studies and fault-less in his behavior toward them. Everything about him indicated that he would develop into a notable servant of Theological letters and a valuable worker for the Church. Thus, it was that, on completion of his studies in Athens, he moved to Great Britain, where he pursued post-graduate studies, initially at King's College, London and then at Oxford, under the outstanding Lady Margaret Professor, F. L. Cross, at Christ Church. He was, at the same time, a member of Saint Catherine's and Wycliffe Hall, where he was in residence. He submitted a thesis on "The Sacramentary of Saint Serapion of Thmouis" and was awarded a post-graduate B. Litt. degree.

While in England, he engaged in intense theological, ecclesiastical and pastoral activity, despite his many academic occupations. Deeply conscious of his Orthodox Theological and Ecclesiastical mission, he served tirelessly in the fields of his theological and priestly responsibil-ity, greatly respected and loved by the local Greek communities and also by those of other faiths, particularly in Anglican circles. He lectured by invitation on Orthodox Theology, worship and life to the university communities in Oxford and Cambridge, as well as at Trinity College, Dublin. Apart from these official occasions, however, he bore witness daily to the Orthodox faith, with tenacity, and love, rejecting fanaticism and exclusivity, so that the faith became welcome to his interlocutors and he himself well-liked and highly-regarded by them, with his gift of conversing and discussing graciously.

In the summer of 1955, when he was still in England, he visited Switzerland, where he attended a course for post-graduate students of Theology at the Ecumenical Institute of Bossey, near Geneva, which forms part of the activities of the World Council of Churches.

After England, he moved to Frankfurt-am-Main (1957–8), where he also pursued his post-graduate studies, researching in the libraries of Mainz, Heidelberg and of the Roman Catholic Theological School at Offenbach.

On his return to Greece, in 1958, he was proclaimed Doctor of Theology, by the Theological School of the University of Athens, having submitted a doctoral thesis on the subject "The Anaphora of the Liturgy of Saint Mark." Thereafter, in the academic year 1960-61, he was elected Assistant Professor (Docent) in Liturgics and Homiletics in the Theological School of the Aristotle University of Thessaloniki, submitting a thesis on his appointment entitled "The Anaphora of the Liturgy of Clement." From this year dates his multi-faceted career as university teacher.

While he was Assistant Professor at the University of Thessaloniki, he was invited by Patriarch Athenagoras of blessed memory, who held him in high esteem, to take over as President of the Theological School at Holy Cross, Brookline, Boston, and of the Greek College of the Holy Archdiocese of America, which is also located there. He remained there as President and teacher between the years 1963–1966. During this time, the School library was renovated, the beautiful Byzantine church was completed and the necessary funds collected for the construction of a new wing to be used for boarders, to replace a building which had burnt down. It was by his efforts that the School was accorded university status by the Massachusetts State Educational Authorities, while it was also recognized by the Association of Theological Schools of the United States of America and was granted equal recognition by the Theological Schools of Greece. He worked hard to raise the educational and academic standard of the School, both by attracting distinguished professors, such as the leading Russian Orthodox Theologian, Father George Florovsky, together with the well-known Greeks, Father Demetrios Constantelos, N. Vaporis, S. Harakas and the musicologist and composer Michael Adamis, as well as by organizing courses and lectures by outstanding professors from Greek and American universities, such as Konstantinos Kalokyris, Sp. Vryonis, Konstantinos Giannakopoulos, Nelson et al.

During his academic service in the USA, he gave lectures on matters related to his specialty to Greek Orthodox Communities, as well as to Theological Schools, such as those of the University of Notre Dame, Andover-Newton, Boston, St. John's Boston and elsewhere.

His fruitful period of office at the Theological School in Boston contributed to a strengthening of the links of its students with the home country and to a deeper knowledge among those students concerning Orthodox Theology, so that many of them later became tried and tested workers for the Church and guides of the Greeks in America into the faith and true values of their fathers. For this reason, his memory remains unsullied among them, and the fruit of his labors is reflected in the faces of his students who are now seeing the Greek Orthodox Church of America.

In 1966, he returned to Greece, where he was appointed Assistant Professor in the chair of Liturgics and Homiletics, while in 1968 he was elected to the chair of Canon Law and Pastoral Studies in the Theological School of the Aristotle University of Thessaloniki.

In 1972, at the invitation of the late Orthodox Patriarch of Antioch, Elias IV, he took up the post of Dean and undertook the organization of "Saint John the Damascene," the newly-founded Theological School of the Patriarchate of Antioch, located in the Monastery of Balamand in the Lebanon, where he remained until 1975. During this period, which was exceptionally trying and a drain in his strength, he divided his time between teaching in Thessaloniki and in the Lebanon by turn, spending a fortnight each month in each place. Because of the difficulties caused by the civil war and the hardships occasioned by it in the Lebanon, the school was transferred, on the instigation of His Eminence the Professor, as he now was, to Thessaloniki from 1975 to 1979. Here he continued to provide for the unimpeded studies and the daily needs of each of the Syrian and Lebanese students. A whole pleiad of graduates from that time are now hierarchs and officials of the Antiochian Church, men who look to him with gratitude and filial love, as their spiritual father in both the broader and more particular meaning of the term. The greatest benefit for the Church from his time in this office was the cementing of closer relations between the two sister Churches.

Nor or it to be overlooked that, as well as organizing the School successfully, he also managed through his own efforts, to have it recognized as a University School of Higher Learning, both by the authorities in the Lebanon and by the Orthodox Theological Schools of the Universities of Greece.

As Professor, he served as Senator in the University of Thessaloniki in the academic year 1976–7 and as Dean of the Theological School of the same University in 1977–8. During his time as Dean, the foundations were laid and the financial and technical plans drawn up by the University authorities for the construction of a university chapel in the Theological School. It was also due to his efforts that, despite opposition, legislation was passed to ensure that only those students who wanted to study Theology were to be admitted to the Theological Schools of the country, not those who happened to be enrolled by computer analysis of their marks in the general university entrance examinations but who had no orientation either toward the Church or toward Theology.

Unfortunately, however, this law was nullified by a Bill passed in 1982, which reintroduced the old, fruitless situation, so damaging to the religious training of young Greeks and to the life of the Church.

In 1982, he was elected Vice-Rector and then Rector by the full Convocation of professors of all Schools of the University for the academic years 1981–3. It ought to be noted that he is the first and only Bishop and University Professor to have been elevated to this highest office in a university since the establishment of the modern Greek State.

In these posts, and despite greatly adverse circumstances, he worked for the smooth and unimpeded running and administration of the University, together with the scientific centers and institutes associated with it, as well as for the extension of its structural installations. Thus, the University Neurological Clinic of the AHEPA. Hospital was completed, as were the buildings of the Dental School and of the School of Physics and Mathematics, while the university farm was given additional support, and so on. As regards the Theological School in particular, a reading room was built on the ground floor and the original building was extended by the addition of a new wing which housed an amphitheatre, rooms for studying, and offices for the teaching staff. The matter of the construction of the chapel was also pressed further. It was due to his efforts as Rector that the Ceremonial Hall of the University was decorated by a sizable and beautiful mosaic, which occupies the whole of one side of the hall, and which was created by the wonderful artist Ioannis Kolefas. It represents Saint Demetrios in the center, in the midst of a series of characteristic scenes from the life of the city of Thessaloniki throughout the ages. Bringing this work to completion meant overcoming many difficulties and obstacles, such as the open and concealed opposition on the part of circles who were motivated by an ideology, contrary to that which had been lived by and had commanded the loyalty of the city throughout its long history. These circles focused their opposition on the promotion and perpetuation of the figure of Saint Demetrios as the emblem of the University of Thessaloniki.

In keeping with his position and his principles, the Bishop and Professor bowed to the demands of his conscience and the dictates of his duty toward the interests — in the good sense — of his high rank, and, wishing to avoid compromise aimed at his own benefit (as is commonly the case in such situations with people who skillfully embellish their concealed, self-seeking, intentions), he resided his position as Rector, together with the Pro-Rector, the late Professor I. Hatziotis and the Vice-Rector, Professor Lysimachos Mavridis, in disagreement over university policy, as inaugurated by Law 1268/82, refusing to break the law, although he was under pressure to do so by the government of the day, in pursuit of its own party-political ends.

In 1982, he represented the Rectors of Greek Universities at a Forum in Belgrade of the Rectors of Balkan countries, held under the aegis of UNESCO. From 1983 to 1996, he served as director of the Section "Law, Life and Diakonia of the Church."

He has been invited to lecture on matters of his specialty and Orthodox Theology, in Universities and well-known intellectual Institutions, Orthodox, Roman Catholic and Protestant in both Western and Eastern Europe, such as the Theological School of the University of Bonn, the School of Law of the University of Vienna, the Orthodox

Theological School at Presov in Slovakia, the Theological Academy of Minsk in Belorussia, the Pro Oriente Institute of Vienna, the Patriarchal Centre of the Ecumenical Patriarchate at Chambesy in Switzerland, at the Dumbarton Oaks Center for Byzantine Studies in the USA and many other places. He was also invited to organize a Seminary for the Orthodox chaplains of the American Army in Germany (Bonn, 1990), on matters of Orthodox Theology, Liturgics and Pastoral Care. Together with Professor Ioannis Foundoulis and at the invitation of His Eminence Avgoustinos, the Metropolitan of Germany, he organized a training Seminar in Bonn on matters of Liturgics and Ritual for the priests of the Holy Metropolis of Germany (1992), while he has also taught Canon Law for a number of years at the Open University of the Municipality of Thessaloniki. He has also lectured, by invitation of the Church hierarchy, on matters related to his dual role, at Conferences of the Holy Metropolitan dioceses of the Church of Greece.

2 CHURCH SERVICE AND OTHER ACTIVITIES. When Evangelos Rodopoulos had completed his studies at the Theological School of the University of Athens, he was tonsured monk at the Holy Monastery of Pendeli (June 14, 1952) when he took the name Panteleimon. At the instigation of Archbishop Spyridon of Athens, of blessed memory, he was ordained deacon on June 29, 1952, by Bishop Panteleimon of Argyrokastron (Gjirokaster, in today's Albania) who was well-known throughout Greece for his long struggle for the national rights of the Greeks. He served as deacon for two years in the Archdiocese of Athens, developing rich catechetic and missionary activity in general among the young in that Archdiocese, as he did thereafter on his enlistment in the Army, where he served with the 7th Brigade. He was ordained Priest in Athens on August 29, 1954, by Bishop Dionysios, then of Rogon, later Metropolitan of Kozani, when he was also given the *officium* of Archimandrite. He was then sent as parish priest to Saint George's, in the Kypseli area of Athens. It was soon after this that he left for his post-graduate studies in England. During the course

of his studies abroad, he served as unpaid priest in England at the communities in Oxford, Birmingham and Bristol giving up the little free time he had each week, laboring ceaselessly and traveling long distances and seeking to deal with the various spiritual pastoral and other problems of the Greek diaspora in England, which was as yet not well-organized. Wherever he went, he inspired respect, which his whole bearing evoked, despite the fact that he was then still a young man, as when he later went to Germany for academic reasons and was appointed parish priest of the Greek community in Frankfurt-am-Main. During his time there, among other things, he made representations to the local authorities and managed to persuade them to grant a site in a central park of the city, where he built the church of Saint Andrew to meet the liturgical needs of the Greek migrants who were at that time living in Germany. This replaced the small room which served as a chapel in the Greek Consulate, which had until then been in use for the large number of older Greek emigrants and for students. For the above reasons, it was natural that he should inspire the love and respect of the then ecclesiastical leader of the Western European eparchy of the Ecumenical Patriarchate, Athenagoras, Archbishop of Thyateira and Great Britain, of blessed memory, who originally came from Boston. From this time, he began to become well-known in the Great Church of Christ in the Phanar, both through the Archbishop mentioned above, as well as through distinguished Archbishops of the Throne such as Metropolitan Iakovos of Melite — later Archbishop of America — who at that time represented the Ecumenical Patriarchate at the World Council of Churches in Geneva. The present Dean of the Archbishops of the Great Church of Christ, His Eminence Ieronymos, Metropolitan of Rodopolis, spent the academic year 1956 – 7 in Oxford and was able to appreciate at first hand the virtues and abilities of the young Archimandrite who promised so much for the Church.

While he was in Germany he eschewed the tempting possibilities opening up for him for a career in the West and, having been invited to do so, preferred to return to Greece, where, toward the end of 1958 he was appointed Protosynkellos (Vicar General) at the Metropolis of Thessaloniki and Rector of the cathedral church of the Wisdom of God. As Vicar General, he was the close associate and aide of Panteleimon, the Lord Metropolitan of Thessaloniki, of blessed memory, who had previously been of Edessa and Pella, not only in matters related to the administration of the metropolis, but also in its spiritual and pastoral work. Thus it was that he organized the pastoral work of the parishes, particularly among young people, on an Orthodox ecclesiological footing, through the introduction and application of modern pastoral methods. With the cooperation of parish priests, he organized more than ten parish pastoral centers, summer camps, parish basketball teams and the children's choir of the church of the Holy Trinity, to which he was appointed Rector on his return from America (1966). This choir is considered the best of its kind in Greece and has won recognition well beyond its native land, with a large number of prizes to its credit. As Rector of the cathedral church of the Wisdom of God (1958–1963), apart from using the Orthodox *Typikon* for the Order of the Holy Services, he also made the modernization of the sermons and pastoral work in this parish his concern and founded its pastoral centre. He likewise made use of the church's land holdings, so that it became financially independent in meeting its spiritual and pastoral commitments.

On May 23, 1974, the Holy Synod of the Ecumenical Patriarchate elected him titular Metropolitan of Tyana. His consecration as bishop took place on June 9 in the same year in the main church of the Monastery of the Holy Trinity in the Holy Theological School in Halki. On November 15, 1977, the same Synod elected him as active Metropolitan, to the see of Tyroloë and Serention in Thrace. Once again, we see what was written by Basil the Great about Gregory the Theologian in application: "Not that the place (position) dignified him, but rather that the place was dignified by him" (Basil the Great, *Epistle* 98, PG 32, p. 496ff). Since then he has remained bishop of this see, despite having been offered what many would consider enviable metropolitan dioceses both at home and abroad.

With the title of bishop of a see which is in today's Turkey, though part of the ancient homelands of the Greeks, he organized an association of people from Tyroloë living in Thessaloniki. He is the honorary president of this association, and every year celebrates a Divine Liturgy on February 10 in honor and memory of Saint Haralambos, the patron saint of Tyroloë, as he does in New Tyroloë on the River Strymon on the Sunday of the Myrrh-Bearing Women. On this occasion a universal feast is held, which thus brings together all the scattered children of the former homeland and fans the smoldering ideals and faith in the hearth of the Church, around the Communion Table, and in the Mother Church, the homeland extending into eternity.

Broadening his spiritual activities in Thessaloniki, he also became head of the branch of the "Greek Light" Christian study association of women intellectuals.

In 1964, he was sent by the Ecumenical Patriarch to Rome, as an observer at the Second Vatican Council where, as the leading member of the Orthodox Church delegation and on behalf of all the non-Roman Catholic observers and all the international ecclesiastical organizations and church missions, he addressed His Holiness Pope Paul VI at a private audience in the Sistine Chapel.

In the 1970's he took part, as a member of the delegation of the Ecumenical Patriarchate, in the meetings of the Pan-Orthodox Preparatory Committee of the Holy and Great Synod, as well as those of the Pan-Orthodox Preparatory Committee of Theological Dialogue between the Orthodox and Roman Catholic Churches.

In that same decade, the 1970's he sat, as the only Orthodox observer/advisor, on the Pontifical Committee for Drafting the *Lex Fundamentalis* of the Roman Catholic Church, which met over a series of years under the chairmanship of Cardinal Pericles Felici.

In the years 1973–4, both before and after the Turkish invasion of Cyprus, he undertook the delicate and most important mission of bringing peace and the restoration of unity to the Church of Cyprus.

In 1983 he was appointed by the Patriarch to be a member of a three-man exarchy, together with Metropolitan Kyrillos of Chaldia and Konstantinos of Derka to handle problems which had arisen in the Church of Crete.

Recently, in 1996, he led the delegation from the Ecumenical Patriarchate in talks with the Patriarchate of Moscow aimed at solving the so-called Estonian problem and restoring relations between the Patriarchates, which had become strained because of this. In both tasks he was successful. Earlier in the same year (February 21–22, 1996), he took part in a three-man delegation from the Ecumenical Patriarchate, together with Metropolitans Geron Joacheim of Chalcedon and Meliton of Philadelphia, which went to Estonia, bearing the Patriarchal and Synodical Act which enabled the autonomy of the Orthodox Church there and installed Archbishop Ioannis of Karelia and All Finland as *locum tenens*. The delegation was received by and had long discussions with the President of the Republic, Mr. Lennart Meri, the Prime Minister, Mr. Tiit Vahi, the Minister for European Affairs, Mr. Endel Lipmaa, the Minister of the Interior, Mr. Kaido Kama and with clergy and laity on the staff of the Church in Estonia.

He has served a member of the Central Committee of the World Council of Churches, of the National Council of Churches of the United States of America and has attended many conferences and meetings of an inter-denominational as well as academic nature. In this connection, he served from 1978 to 1983 as Vice-President, and from 1983 to 1991 as President of the academic Society for the Law of the Eastern Churches, based in Vienna, while from 1991 he has been honorary president thereof. He was also chairman of the administrative board of the Patriarchal Institute of Patristic Studies, which is located in the Holy, Patriarchal and Stavropegic Vlatadon Monastery in Thessaloniki (1985–89). As chairman of this Institute, he restored its finances so that it was able to meet its goals, and housed it in the new building complex of Vlatadon Monastery (1989). He also improved, as far as possible, its administration, although in doing so he encountered opposition from those whose interests were being encroached upon. He also served as chairman of cultural associations and a member of administrative boards of agencies of higher education.

He is president, on the Orthodox side, of the Joint Commission for Theological Dialogue with the World Association of Reformed Churches, which, because of their Ecclesiological structure, is the most of the continuing dialogues with non-Orthodox Churches. By his careful and delicate handling of these talks, he has managed to ensure a positive orientation on their behalf toward the teaching of the historical Churches, an achievement acknowledged by representatives of the Orthodox.

He is also chairman of the Organizing Committee of the annual, academic symposium on the general subject of "Christian Thessaloniki", held within the framework of the "Demetria" festival, as well as being Abbot of the Holy Vlatadon Monastery (1985). As Abbot, he was responsible for the complete re-organization of the Monastery, and of its dependencies, having its rights of ownership over them recognized. These, such as the dependency of Our Most Holy Lady the Laodigetria, had previously been challenged. He completed the building complex of the Monastery, totally renovating the dilapidated Abbot's Quarters (1985) and building the wing which houses the Patriarchal Institute of Patristic Studies (amphitheatre, offices, library etc. (1989) as well as the third wing of the Monastery, which houses the new Sacristy-Museum, organized in exemplary manner, a hall for receptions and the bookshop. He also organized the Theological Boarding Wing of the Monastery, which hosts Orthodox post graduate and undergraduate students of Theology from abroad, though not to the exclusion of the non-Orthodox. 24 students from 11 countries were living there in the year 1995 – 97, 30 in the year 2005 – 06, and in this way the Theological Boarding Wing of the Monastery has proved to be a Pan-Orthodox Centre for the cultivation of spiritual unity and fellowship among the future spiritual leaders of the Orthodox Church. He is vice president of the Patriarchal Institute of Patristic Studies which is in the Monastery and an honorary member of the Administrative Board of the Pro Oriente theological and ecclesiastical institute, centered in Vienna. He presides at present over the Supervisory Committee of professors of the Ecumenical Patriarchate Internet website, which was recently established in Vlatadon Monastery through which it "now has the possibility of linking up with Orthodox all over the world and all these interested in the Ecumenical Patriarchate and its Institutions. In this way, the first Church of Orthodoxy will be able to make contact with a community of some three hundred million faithful," as he himself declared at the inauguration of the site, which was welcomed as a significant event by the official Church press in Greece.[2]

Despite his many commitments and the press of his duties, as academic and bishop, which he discharges with most responsible activity and therefore does not have the luxury, enjoyed by every other university teacher, of dividing his time between library and chair, he has nevertheless presented a considerable written *oeuvre* on matters of Canon Law, Liturgies, Pastoral Care, Inter-Church Relations, as well as expert opinion on critical, current matter of Church life, when requested to do so by the Ecumenical Patriarchate and the Church of Greece. Apart from this, he has also written speeches, talks, lectures, essays, biographies and much else, in English, German and Greek. His works number about one hundred and consist of books, monographs and articles published in periodicals and *Festschriften*.

In recognition of his important contribution to the discipline of Theology and to the Church, he has been awarded honorable distinctions, decorations and medals by the Patriarchates of Alexandria, Antioch and Moscow, the Vatican, the Archdiocese of Thyateira and Great Britain, honorary doctorate by the University of Sibiu, Romania, Holy Cross, Brookline, the Metropolitan dioceses of Thessaloniki, Neapolis and Stavroupolis, Nea Krini and Kalamaria, the Municipality of Thessaloniki and the City of Niagara in the USA, by Organizing Committees of International Conferences, the Greet Armed Forces Staff College, the Union of Greek Writers and so on.

---

[2] *ΕΚΚΛΗΣΙΑ*, April 1, 1997, no. 6, pp. 286 – 7.

His Eminence the Metropolitan of Tyroloë and Serention, Professor Panteleimon Rodopoulos, an outstanding ecclesiastical personality today and one of the leading hierarchs of the Ecumenical Patriarchate and the Orthodox Church in general, is honored and respected for his high personal standards, his academic merit and his deeply ecclesiastical outlook by all those who know him and by all those who are able to judge and, evaluate his talents and his character. Such were the Ecumenical Patriarch Athenagoras, majestic in his dealings, who sent him as President to the Theological School of Boston, the Greek-educated Orthodox Patriarch of Antioch, Elias IV, at whose invitation he ran, organized and taught at the newly-established Theological School of his Patriarchate at Balamand in the Lebanon, the Ecumenical Patriarch Demetrios, now at rest with the saints, who appointed him to his episcopal Throne, his long-standing collaborator, Archbishop Iakovos of America, who tended the Church of America to bountiful fruition, exhausting his substance in the service of the Greek Nation overseas and stamping two generations with his personality, the Archbishop of Athens, Serapheim, who repeatedly had recourse to Metropolitan Panteleimon of Tyroloë for expert opinion on serious Church matters and many others. He also enjoys the same honor from non-Orthodox ecclesiastical personalities — Roman Catholics, Anglicans and Protestants — with whom, because of his mission, he has come into contact and has conversed with at meetings, and conferences and on private occasions.

The responsible positions and extremely delicate missions with which the Mother Church entrusted him were undertaken with a high sense of responsibility and seriousness, and he served the Church, the Mystical Body of Christ, as if serving before God with no thought of self, no reckoning and no expediency. Rather, he always looked to Him, the eternal, world-saving Interest, and not to any personal ambition or gain.

Panteleimon of Tyroloë, a true aristocrat from a family with tradition and breeding, has never permitted himself any relaxation of *noblesse oblige* throughout the course of his life and has remained faithfully at the post to which duty has called him, always aiming at executing everything assigned to him in the best manner possible. With these criteria, he has retained this dignified stance throughout the trials which have befallen him and which have been no strangers to him in either of his positions. It is a peculiarity of the envious that they have not the ability to rise to the stature of those above them and that they find solace in attempting to reduce them to their own measure. These instances he has met with generosity of spirit and silence. No stranger to praise for the good works he has performed, he is also familiar with virulent ill-will directed against him. He is well able to stand against the base things of this world and to avoid being worn down by the whirl of business and other affairs, so harmful for the spiritual life, of the current, low level of our daily round. The scale and measure of his actions is to serve the aims he set himself from his youth up and to which he has devoted his life as a faithful laborer in the Church.

In general, His Eminence the Metropolitan and Professor, combining as he does, by definition, theological formation and a firm ecclesiastical outlook with a broader humanistic training and cultivation, a man who is adamant on matters of principle but amiable to one and all, of high personal standards and nobility of manner, of directness and integrity of character, discrete in his ways and gracious in company, traditional in his positions but with a broadness of perspective, is by no means a personality formed by chance. The discipline of Theology and the Church — particularly the Ecumenical Patriarchate — can be justly proud of having in their ranks a hierarch and academic teacher such as Metropolitan Panteleimon of Tyroloë and Serention.

Athanasios K. Arvanitis, D.D.
Former General Director,
Ministry of National Education and
Religious Affairs of Greece

LaVergne, TN USA
28 December 2009
168239LV00003B/98/A